THE AMERICAN SOUTH SERIES

Edward L. Ayers, *Editor*

Slave in a Box

The Strange Career of Aunt Jemima

M. M. MANRING

University Press of Virginia

■ *Charlottesville and London*

THE UNIVERSITY PRESS OF VIRGINIA

© 1998 by the Rector and Visitors of the University of Virginia

All rights reserved

Printed in the United States of America

First published February 1998
Second paperback printing June 1998

∞ The paper used in this publication meets the minimum requirements of the
American National Standard for Information Sciences—Permanence of Paper
for Printed Library Materials, ANSI Z39.48-1984.

Library of Congress Cataloging-in-Publication Data
Manring, M. M., 1962–
    Slave in a box: the strange career of Aunt Jemima /M. M. Manring.
      p. cm.—(American South series)
    Includes bibliographical references (p.   ) and index.
    ISBN 0-8139-1782-4 (cloth: alk. paper). ISBN 0-8139-1811-1 (paper)
      1. Jemima, Aunt. 2. Advertising—Social aspects—United States—
History—20th century. 3. Afro-American women in advertising—
United States. 4. Stereotype (Psychology) in advertising—United
States. 5. Quaker Oats Company. I. Title. II. Series.
    HF5813.U6M25   1998
    659.1 '664753—dc21   97-33355
                                           CIP

Contents

Illustrations

Acknowledgments

I am grateful to Dave Roediger of the University of Minnesota, who suggested this subject to me years ago and whose help and insights have been invaluable. I also wish to thank Henry Hager of the University of Missouri for his guidance, particularly in the area of advertising. David Lendt, Timothy Fall, Jennifer Greathouse Fall, Randy McBee, Julie Willett, and Kim Schreck read parts of this manuscript at one time or another, and I thank them for their observations.

This book would not have been possible without the help of the staff of the Hartman Center for Sales, Advertising, and Marketing History at Duke University. Its advertising archives, especially the collected papers of the J. Walter Thompson Company, are unmatched. The staff of the Western Historical Manuscripts Collection in Columbia, Missouri, provided guidance to their valuable collections. Thanks also to Lynn Burkett, who generously provided me with a copy of the original and rare Aunt Jemima pamphlet.

Some of the material in chapter 5 originally appeared in "Aunt Jemima Explained: The Old South, the Absent Mistress, and the Slave in a Box," *Southern Cultures* 2 (Winter 1996): 19–44.

Thanks most of all to Michele McFadden, who is pleased that I am finally finished with my "book report."

SLAVE IN A BOX

The Strange Career of Aunt Jemima

1 Cracking Jokes in the Confederate Supermarket

> Before . . . our joy at the demise of Aunt Jemima and Uncle Tom approaches the indecent, we had better ask whence they sprang, how they lived? Into what limbo have they vanished?
>
> —James Baldwin, *Notes of a Native Son*

In 1955 in his *Notes of a Native Son*, James Baldwin asked "whence" Aunt Jemima "sprang," and "into what limbo" she and her male counterpart, Uncle Tom or Uncle Mose, had "vanished."[1] How are we supposed to answer Baldwin's question? Who could have created Aunt Jemima, and for what reason? She began as a white man, in drag, wearing blackface, singing on the minstrel stage. She became a face on a bag of pancake flour, then a real-life ex-slave who worked in a Chicago kitchen but cobbled together enough reality and fancy of life under slavery to entertain the crowds of the 1893 World's Fair. Next, advertising copywriters and one of America's most distinctive illustrators brought her to life in the pages of ladies' magazines, although the print version was still shadowed by a succession of real-life Aunt Jemimas who greeted the curious public at county fairs and club Bake-Offs. Then, in the era of the Civil Rights movement and Black Power, she grew into a liability, someone to be altered to meet the times and explained away with no small amount of embarrassment. Finally, instead of vanishing into the limbo

Baldwin described in 1955, she rebounded forty years later as a television advertising icon, a black spokeswoman redeemed by having another, more up-to-date, black spokeswoman speak for her. How did she spring back? Why does she persist? Aunt Jemima's strange career defies easy explanation, despite the increasing attention she has received from historians of marketing, journalism, advertising, and literature during the past decade. She has a confusing history.

One way to answer Baldwin's question is to ask, in turn, Who cares? At a single glance—the way most people see Aunt Jemima, after all—she seems an insignificant relic. How much meaning can we derive from a cartoon face on a pancake box? It is possible to view the mammy's picture as at best benign and at worst a silly, outdated joke that no longer carries any of whatever meaning it previously held. The slave population represented by Aunt Jemima, we are reminded, freed itself in the wake of the Emancipation Proclamation. The woman's face and dress have changed significantly since she began her career, supposedly no longer bearing any meaningful resemblance to an earlier image that traded heavily on her slave origins and ways. And further, Quaker Oats, the company that owns the line of Aunt Jemima products, no longer trades on that image, preferring to cast Aunt Jemima as a modern woman, to the extent that it characterizes Aunt Jemima as anything at all. She does not speak or move in the television or print advertisements; nowadays she is simply a label, not meaning anything other than to identify a particular brand, and kept because customers recognize the name and symbol the same way they recognize Coca-Cola's "Dynamic Ribbon" typeface or Budweiser's ornate label. It is an admittedly stupid joke that has lost its offensiveness and thus lost its meaning beyond what marketers call "trade dress," the way a package is designed, and "brand equity," the extent to which the name and design attract and hold consumer loyalty. In the average American supermarket, the argument goes, approximately thirty thousand products vie for our attention during the half hour we spend shopping for goods.[1] Why concern ourselves with a faded joke on a box of ready-mix pancake batter?

I call Aunt Jemima a joke because Aunt Jemima was the butt of jokes in minstrel shows and print ads but also because the term clarifies a basic argument about how her image should be interpreted. The meaning of jokes, or the dispute over whether jokes have meaning in the first place, parallels the question of whether a figure such as Aunt Jemima has any meaning. One way to look at a joke is commonly termed "incongruity theory," an idea put forth at least as early as the eighteenth century by James Beattie, who wrote that "laughter arises from the view of two or more inconsistent, unsuitable, or incongruous parts or circumstances, considered as united in one complex object." The essayist Elliott Oring explained what Beattie was talking about by reminding us of an old joke about the kangaroo buying an expensive drink in a bar. The bartender tells his marsupial customer that he does not see many kangaroos ordering drinks in his bar. The kangaroo replies, "At four seventy-five a drink, I can see why." As Oring explains in exhaustive detail, a successful incongruity, the basis of most riddles, requires a great deal of cultural knowledge on the part of both the joke teller and his audience: Kangaroos do not speak and do not order cocktails, and $4.75 is a lot to pay for a drink.[2] But more important, while a joke depends upon the teller and listener's ability to access pieces of implicit information, jokes themselves do not mean very much. A kangaroo in a bar, a smiling black woman on a pancake box, both are meant to be passingly pleasing; kangaroos are not defamed by such an innocent association, an incongruity meant to make us smile. A joke is just a joke except in the respect that it reveals common cultural knowledge, and jokes are not meant to be examined in such a way, just enjoyed. A good joke, by its very nature, collapses if it requires any such explanation to the humorless. If a sales clerk has to explain why a smiling black woman is on a pancake box, you probably are not going to buy the product anyway.

In his 1905 book *Jokes and Their Relation to the Unconscious*, Sigmund Freud argued that jokes are aggressive, articulating the unconscious motives that underlay them. Thus the father of psychoanalysis typically emphasized the teller of the joke rather than the techniques of joke telling, unlike Beattie and incongruity theory. As Oring observed, Freud's psychoanalytic approach and its emphasis on aggressiveness were in line with earlier observations concerning the meaning of humor, such as Thomas Hobbes's belief that laughter was the result of a sudden realization that one is superior to another (who is the object of the joke). Thus a joke could be more than the simple pleasure of a cultural incongruity and, in Oring's words, "actually spawns such eminency [of the joke teller] through the regular and deliberate diminution of others." Jokes are masked assaults against real individuals and groups in society, socially sanctioned because they serve aggressive emotions in a safe way, one that does not embarrass or offend the particular audience that is the joke's recipient.[3]

When a joke crosses a line of safety—such as the actor Ted Danson's decision to wear blackface and tell watermelon jokes at a 1993 roast of the actress Whoopi Goldberg—it is perceived as something more meaningful and, in this case, repulsive than a mere joke and is not funny.[4] Another relatively recent and more wide-ranging example of the hostile humor identified by Freud is the elephant joke cycle of the 1960s, which Roger Abrahams and Alan Dundes examined in their 1969 article "On Elephantasy and Elephanticide." Elephant jokes were a series of especially absurd incongruities in the form of questions and answers, like these:

Q: What's big and gray and comes in quarts?
A. An elephant.

Q. How do you know if an elephant is in the bathtub with you?
A. By the faint smell of peanuts on his breath.

Q. How do you keep an elephant from stampeding?
A. By cutting his 'tam peter off.

The authors sought to explain the elephant joke as something that helped whites express their fears and fantasies in a time when traditional racial barriers were under attack, during the Civil Rights and Black Power movements, and when greater attempts were made to integrate schools, workplaces, and other public spaces. The elephant was a safe harbor to say things about blacks that were formerly expressed in increasingly forbidden, explicit humor:

Q. What do you call a Negro with a Ph.D.?
A. Nigger.

Abrahams and Dundes interpreted these jokes as disguising racism rather than merely celebrating incongruity. The "big and gray and comes in quarts" line is a reference to the supposed mammoth nature of black sexuality. The joke about bathtubs and breath hints at black intrusion into the most intimate areas of white life. The stampeder joke hides the aggressive desire of whites to control and emasculate black men. This was too much for Oring, who wrote that "there is no reason to view [the Civil Rights movement] as the single force conditioning the joke cycle"; he concluded that "much more than the relations between the races was being turned on its ear" in these riddles. Oring believed the elephant joke arose in the wider countercultural movement, with its sit-ins, strikes, and demonstrations on university campuses, which the jokes reflect through their blatant challenge to conventional reason and their intrusive sexuality.[5] The point is, however, not whether the racial explanation or countercultural analysis is correct (both seem plausible), but that even a view of jokes as incongruous does not assume that jokes are meaningless. Even if the elephant jokes, for example, do not mask a hostile impulse toward blacks, they might still be a sign of some other aggressive challenge toward societal mores, surfacing in an innocuous and even silly way.

So the argument is not about whether jokes mean anything, but what jokes mean, bringing us back to Baldwin's question: What is the meaning of Aunt Jemima? The question is really whether Aunt Jemima is merely incongruous—a relic that persists on pancake boxes, a now-harmless joke that nobody gets anymore, anyway. This is a historical inquiry. Aunt Jemima might have been one kind of joke on the minstrel stage and another in print campaigns, a message that was altered from the 1890s to the 1980s as the circumstances around her changed. Just the same, there must be something at the core to explain her staying power over a century of dramatic and sometimes subtle changes. However incongruous the picture of a slave woman on a box of modern processed food might seem, there must be a way to explain her presence that is causal rather than casual. The reason she is still on the box could be the same reason she was put on the box in the first place; the reason she has changed so much could be the same reason she has stayed the same in so many ways. If her essential persuasive power was exhausted over time, she would have been discarded, not altered. Or more directly, if she did not help sell hundreds of millions of dollars' worth of processed foods every year, somebody or something else would be on the box—unless we accept the idea that there is not an important relationship between what is on the box and what is inside it.

The relationship between what is on the box and what is within it has never been a casual one, at least not since the advent of mass production and consumption. As Thomas Hine has noted in *The Total Package: The Evolution and Secret Meanings of Boxes, Bottles, Cans, and Tubes*, some products would be impossible if not for packaging, a phenomenon he calls the "Aunt Jemima Effect," because the pancake flour is a combination of separate, familiar products formerly sold unpackaged. Other examples of the "Aunt Jemima Effect" would be those small crackers with peanut butter that languish in vending machines or the McDonald's McDLT, whose dual clamshell package "kept the hot side hot and the cold side cold." The relationship between the product and the package, however, goes beyond mere functionality; to a great extent the package creates the product's personality and in turn enables the consumer to establish a relationship with a stranger: the distant producer of a mass product. Some of the most powerful and consistent relationships are simple enough to be maintained by designs on small packages, such as the box for Marlboro cigarettes, which few of its regular customers can describe offhand, but all can recognize instantly (which is the reason it is the most valuable brand name in the world). Other relationships are more complex. For instance, test marketing has demonstrated that people recognize the Tide detergent box even when all its typographical elements and colors are hopelessly scrambled.[6]

If we want to see the product-consumer relationship in action, we have only to head for one of the most American of places: the supermarket. One of the unique privileges of being an American is shopping in the veritable cornucopia of food and related stuff known as the supermarket, the place where 30,000 products meet the consumer for 30 minutes, each specially designed to stand out in some special way to a special person. What is interesting about the supermarket, of course, is that so little seems to be transpiring even as so much calculated behavior is going on, endlessly, as some products are selected and others are not, some marketing plans are realized and others crushed. Billions of dollars ride on the sum of millions of apparently innocuous acts; millions are spent by research firms to test typefaces, colors, and images, sometimes videotaping consumer responses in stores, sometimes in controlled tests using a tachistoscope, a slide projector with a rapid shutter speed designed to measure instant recognition.[7] The designers of supermarkets have learned that most of us shop 2.2 times a week. They know that if they slow the store's music down enough, our eyes will blink only 14 times a minute, as opposed to the normal 32 times a minute. They have figured out that the best angle to view products on shelves is 15 degrees below the horizontal, and you probably will stand four feet away, on average, from whatever product you are seeing.[8]

In that environment, if you choose to believe that the "joke" that is Aunt Jemima is not some highly analyzed transaction, you may, but the only remaining question would be, Who is kidding whom?

The Confederate Supermarket

Nothing special seems to be going on in the average American supermarket. Everybody does what everybody else is doing—wandering past rows of cartoon characters on cereal boxes, fixating on a list, hovering over a folding table as a preternaturally friendly woman prepares a free sample of microwavable Vienna sausage. I can devote a considerable amount of mental energy to deciding whether the 48-ounce size of detergent is preferable to the 96-ounce size, or whether picante sauce is a justifiable expense. Shoppers do not come to the supermarket to think about Aunt Jemima's deeper meaning; they have other things—prices, schedules, traffic—on their minds. I do not see those 30,000 products there in the 30 minutes I spend; I see the things that are on my list or catch my eye. (I wonder how James Baldwin would react here.) It is a singular experience rather than an examination of a bunch of individual items, which, conversely, is why packaging experts go to so much trouble to make their items stand out. It is possible to get through the whole trip without concentrating on anything more than keeping the number of products in the cart low enough to secure passage through the express line (I put the picante sauce back). While I wait in line, another hundred sets of eyes are fixed on Wesson oil, a hundred sets of hands fumble through business-size envelopes stuffed with coupons clipped from the Sunday newspaper. It is all very mundane. And perhaps that is the way it should be. We do not need to spend every waking moment thinking about the International Monetary Fund or the latest ballot referendum. In my experience the supermarket is an excellent refuge from thinking about things like the Confederate Memorial movement.

Or, more accurately, it seems to be. We pass by a weird sort of Confederate memorial, in a sense, every time we push our carts down that aisle with the breakfast items—ersatz maple syrup, Pop Tarts, powdered stuff in boxes. Looking out at us, at about eye level, is one of those seemingly unexplainable relics, something that has been around so long, put to such ordinary use, that it seems not to require much explanation anyway. The black woman on the box of Aunt Jemima pancake mix still smiles at us in much the same way she did in 1920. She has changed her hair, added some jewelry, and lost some weight, but she has not gone anywhere since the turn of the century. Maybe she keeps sticking around because she is more successful than ever, with her face on about forty products, accounting for an overwhelming lead in market share in the ready-to-prepare breakfast category, with sales of more than $300 million annually. But that is not much of an explanation for why she is there. It tells us she still works for Quaker Oats, her owner, in some way, but it does not explain how she works and why people originally decided to put her there. The presence of a statue of a Confederate general in a park probably does not explain the decision to take a walk in the park; we can pass by with scarcely a thought as to what a weather-beaten, green-copper man is doing on a horse, surrounded by Frisbee throwers and pic-nickers. The people who put him on that horse had big ideas about what he was doing there, no matter how ordinary he seems today. And even those who might object to everything the man depicted in the statue stood for, if it happens to occur to them, stop far short of suggesting that the green-copper equestrian should come down after all these years. He has become part of the scenery.

Those old statues were not solely commemorating the Confederacy, as Gaines Foster has shown, but were a way of interpreting the "Old South" as a whole, forming a public memory of a time, social order, and place—for white men, white women, black men, and black women. The purpose of constructing social memory through Confederate memorials was not simply a nostalgic look back but a way to come to terms with the realities of the postbellum South—dealing with defeat and building social unity during a time of transition. The Virginians who squabbled over the proper way to memorialize Robert E. Lee in the 1880s, for example, had held a variety of opinions on the possibility of a Confederate victory or on the abilities of commanders like James Longstreet, but in commemorating Lee they employed the Confederate tradition to cele-brate the prewar culture. A great many assumptions could be bound up in the forging of a statue, ideas about deference, religion, duty, and white supremacy.[9]

Not everybody gets a statue, of course. Other icons of the Old South ex-plain as much about their creators' worldview—their ideas about race and class and gender and order—as statues of Confederate commanders, but they were not cast in bronze or iron. One of them is the mammy, a female slave who in postwar literature and diaries took on special importance. She was depicted as genuinely loving her masters and mistresses, thus providing a justification for slavery. She was sometimes remembered as a maid-of-all-work, someone who not only cooked in hot, detached southern kitchens, keeping a fire burning steadily all day, but also served as a nursemaid, physician, and counselor. The ex-tent to which any slave did all these things is the subject of some dispute among historians of slavery. Some of them cling to the maid-of-all-work, emphasizing her loyalty and authority in plantation households; others point to the evidence that shows no single slave did all those things, nor did her master and mistress want her to do them. None of them takes the female slave out of the kitchen, however, and her place in the kitchen is the key to understanding her place in white southern ideology, both male and female, antebellum and postbellum. Black women in the kitchen kept white women out of it, defining not only the proper place of black women but of white women as well. Gender roles were defined by what different women did, and what they did not do; feminine virtues were defined by task. Robert E. Lee, as a Confederate memorial, was an idea of exemplary southern white manhood. The mammy was an idea about exemplary southern black womanhood, and an important one even after the decline of the Confederate Memorial movement. As late as 1923 the United Daughters of the Confederacy tried, but failed, to build the mammy her own national memorial in Washington, D.C.[10] She might not have gotten her statue, but her legendary role in the kitchen retained its resonance; it was a place for black women, a place where Robert E. Lee arguably would have been at a loss. The mammy would be remembered in different ways. Appropriately, she remained in the twentieth century what she had been in the nineteenth century—a black woman bought and sold.

So if we cannot find mammy by looking at statues, we need to look elsewhere—toward that black woman who is looking back at us from the supermarket shelf. And in doing so, we bring together themes in the history of the South, women, business, media, and African Americans in a way that explains the origins and persistent appeal of one of America's advertising icons, all the cultural information that underlies the seeming incongruity of a black woman on a box of pancake mix, or the unexplained motives behind the joke. Just as others have done, I am putting Aunt Jemima back to work, this time in an effort to historicize the popular image of mammy.

In chapter 2, I study the development of the popular image that formed the basis for Aunt Jemima. The slave woman called "mammy" has become the focus of growing interest among historians in the past three decades. Much of what was assumed to be common knowledge about her is now in dispute—how she worked, why she worked, and even whether she actually existed. Not only historians but novelists and diarists were responsible for fleshing out the image of mammy, and thus any account of her career also requires a study of fictional works as well. The southern mammy exemplified by Aunt Jemima, I argue, was a well-established and well-understood idea long before her image was pasted on a box of pancake flour. From her beginnings in southern plantation reality and literature, the mammy was a sexual and racial symbol that was used by men and women, North and South, white and black, to explain proper gender relationships, justify or condemn racial oppression, and establish class identities (for both whites and blacks). I explain the way historians have treated the mammy both as a real person and as a largely imaginary symbol of white male ideology in the Old South and demonstrate the ways that writers of fiction, North and South, used her to explain differing ideas about race, class, and gender, starting with the years after the Civil War and ending about 1970. This review of the literature considers both the historiography of slavery and the importance of popular fiction in creating the mammy image to which Aunt Jemima is an heir. There is an inherent difficulty in balancing the two, because many historians consider her largely a fictional person, and many novelists who included mammies in their works, such as Thomas Nelson Page and Thomas Dixon, considered themselves to be faithful reporters of southern history.

Some of these books are about the Old South, some about the New South, and most of them focus on the nature of slavery, from numerous angles. All touch upon mammy in some way, explaining the world black women lived in, both in slavery and freedom. They tell us how the world either stayed the same or changed, and what ideas white people held about mammy, as well. Some, like Deborah Gray White and Catherine Clinton, question mammy's existence and go so far as to regard her as a myth even among those who lived in the Old South. Others, like Eugene Genovese and Donald Blassingame, see her as a real person. All of them, one way or another, describe what she might have meant to white people—as living justification of the correctness of slavery, as a carrier of black political sensibility after slavery, as an "uplifter" of white southern womanhood, or as a combination of those and other things.[11] One of the conclusions I have reached is that mammy, whatever she was, has been as useful a servant to historians and novelists as she was to her southern masters; that is, she helps Eugene Genovese's class analysis as much as she happily works in Thomas Nelson Page's racial paradise. The variety of views on mammy demonstrates historiographical changes over the century, but it also shows the utility a black image has had in white minds, black minds, male minds, female minds. She was above all, and continues to be, a useful person.

In chapter 3 I show how one of the popular images of Aunt Jemima, the white man dressed as a black woman on the minstrel stage, inspired the adoption of the mammy as a trademark. To understand the "discovery" of Aunt Jemima by an aspiring food manufacturer, one must understand not only the racial, gender, and class ideology wrapped up in minstrel shows but the growth of an American industry that promised to prepare, package, and deliver ready-mixed foodstuffs in the late nineteenth century. Aunt Jemima pancake mix did not arise simply because of the mammy's inherent utility as a trademark but because the logistics and economics of food production created an opportunity for nationally marketed products. Thus what is often described as a coincidental meeting between the mammy and an entrepreneur in a St. Joseph, Missouri, minstrel hall was actually the confluence of major trends in American popular culture and economics, not much of a coincidence at all.

The fourth chapter addresses the rise of the American advertising industry in the first two decades of the twentieth century, and how its attempts to persuade American families to use new products increasingly targeted consumers' self-image, their doubts and their aspirations. This topic has been addressed by numerous historians and sociologists, but I am convinced that one of the trends in American advertising which has largely escaped their notice was the power of the South—in particular, the plantation South—as a symbol of white leisure, abundance, and sexual order. The utility of such an image is that it directly addressed the dilemma that white households faced as the overall servant population decreased and, simultaneously, the percentage of black domestics increased. America's long-standing "servant problem" was becoming a "black problem." In several advertising campaigns, especially the one for Maxwell House coffee, the South was connected with a product and portrayed as a place in which elite white men and women were above laboring for their sustenance. They were instead depicted as feasting, dancing, and celebrating their (white) culture as black servants handled the service that made all the revelry possible. At this juncture we encounter James Webb Young, a mercurial advertising man for the J. Walter Thompson firm, who skillfully employed images of black labor and white leisure not only to persuade white consumers—both men and women—to try new products but to make national brands synonymous with national reconciliation after the Civil War. White southerners knew how to eat and celebrate; Yankees knew how to manufacture and distribute. Both could live in harmony as long as African Americans waited tables and fed the kitchen stoves. A "southern" ideal of racial order and leisure was married to a "northern" approach to enterprise.

Chapter 5 details the Aunt Jemima advertising campaign after World War I, when Young's agency revamped and expanded the reach of the product's national effort. This is how the campaign was designed to work: It first established a time and place—a large plantation in Louisiana, either just before or after the Civil War. The manner in which the ads told a story that straddled the war established the continuity of the product, from its Old South origins to its development in the industrial North. At the plantation we meet Colonel Higbee, the aging, dignified, and bearded owner of a collection of slaves, most notably Aunt Jemima, who tend to his huge white-pillared mansion. We also meet an unending stream of white relatives and guests who arrive for Christmas and Thanksgiving dinners and dances and friends who just "happen in" from hundreds of miles away. They gather for huge banquets and share long stories, and they sometimes stay for weeks. The central character in all the revelry—the person who makes it all possible—is Aunt Jemima, the deliverer not only of unending stacks of pancakes but fish and fowl and all the other wonderful things they eat. (Presumably, she and the rest of the slaves are slaughtering the animals, cleaning up the dishes, and emptying the chamberpots as well.) The missing character is the southern mistress, for Colonel Higbee is not complemented by a lady of the house, and the tableaux presented in James Webb Young's advertisements for the pancake mix invited real, living white housewives to join in the fantasy of Colonel Higbee's plantation, figuratively to buy into the woman known as Aunt Jemima—the slave in a box. In the ad campaign's strategy, white housewives were not supposed to aspire to be the black Aunt Jemima as they might have aspired to be the white Betty Crocker. They were offered the opportunity to have Aunt Jemima, securing a type of femininity, whiteness, and class uplift through the display of a popular image of black womanhood.

The analysis of ads in chapter 5, however, requires this disclaimer: No historian can say with absolute certainty why the Aunt Jemima campaign worked, because the voices extant are largely those of the creators of the campaign, not the targets. We can easily establish what James Webb Young intended to do in designing the ads, and we can judge that the campaign in both its creative concept and its increased exposure for the product significantly improved sales of Aunt Jemima's mix. The type of market research that might have told us whether and to what degree white housewives bought into Young's fable is not extant—and there is no evidence that Young or his colleagues attempted to collect such data. Even today, with more advanced techniques for interrogating consumers and tracking their behavior, advertisers are sometimes unable to determine precisely why a campaign failed, or even why it succeeded. As the authors of one of the most recent advertising school textbooks wrote, "If we are to begin to understand advertising in contemporary society, then, it is essential that we constantly keep in mind the frequent uncertainty of the process."[12] So while I argue in chapter 5 for the interpretation of the ads I have given, I also note other possible interpretations of the images that might have appealed to women.

The sixth and final chapter follows Aunt Jemima's image into contemporary times, as the seemingly benign character increasingly became the focus of anger from African Americans. As the limited market research regarding African-American consumers in the 1930s established, blacks were always repelled by Aunt Jemima. In the 1940s and 1950s, the term *Aunt Jemima* was converted by them—especially among boys "playing the dozens"—into a form of insult, a simultaneous attack on masculinity and racial solidarity that would surface in debates during the Civil Rights and Black Power movements. Local chapters of the NAACP would concentrate on blocking appearances by actresses depicting Aunt Jemima in an effort to ensure that whites understood that the woman in the bandanna was an insult. Finally, I review the ways in which Aunt Jemima's owners attempted to respond to protests by altering her image, instead of dropping it, and speculate on the prospect that she can continue to be useful as an advertising trademark in the twenty-first century.

There are two reasons why Aunt Jemima is a worthwhile subject and not just an old joke. The first is that there is no other source that explains racial imagery this way, bringing together the Old South myth, the New South creed, the history of slavery, women's history, African-American history, and the history of advertising in a way that coherently explains how they all intersect. Aunt Jemima's history uniquely demonstrates the ancestry of one of our time's everyday objects, a box on a grocery shelf that can only be understood by looking at how American manufacturing and marketing developed around World War I, and how its advertising was linked to events even earlier on the minstrel stage and the southern plantation. Aunt Jemima might seem an unlikely guide through American history, but often the best way to investigate a household is to knock on the servants' entrance instead of the front door.

Recent works have attempted, with different measures of success, to explain what Aunt Jemima means to America, but they seem generally to take a viewpoint lacking historical context. The book *Celluloid Mammies and Ceramic Uncles*, while providing an excellent survey of racial imagery in American popular culture, from minstrel shows to the movie *Little Shop of Horrors*, does not discuss where Aunt Jemima came from, or why she works in the imagination of racists (they're just racists; that is all). *The Myth of Aunt Jemima*, a recent collection of useful essays on southern women, only mentions Aunt Jemima in its title, which at least demonstrates that the name still has some sort of instant recognition that does not have to be explained, especially if one is discussing southern black women. Likewise, Kenneth W. Goings's *Mammy and Uncle Mose: Black Collectibles and American Stereotyping* is a valuable guide to the large number of black collectible items that are being traded in increasing numbers, but its focus is mostly on the history and trade of the items themselves, for he does not aim to explore the Aunt Jemima story in depth. The most recent and best work on Aunt Jemima is Marilyn Kern-Foxworth's *Aunt Jemima, Rastus, and Uncle Ben*, a general history of racist images in advertising. Kern-Foxworth, a journalism professor, provides a wide-ranging and at times deeply personal survey of how images dating from slave advertisements persist in contemporary society. In doing so, she also offers the most complete history of Aunt Jemima to date. What Kern-Foxworth does not attempt to do, however, is explain in detail the mechanics of the Aunt Jemima campaign—why, at a certain place and time, it worked and how it was sustained over time. To do so, one must historicize the image and look at what was going on in the world outside the box.

Some historians have done just that, although not with Aunt Jemima advertisements. In *White on Black: Images of Africa and Blacks in Western Popular Culture*, Jan Nederveen Pieterse surveyed the development of Western stereotypes of black people over two centuries. In his analysis of European and American advertising, he noted similarities in advertisements for familiar products such as tobacco and coffee on both sides of the Atlantic, many of which featured smiling darkies (like the eponymous emblem of Darkie toothpaste) and cartoonish pickaninnies. Many advertisements made direct references to color, none more so than advertisements for soaps, which in the late nineteenth century and early twentieth century repeatedly implied that blacks could "wash themselves white" with the product. One 1910 ad for a brand of soap produced in the Netherlands depicted a grinning white child telling his black counterpart, "If only you too had washed with Dobelmann's Buttermilk Soap." The intent of the advertisements was not to indicate that blacks truly could wash away their color, Pierterse pointed out, but to amuse whites by confirming in a cartoonish way that "educating and civilizing blacks [was] a vain labor, just like trying to wash them white."[13] Pierterse demonstrated how one could crack—in this sense, meaning decode—the jokes advertisers cracked with their target audiences.

Pieterse's objective was to demonstrate how the growth of advertising and mass production was interwoven with color, class, and gender hierarchies under European colonialism; how the world outside products shaped the ways that products were pitched to consumers. More recently, Anne McClintock, in *Imperial Leather: Race, Gender and Sexuality in the Colonial Context*, broadened and sharpened aspects of Pieterse's analysis by demonstrating the intersection of commodity racism and commodity sexism that "racialized domesticity," again largely through an analysis of turn-of-the-century British soap ads. During the 1880s and 1890s Monkey soap was advertised with an illustration of a monkey holding a frying pan, with a large bar of the soap before him. The soap's motto promised to do away with women's labor: "No dust, no dirt, no labor." As McClintock described, the seemingly incongruous combination of soap, monkey, and frying pan was an attempt to represent domesticity without depicting women actually at work:

> The Victorian middle-class house was structured round the fundamental contradictions between women's paid and unpaid domestic work. As women were driven from paid work in mines, factories, shops and trades to private, unpaid work in the home, domestic work became economically undervalued and the middle-class definition of femininity figured the "proper" woman as one who did not work for profit. At the same time, a cordon sanitaire of racial degeneration was thrown around those women who did work publicly and visibly for money. What could not be formulated into the industrial formation (women's domestic economic value) was displaced onto the invented domain of the primitive, and thereby disciplined and contained.[14]

McClintock, like Pierterse, also offered examples of advertisements in which blacks were depicted as using soap products in an attempt to wash away their skin color. It is important to note that McClintock described a situation considerably different from the circumstances that surrounded Aunt Jemima's development; the soap ads were developed in a time in which British women were exiting paid employment, while Aunt Jemima advertisements came as more women entered paid employment other than domestic work. However, in both cases the aim of the advertisements in question was to remove every trace of white female labor by employing blacks to represent the product. Pierterse and McClintock seem to point the way toward understanding Aunt Jemima: Look at the ads but look at the world around them also. That is the way to crack the code underlying the innocuous joke.

The second reason to pursue this subject is not what it says about the past but about the present. In an age of supposedly rampant political correctness, in which our sensibilities allegedly have been strained to an incredulous degree, there remains a picture of an antebellum slave, a minstrel show figure, a (formerly) bandanna-wearing "aunt," on a very popular line of processed foods. This strikes me as very interesting. Either Aunt Jemima has escaped our attention, or perhaps her existence is evidence that the times are not as politically correct as they are assumed to be. It is possible to argue that a face on a pancake box is a rather trivial source of information on our time, but I disagree. The things we see and use every day—and even more to the point, ignore—tell us much about ourselves. They are, to use one of Baldwin's phrases, "the evidence of things not seen." The figures that are made ordinary, those subtle stereotypes, in some ways are the best indicators of what our values are. We might pass by Aunt Jemima without thinking, just the way we might walk by a Confederate memorial without thinking about who put it there, and why. But I believe there is a usefulness in asking this convoluted question: When we are not thinking, what are we not thinking about? Understanding the way the mammy was merchandised, and the way she is still bought and sold today, might teach us a great deal about our past and our present, not only how times have changed but how they have remained the same.

That is an appropriate enough answer to Baldwin's question, for now. The author and essayist himself struggled to come up with a solid explanation for why Aunt Jemima sprang into the white mind. His own description of her personality, and that of Uncle Tom, was complex and yet typically still searching for some elusive conclusiveness: "They knew us better than we knew them. This was the piquant flavoring to our national joke, it lay beneath our uneasiness as it lay behind our benevolence: Aunt Jemima and Uncle Tom, our creations, at the last evaded us; they had a life—their own perhaps, a better life than ours—and they would never tell us what it was."[15] That is because Aunt Jemima and Uncle Tom lived their lives in the fantasy world of whiteness, the only place where they were possible, even though they invaded the world of Baldwin and every other black American. Can you explain Aunt Jemima to a black person in a way that makes her seem benign, comforting, or any of the other things she has been to a white person?

Baldwin's final observation about Aunt Jemima came on his deathbed in Paris in 1988, as his biographer and friend David Leeming described. Baldwin asked Leeming to travel from the United States to visit him with a few artifacts from America: boxes of Aunt Jemima pancake mix and syrup. Leeming wrote that after he unwrapped the package, Baldwin laughed and said, "We can't escape our culture." It is important to remember that Baldwin, throughout his work, essentially defined "our culture" as being both black and white: White people cannot escape "our culture" either. Aunt Jemima is as much the problem of white people as she is of blacks. The punchline to Leeming's story, though, goes like this: Baldwin, consumed with cancer, woke up later that day and asked for pancakes. He ate them and shortly after had to be carried to the commode to vomit them. Leeming wrote, "My suggestion that it was 'Aunt Jemima's revenge' brought miserable laughter."[16] Certain jokes are funnier for some people than others, of course.

2 Someone's in the Kitchen: Mammies, Mothers, and Others

I've seed the first en de last. Never you mind me.
—Dilsey Gibson in William Faulkner,
The Sound and the Fury

A shadowy figure works within the kitchen walls of the southern plantation household of history and fiction. Most people acknowledge her presence, but their memories of her appearance and actions vary widely. She might have been an obsequious servant who lived to meet her master's beck and call, or she could have been an embryonic black militant. She might have raised, even nursed, her master's children at the expense of her own, or she might have used her position to protect her family. Just as often as she is described as her mistress's most trusted lieutenant, she is relegated to the role of comic relief. She is sometimes said to be a key to understanding the rules of sex and race in the Old South, but those who claimed to love her the most might have considered such a statement to be ludicrous. And although she is undeniably southern in origin, she maintains her essential characteristics when she travels north.

The mammy is the historical basis for Aunt Jemima, the happy, devoted, simple woman who filled ad pages in the early twentieth century. One cannot understand Aunt Jemima's appeal—the heartstrings she was designed to pull—unless one also understands the mammy's value as a popular icon. The problem with studying the mammy's long and complex career in the American imagination, however, is that different people have described her in markedly different ways. There is a traditional picture, the stereotyped silly, happy slave totally devoted to the service of her white family. But historians and novelists have disputed the reality of this image, some seeking to explain all that apparent servility some other way and others seeking to disprove that any such person ever existed.

The problem is that the real woman who would be the basis for Aunt Jemima seems trapped in the amber of southern history, her image well maintained but the reality of her life open to interpretation. It is indisputable that there were slave women called "mammy," that these women supervised other house slaves, cooked, and watched children. It also is indisputable that even children and housewives of postbellum America fondly remember a woman called mammy, who played much the same role. But even those who are absolutely certain that they know the person called mammy have trouble explaining everything they think she did. She has been assembled into a historical and literary figure by historians and writers ordering from such a virtual Chinese menu of traits—sycophancy, loyalty, girth, nurture, passion, stupidity, sacrifice, selfishness, piety—that any two versions of mammy can seem unlikely residents of the same universe. While someone called mammy persists in our library books and on our television sets and theater screens (not to mention pancake boxes), the images vary depending upon who describes her. When people describe mammy in novels, histories, diaries, or oral accounts, her meaning changes to fit the way they understand the world. As much as she is universally understood as a servant literally, she also is a servant in an abstract sense. The mammy was a servant, for example, of writers who wished to describe slavery as a humane institution, and she also helped those who have tried to broaden our understanding of the tragedy of slavery.

The purpose of this chapter is not to uncover the absolute, single historical truth about the mammy but to demonstrate how others tried to explain her and what a malleable figure she has been in American history. Her person represents a territorial struggle in our country's writing, with depictions changing with evolving ideas about race, men, women, and class. Writers and historians sought to demonstrate the truth of their worldviews by explaining how she might have fit in. If the mammy had not possessed such a strong hold on American literary and historical imagination, Aunt Jemima never would have become a powerful advertising trademark. Various descriptions of mammy usually reflect what an author has to say about some larger issue. The cumulative efforts of writers and historians created the literary and historical mammy, a nest of internal contradictions, by contributing important pieces to the puzzle but leaving out others. This is not to say that some accounts are correct, and others are not—almost any individual depiction or observation can be corroborated by someone's memory—but that most are missing something that comes with considering a group of people under a supposedly all-encompassing stereotype such as the mammy, regardless of whether the depiction of that group is positive or negative. Depending on the author's location, accounts of mammy range from simplistic white supremacy, to arguments that subsume race within class, to interpretations that deny her very existence. No matter what historians, novelists, diarists, and advertising executives did, they breathed life into the sometimes beloved, sometimes hated southern mammy. Or rather, they took the lives of real persons and simplified them into their preferred versions of a historical stereotype.

A discussion of the mammy begins and ends with how slavery has been remembered. Depictions of her turned not simply on whether the authors approved or disapproved of the peculiar institution, however, but on how they viewed the entire social order of the slave South and its implications for men and women of both races and all classes. In the late nineteenth century, historians, diarists, and novelists set a standard for depicting the woman in question, one that persisted through most of the twentieth century. As a new generation of writers began to reexamine slavery more critically after the 1960s, however, questions about how mammy fit in remained a key. She was always a useful person in slaveholding households; she would be useful to a century's worth of writers as well.

Justifying and Unjustifying Slavery and Jim Crow

Mammy's origins are found not only in studies of antebellum society but in the ways different people attempted to describe the postemancipation South. As Patricia Morton and many others have noted, turn-of-the-century historiography assumed a particularly racist character as a "pillar of Jim Crow's defense."[1] Black women as well as men were the targets of white male authors, but the chief image of black women was the lustful Jezebel, not the loyal mammy. Jezebel, who supposedly lured white men into interracial sex, was a woman turned loose on southern white men now that they no longer owned her.

In 1889, the year that the hideous smile of a cartoonish mammy first appeared on a sack of pancake flour, Philip Alexander Bruce published *The Plantation Negro as a Freeman*. Bruce linked the savagery he saw in black males with the failure of black mothers to instill proper moral values in their children. The female former slaves "molded the institution of marriage," and "to them its present degradation is chiefly ascribable."[2] Although the argument seemed to be over the nature of motherhood in general—white and black—Bruce made the nature of motherhood something explainable by the nature of race. James F. Rhodes, who condemned slavery, nevertheless took the view that slave women were inherently licentious, even after they were freed, and spelled out the consequences for whites. In his *History of the United States*, published in 1892, he depicted slave women in general as welcoming intercourse with their masters, eager to sire children of mixed blood. The charms of the slave woman led masters to contaminate their race and create an affront to "noble and refined [white] women." Because it allowed white male authors to explain slave rape and the resultant children of mixed race in a way that shifted responsibility to the black woman, the Jezebel theme had a long career, despite scholarly disputes over whether the slave woman was really such a "good breeder."[3]

As late as 1941 W. J. Cash, in his landmark *The Mind of the South*, wrote that the slave woman had been taught "easy compliance" in sexual liaisons. She had been "torn from her tribal restraints" enforced by black men and white men, apparently irreparably. Although Cash's work marked a new stage in the criticism of the antebellum South, including an attack on "florid notions" about the sexual purity of white plantation women and ridiculing ideas that placed them on a pedestal above passion (perhaps their own "tribal restraint"), he depicted black women in the Jezebel tradition.[4]

At the same time that Jezebel reminded whites of the importance of maintaining the color line, however, the historical legend of the mammy was blossoming, too. Unlike Jezebel, who represented the nightmarish consequences of lascivious black women free to tempt white men, she affirmed the other side of the story, how black women behaved when under proper white control. Her story dovetails neatly with another historical image developed after the Civil War—a fable born of what the historian Joel Williamson has termed the "white reconstruction" of the 1880s, a time when the "essence of the old order, the sense of Southernness and whiteness," rose out of the ashes of the federal Reconstruction of 1865–77. Those who held what Williamson calls a "conservative" view sought to reconstruct race relations along the lines of the prewar South, reviving paternalistic appeals and calling for the "ungrateful children" of Africa to return, if not to slavery, then to their former place as charges of white masters. The conservative view Williamson describes was not unprogressive; in fact, it was adopted by those who wished to promote a "New South." The term *New South* is admittedly ambiguous, one shaped by contemporaries and "useful as a propaganda device to influence the direction and control of Southern development." It was a rallying cry for postwar redeemers who seized the term to build support for a bewildering number of causes, from southern communism to social Darwinism; in other words, it was used for whatever type of new society reformers believed would best suit their backward region.[5]

The importance of the New South for this discussion, however, is that it necessitated the invention of an Old South, a romantic fable of "white reconstruction" that prevailed (and to some extent still prevails) on both sides of the Mason-Dixon Line. The Old South was a nearly perfect land, "studded with magnolias," filled with sprawling plantations, and populated by beautiful women and courtly gentlemen, whites who led lives of leisure. The work that had to be done was performed by black slaves, who were "lovable, amusing and devoted." Spokesmen for the New South, regardless of the particular program they advocated, rarely failed to praise the golden era that had passed with the Civil War and Reconstruction. They drew on deeply held beliefs about their culture and the North's established in literature and politics during the long debate over slavery—the idea that the nation was populated with "Cavaliers and Yankees"—that could not be erased by the loss of the Civil War. A commitment to progress was linked to nostalgia for a world that never existed, even among northern advocates of a New South. A call for change required reassurance that old values were not being put aside, that in fact progress was rooted in an understanding and approving look at the past. As C. Vann Woodward noted in *Origins of the New South*, "The deeper the involvements in commitments to the New Order, the louder the protests of loyalty to the Old." These protests went beyond politics and were evident in literature, music, and journalism and in organizations such as the Kappa Alpha order and various associations of the Sons and Daughters of the Confederacy.[6]

The mammy was a key ingredient in the Old South fable because of her role among its happy, devoted slaves. As the servant and biological opposite of the delicate, pure, ultrafeminine southern woman of the Old South, the large, strong, sexless mammy provided a needed contrast. As "the foremost Big House slave," she not only complemented white womanhood but served as the home's domestic manager. She was more than a servant of white folks; the mammy of the Old South mythology was a collaborator in their society, a reassuring figure who, despite her breeding, comforted her white betters, offered advice, kept black males in line, and put hot food on the table. However the image of the mammy might not have squared with reality, it soothed white guilt over slavery and uplifted white womanhood through sheer contrast and by keeping white women out of the kitchen. She saved them from work but also from worry and seemingly cleared up tensions between white men and white women, between masters and servants, by clarifying sexual and work roles as well as racial lines. The ultimate proof of the mammy's staying power as a popular emblem of the Old South might be the Black Mammy Memorial Association, a Georgia women's group that in 1910 sought to establish a vocational school to train black women in the "spirit of service" of mammydom—to make them just what they used to be, according to popular myth, and thus implicitly to make white men and women just what they used to be, too.[7] The image of the mammy reflected the desire and the reality of white male efforts to keep both black and white women under their control; at the same time, it also revealed what white men and white women tended to think about each other, and black men, too.

The "peak time for the glorification of the mammy," however, came long after Reconstruction or the early days of the New South movement. In her essay "The Development of the Mammy Image and Mythology," Cheryl Thurber noted that southern memoirs mentioned mammy most from about 1906 to 1912. Before 1906, Thurber wrote, mammies, as either fictional characters or real people, were used to describe "specific incidents in the life of a specific individual." But from about 1906 to the mid-1920s, "general odes to her virtue" were more the norm, as writers "tended to glorify the mammy in the abstract, as the idea rather than as a person."[8] Even as actual memories of the Old South were dimming, the popular myth of the mammy's world grew—or perhaps, one might speculate, the popular myth grew because the actual memories had grown dim. But if actual memories were few, there was a reality that transported mammy beyond the Old South: the presence of black women in New South households, for virtually the only source of employment for black women, South and North, was domestic work; black women would even replace white immigrants as the primary source of domestic servants in the North in the early twentieth century.

The problem with separating popular myth from history becomes evident when we consider the degree to which history itself has been popular myth. The most prominent turn-of-the-century historians might have been expected to determine whether the mammy was a real historical figure or to what extent the image shaped by New South boosters was simply a creation of Old South masters and mistresses. They might have asked whether the mammy worked to obscure other dramas in southern society. Instead, they continued to cast the mammy in a romantic light, using her as a vessel to express their approval of the Old South—and its racial and sexual hierarchies—and to call for a new one. They did not challenge the masters' fond memories of a loyal servant or the postwar image of a magnolia-studded paradise—the paradise where, according to advertisements, Aunt Jemima lived.

In *The Old South*, published in 1892, the historian and novelist Thomas Nelson Page praised the mammy as a "universally beloved" and "honored member" of the white family, second only in authority to "that of the mistress and master." Page especially emphasized the mammy's loyalty to white children, even if that loyalty came at the expense of paying attention to her own. U. B. Phillips's *American Negro Slavery*, though more scholarly in presentation, picked up all of Page's themes concerning the mammy. The book, published in 1918, affirmed that "the [white] children supplied" all the proof needed of the mammy's exalted position. (Phillips did not look for proof from black men, women, or children.) She was, in other words, a racial property acceptable because the prize of motherhood—nurturing, receiving, and returning love—was really the thing owned. Phillips argued that black and white lives were intertwined, paradoxically, because everyone understood how they were separate. The mammy is particularly important in this regard because, although Phillips did not directly say so, the aged mammy was no sexual threat, and apparently she was free from sexual exploitation by white men.[9] (Jezebel was afoot to explain why that phenomenon occurred.) In *American Negro Slavery* the happy mammy was a symbol of proper order, living proof of the racial and sexual harmony that results when blacks and whites occupy their separate and well-understood roles, and a denial of any conflict between masters and mistresses as well as blacks and whites. What better spokesman for the age of Jim Crow, one might ask, than Phillips?

In his novel *Red Rock*, Page touched on the mammy's dilemma in a white world turned upside down by Reconstruction. Throughout the 1899 novel (which was the fifth best-selling book of the year),[10] the characters are predictably drawn: All the Radical Republicans are evil, the freedman is treacherous, and the noble Gray family, which resides on the Red Rock plantation, is full of honorable men and virtuous ladies. Page goes so far as to hint that Red Rock is somewhere near the original site of the Garden of Eden, and one of his southern gentlemen, Steve Allen, is a Christian martyr fed to carpetbagging lions. The mammy is a minor character in *Red Rock*, but Page uses her early and effectively to establish what good-hearted blacks hope for after emancipation. In 1865 a slave owner returning from Appomattox attempts to set a wage scale for his slaves but is rebuffed by Mammy Krenda, who is afraid he will charge her room and board, and who wants to know whether her mistress also will be receiving wages. Page's fiction is no different from his history (which could be regarded as mostly fictional, too); mammy would be lost without her white family. But as important as the idea of family, black and white, is to Page, it is not clear just how much the white family would be lost without its black mother. Even though a reading of *Red Rock* clearly shows how much Krenda and her white family are allied—against those who would disorder the South, northerners, and even other blacks—we do not see this member of the ideological family as a member of the real family. She is a racial dependent when slavery passes, not a mother, regardless of how strong her ties to the white children of the household were. Much Reconstruction literature, of course, is crudely polemical and concentrates on the planter class and its former slaves instead of, for instance, the yeoman, but it could be argued that Page's mammy, like the rest of the people in the book, is exceptionally one-dimensional. As one of the author's biographers noted, "Character delineation is certainly not the most impressive aspect of Page's fiction."[11]

It is important to mention that people do remember women in some respects like Mammy Krenda, who would have refused pay to maintain her place in the order. For example, Hazel Lambert, born in 1893 to a Mississippi household of black servants, is included in Susan Tucker's collection of oral histories of domestic servants. Lambert describes the time a mammy (she uses the word), "Cookie," was found to have a "20-pound tumor" in her stomach and was hospitalized for a month. Lambert said she and her husband visited Cookie every day but replaced her in the kitchen. The day after Cookie was released from the hospital, Lambert's husband stepped out to get the paper and found her sitting on the stoop. As Lambert described it: "He said, 'Cookie, what's wrong?' And she said, 'Nothing. I've just come to help.' And so we said, 'Well, we can't pay.' And she said, 'Who's talking about money?' She was just so grateful. And so she stayed and she cooked."[12] Both Page and Lambert were full, as Tucker notes, of the "happy days of the Old South," particularly the racial order it included. It did not occur to Page or to Lambert that the mammy might have been motivated by more pressing concerns than maintaining racial order—the immediate need to feed and shelter herself and her family, for instance, or a bond of real empathy with a white person in the household. It never occurred to either that the mammy might have been been playing a role to suit her own purposes.

Thomas Dixon improved on Page's "rape of the South" formula, moving the plot more quickly, avoiding unnecessary detail, adding more sensational violence, and ultimately selling many more books.[13] The Radical Republicans suffer even a worse fate than in Page's novel, since Simon Legree of *Uncle Tom's Cabin* is reintroduced as one of their leaders. In *The Leopard's Spots* (1902) and *The Clansman* (1905), however, the mammy plays the same role, except that she is perhaps less noble and more stupid, as are all his newly freed slaves, even the "loyal" ones. Still, Dixon's mammy protects the white household she knows. In *The Leopard's Spots* vagrant freedmen are ransacking the North Carolina home of the hero and Klan leader Charles Gaston. Gaston's mother sees "a great herd of negroes trampling down her flowers, laughing, cracking vulgar jokes, and swarming over the porches." She hears footsteps in the hall and perceives the "unmistakable odor of perspiring negroes." Mrs. Gaston faints in anticipation of meeting that fate worse than death. Then, "there was a sudden charge as of an armed host, the sound of blows, a wild scramble, and the house was cleared. Aunt Eve with a fire shovel, Charlie with a broken hoe handle, and Dick with a big black snake whip had cleared the air." The shovel-wielding Aunt Eve has joined the men in the rescue effort, like Mammy Krenda, a protector of a white family. She stays on the front steps, shaking her shovel, and yells, "Des put yo big flat hoofs in dis house ergin! I'll split yo heads wide open! You black cattle!" Sadly, Aunt Eve does not intervene in time to save Gaston's fragile mother, who is literally mortified by the threatened attack. The mammy of *The Clansman*, as well its more famous film adaptation *Birth of a Nation*, is much the same, happy to have a properly ordered relationship with a white family and serving as a counterpoint to the uppity mulatto from the North, Silas Lynch, as well as the rapacious southern-born black brute, Gus. When Aunt Cindy learns that her husband, Uncle Aleck, has purchased forty acres and a mule from a "gubment" agent, she, like the rest of the white family, eyes him with contempt and mocks him when the deed turns out to be phony.[14] Throughout his work Dixon describes black women ready to protect white women from black men, black women who join white men to ridicule black husbands, and black women who have intense, personal stakes in membership in white families. They serve a family by serving the master's racial and gender supremacy. But the mammies do not do so because of some bond that transcends the racial line; they are more like domesticated animals who bark when wolves come to white families' doorsteps. Dixon's general call for white supremacy shapes the mammy's characterization. Unlike Page or Phillips, he does not depict her as a superhuman earth mother for two races; his sentimentality is reserved solely for whites. The image of Aunt Jemima in advertising campaigns would be more like Mammy Krenda of *Red Rock* or the women depicted in Phillips's allegedly historical research than Dixon's Aunt Eve. Sentimentality about mammies and support for white supremacy were not mutually exclusive and would be a hallmark of Aunt Jemima ads; as a white supremacist, Dixon was exceptional for his relative lack of sentiment toward black servants.

Not all of Page's and Dixon's contemporaries in fiction writing, however, held such narrowly paternalistic or white supremacist views. Mark Twain's first contribution to the *Atlantic Monthly*, "A True Story, Repeated Word for Word As I Heard It," gives the lie to the image of the happy servant. This early work of Twain's is important for at least two reasons. First, it makes the mammy the subject of her story rather than a stock character, stating her account the way that she told it and allowing her frustrations to come to the surface with tremendous persuasive power. Although Twain narrates the story, framing it with a white male voice, the structure intentionally emphasizes his ignorance and surprise at the woman's tale. Second, considerable evidence exists that Twain was directly influenced by a black woman in the writing of "A True Story." In *Was Huck Black?* Shelley Fisher Fishkin examines the influence of African-American culture on Twain's prose and explains how conversations with the former slave Mary Ann McCord moved Twain first to tell "A True Story" to friends and then, satisfied with its effect, to write it down. Twain's own journals display his painstaking effort not only to pass on the facts of the mammy's tale but to duplicate her manner of speaking—as the title indicates, "word for word as I heard it."[15]

Twain's Aunt Rachel is introduced by "Mr. C———" (Mr. Clemens?), an educated white man who ostensibly narrates the tale, although most of it is in Rachel's voice. As he observes the mammy, "mighty of frame and stature," singing and laughing through her work, he innocently and ignorantly asks her, "Aunt Rachel, how is it that you've lived sixty years and never had any trouble?" Rachel, who can hardly believe Mr. C——— is serious in asking, spends the rest of the short story detailing her life as a slave, her separation from her family, her sale at an auction in Richmond:

> Dey put chains on us an' put us on a stan' as high as dis po'ch—twenty foot high—an' all de people stood aroun', crowds an' crowds. An' dey'd come up dah an' look at us all roun', an' squeeze our arm, an' make us git up an' walk, an' den say, "Dis one too ole," or "Dis one lame," or "Dis one don't 'mount to much." An' dey sole my ole man, an' took him away, an' dey begin to sell my chil'en an' take dem away, an' I begin to cry; an' de man say, "Shet up yo' damn blubberin'," an' hit me on de mouf wid his han'. An' when de las' one was gone but my little Henry, I grab' him clost up to my breas' so, an' I ris up an' says, "You sha'n't take him away," I says; "I'll kill de man dat teches him!" I says. But my little Henry whisper an' say, "I gwyne to run away, an' den I work an' buy yo' freedom." Oh, bless de chile, he always so good! But dey got him—dey got him, de men did; but I took and tear de clo'es off of 'em an' beat 'em over de head wid my chain; an' dey give it to me, too, but I didn't mine dat.

Eventually, Aunt Rachel is reunited with Henry, but after the harrowing description of her life, she tells Mr. C——— that "I hain't had no trouble—an' no joy!" "A True Story" was described by the *Atlantic Monthly* as a "humorous sketch," something, as Fishkin notes, it clearly was not, and it confounded the reviewers who nonetheless recommended it for the compelling story and skillful use of dialect. Twain as "Mr. C———" uncovered the sorrow beneath the surface, the woman's will to endure tremendous hardship, by simply asking and then by letting her tell the story in her own words.[16]

Twain's Aunt Rachel might have been the basis for Aunt Roxy, a character he was to develop later in the novel *Pudd'nhead Wilson*. Roxy, as one critic has noted, fits uneasily into any classification or category. She is at times loving and compassionate, deceitful and dishonest, accommodating and subversive, transcending stereotype and moving most of the plot of *Pudd'nhead*, which was published in 1894. Twain's Aunt Roxy was a departure from conventional mammies in her physical appearance: "From Roxy's manner of speech, a stranger would have expected her to be black, but she was not. Only one-sixteenth of her was black, and that sixteenth did not show." Twain went so far as to emphasize Roxy's beauty, at least by white conventions, writing that "her face was intelligent and comely—even beautiful." But most impressively, Roxy is the central character of *Pudd'nhead Wilson*; the title character is secondary, as the traditional stock character of the mammy takes center stage throughout.[17]

The light-skinned mammy switches her infant "black" son with her master's "white" child in order to keep him from being sold down the river. She gains her freedom and becomes a maid on a steamboat, but ultimately returns to slavery in order to help her son out of financial trouble—and winds up being sold down the river herself. In the end she confronts the ungrateful child, who later is revealed not only as an imposter but a murderer when the baby switch is discovered in court. The complicated plot of *Pudd'nhead* enabled Twain to explore questions of human identity, as the "white" child who is swapped with the "black" infant grows up with the mannerisms of a slave, while the imposter, Roxy's son, is "white" until the moment his true racial identity is revealed in court, and then he, too, winds up being sold down the river. Roxy is enigmatic, but what is most striking about Twain's depiction of her is the manner in which her character, created at the height of Jim Crow laws and lynchings across the South, defies supposedly rigid standards of racial identity, is often depicted as intellectually superior to the whites around her, and moves the plot throughout—although for most of the book, everyone is oblivious to her actions. Twain took the stock character employed in the background of a happy and orderly South—the South of Dixon and Page—and made her story the story, complete with motives none of the master race even guessed. Roxy, like Rachel, is the mammy as a survivor, negotiating an existence between truths and lies, only superficially the loyal woman of southern wishful thinking.[18]

Lifting Them Up, Holding Them Back

White male authors like Phillips, Page, Dixon, and Twain did not have the last word on the mammy. Black and mixed-race writers offered opinions about her in a completely different context. In particular, they asked what the mammy meant to her race, especially in the African-American struggle for economic and social advancement. Some saw the mammy figure as literally the sheltering mother of a people on the rise, while others depicted her as a person blacks had to leave behind on the path to equality.

Carter G. Woodson, arguably the greatest African-American scholar, while noting that "the Negroes of this country keenly resent any such thing as the mention of the Plantation Black Mammy," paused in 1930 to praise the "Negro washerwoman" as the "towering personage in the life of the Negro." Woodson said the washerwoman gave her life in sacrifice to her race before and after emancipation, abandoning her own children to bear the burden of serving a "despotic mistress," offering compassion to fellow slaves, and helping newly emancipated households step toward economic independence by continued toil in a time when "land was cheap, but money was scarce."[19] Woodson's mammy continued to be the head of the household even after the fall of the Big House. In a way, Woodson said, she employed all the traits she learned in slavery to nurture the black family in freedom. Woodson simultaneously denied that the obsequious house slave had existed while acknowledging other things that white supremacists also found so handy and comforting. Woodson did not wish to acknowledge mammy as a second mother to white children, but he did see her as the mother of her own race, nurturing it to economic empowerment. So while he recognized some of the same traits emphasized by white supremacists, he described the "woman's work" performed by mammy as something different than service to the white patriarchy. An unasked question, at that point, was whether she was in service to a black patriarchy instead.

Eight years later Jessie W. Parkhurst emphasized those same traits even more forcefully. Parkhurst said that the mammy was "an acceptable symbol to whites and an unacceptable one to Negroes," but in many ways the mammy she described could suit either black or white ends. Parkhurst said the mammy had become an important but imaginary figure even in the minds of white southerners who had never met a black female slave. But Parkhurst turned to the children of the planter class, who had "a first hand and personal knowledge" of the mammy, for "insight into what she meant to southern society." Parkhurst, offering no critique of why planter-class children might have retained such memories, or how their remembrances might have been gilded over the years, summarized:

In the plantation household, the "Black Mammy" was self-respecting, independent, loyal, forward, gentle, captious, affectionate, true, strong, just, warm-hearted, compassionate-hearted, fearless, popular, brave, good, pious, quick-witted, capable, thrifty, proud, regal, courageous, superior, skillful, tender, queenly, dignified, neat, quick, tender, competent, possessed with a temper, trustworthy, faithful, patient, tyrannical, sensible, discreet, efficient, careful, harsh, devoted, truthful, neither apish nor servile.[20]

Parkhurst was not seeking to mock the legendary mammy through over-statement of her skills. The mammy, Parkhurst wrote, was a "prime minister" in the Big House and was rewarded for her service with greater personal freedom and a less physically rigorous workload. In addition, her children were protected from punishment or sale. She wielded the greatest authority among slaves and children of both races and "often nursed her master's child at one breast and her own at the other." Later she taught white children "the proper forms of etiquette, of deportment to all of the people of the plantation, the proper forms of address and the proper distances to maintain."[21] Parkhurst's "prime minister" sounds an awful lot like a mother. Parkhurst allowed that the mammy did teach slave children some of their lost culture, such as snatches of African dialect and tales later popularized by Joel Chandler Harris, but she defined the accomplishments of the mammy as enforcing the master's rules, helping the other slaves to follow them, and minimizing punishment when they were broken. The mammy taught white children when to speak and not to speak, how to dress and eat, and told black children what whites expected of them, too.

Explicit throughout Parkhurst's argument is the idea that these rules became especially useful later, when African Americans sought to advance as a class. As Kevin Gaines has shown, such concerns about deportment and hard work were typical among many members of the African-American elite. It should not be surprising that an advocate of black "uplift" might have focused on a strong, disciplined figure that emphasized the merits of hard work and proper behavior. However, Parkhurst and Woodson were atypical in dwelling on an inherently matriarchal figure, when most of the arguments for black uplift centered on the need for stronger male figures heading households.[22] And even more contradictory, while neither Parkhurst nor Woodson wished to admit that mammy actually existed, they were willing to argue that the lessons a mammy must have learned in the Big House helped African Americans rise in the social strata after slavery.

One very prominent African-American novelist, however, sometimes seemed to argue that mammy had learned nothing about a proper class relationship in the years after slavery, and that her old survival strategies needed to be put away. "Thomas Dixon was writing the Negro down industriously and with popular success. Thomas Nelson Page was disguising the harshness of slavery under the mask of sentiment. The trend of public sentiment at that moment was distinctly away from the Negro." That was the succinct assessment of Charles W. Chesnutt, a black novelist who responded to characterizations like Page's and Dixon's in his own work, particularly *The Marrow of Tradition* (1901). The author of *The Conjure Woman, The Wife of His Youth*, and *Frederick Douglass* (all published in 1899), Chesnutt aimed to undermine white supremacy by subtly challenging the idyllic plantation and arguing, like Parkhurst and Woodson, that the former slave had come a long way. Unlike the Parkhurst and Woodson versions, however, the mammy seems more a liability than a savior in *The Marrow of Tradition*. Chesnutt was the grandson of a white North Carolinian and his black mistress, and he was raised in North Carolina during Reconstruction before becoming a relatively prosperous urban dweller. While some of his characters were, as Edward Ayers has noted, "black people of the sort readers expected to encounter in stories about the South," Chesnutt wrote about a wider range of African Americans than any other author of his time. Most prominent was a former slave named Julius, on the surface the archetypal superstitious darky, who used his storytelling to manipulate his white employers—Uncle Remus with an ulterior motive.[23] But in addition to Julius and the conjure woman, Chesnutt offered alternatives to plantation stereotypes, reflecting differences among blacks of different classes.

In *The Marrow of Tradition*, Chesnutt placed aspiring black professionals, meek former slaves, and radical black workers in proximity, juxtaposing the characters in a fictionalized account of the Wilmington, North Carolina, massacre of blacks in 1898. The most prominent black characters are Dr. Miller, a physician who saves the injured son of a white supremacist in the wake of antiblack violence, and his alter ego, Josh Green, who kills another white supremacist and is killed himself. Miller and Green, respectively, represent the practical, middle-class professional and the heroic but doomed lower-class worker. Representing the third black group, the loyal, simple retainers, is Mammy Jane. As the book opens, Major Carteret's sickly wife is about to give birth, and the silly and superstitious Jane prattles constantly, her comic relief breaking the tension not only for the reader but for the doctor and husband.[24]

Later, after Mammy Jane has suffered a bout with rheumatism, a new, younger black nurse, Miss Livy, arrives to assist, and the archetypal mammy tries to keep the "new Negro" in her place:

"Look a-here gal," said Mammy Jane sternly, "I wants you ter understan' dat you got ter take good keer er dis chile; fer I nussed his mammy dere, an' his gran'mammy befo' 'im, an' you is got a priv'lege dat mos' lackly you don' 'preciate. I wants you to 'memer, in yo' incomin's an' outgoin's, dat I got my eye on you, an' am gwine ter see dat you does yo' wo'k right."

"Do you need me for anything, ma'am?" asked the young nurse, who had stood before Mrs. Carteret, giving Mammy Jane a mere passing glance, and listening impassively to her harangue.[25]

The contrast between the nurses young and old is obvious in demeanor, dialect, and attitude; Miss Livy would never say "gwine ter see." Chesnutt used a variety of ethnic types, including not only traditional Stepin Fetchit males but a Chinese laundryman, to demonstrate the social progress blacks had made, to play what they once supposedly were against what they had become. The mammy is not an exemplar of white values or virtues as much as a signpost the race was passing on its way to more respectable roles, the racist-sexist stereotype sustained in the name of demonstrating a racial group's class progress. Chesnutt sought to tell an almost totally white popular audience the truth about its black neighbors, but at the price of maintaining one of the stereotypes that made Page and Dixon palatable, too. In the end Mammy Jane receives a fatal wound in the race riot that is the climax of *The Marrow of Tradition*. Her last words, as she falls unconscious, are, "Comin', missus, comin'!"[26]

It would be a mistake to view Mammy Jane as merely a parody, as Trudier Harris has observed. Harris argues that what Mammy Jane "says and how she acts in that role reflect the historical pattern of many black women after Emancipation, women who found themselves without identities beyond those of the white families for whom they had spent most of their lives working. To the extent that Mammy Jane reflects a truth that goes deeper than the type, her role is important. To the extent that she illustrates a major obstacle toward self-assertion for many of her contemporaries, her role is equally important."[27] What

Mammy Jane really represents, perhaps, is the differing interpretations that the mammy stereotype could inspire in advocates of black uplift. Woodson, Parkhurst, and Chesnutt describe a woman whose primary characteristics are devotion and hard work, but the novelist left her dying in the street, while the historians depicted her as sustaining a race. They did not disagree over what mammy was like, but their interpretations of the same traits led them to cast mammy in dissimilar roles.

Imitations of Life?

Three works by white women in the mid-twentieth century significantly shaped the mammy image. The authors Fannie Hurst, Margaret Mitchell, and Lillian Smith maintained a mammy that resembled Chesnutt's "buttertongued throwback," but they emphasized the mammy's role as a guidepost on the white woman's path in the social order. In the case of Hurst's book, the mammy's advice is ignored, resulting in tragedy. Mitchell's mammy is present mainly as a foil to Scarlett O'Hara's rebellious spirit—a reminder of that which Scarlett rebels against. And Smith's mammy is evidence herself of dysfunction in the larger social order.

Imitation of Life, Fannie Hurst's 1933 tearjerker, is the sentimental story of a white woman who exchanges her happiness for success in business, and it shaped the popular image of the mammy as black matriarch as much as any single work of this century. It inspired two films—one shortly after its publication and another in 1950. The women who played Hurst's mammy, Aunt Delilah, in the film (Louise Beavers in 1934 and Academy Award nominee Juanita Moore in the remake) set a visual standard for the popular mammy—Christian, stoic, large, loving, good-natured, and magical in the kitchen. She became more of a human figure than her predecessors in film, but more important, *Imitation of Life*, in book and film, constructed a mammy in contrast to the white northern career woman. Instead of speaking for a southern white version of femininity and domesticity, Hurst's Aunt Delilah is a national mammy. Delilah wants a family, a home, a traditional domestic order in her life and her employer's as well. But the white woman, Bea Pullman, seeks a nontraditional fortune in business and puts off domestic bliss until it is too late. The plot of *Imitation of Life* seems odd when we consider the nontraditional life Hurst chose for herself by leaving a safe but suffocating home in St. Louis to become a New York writer who explored the city's underbelly, ate and drank with Jazz Age authors and artists, and, most infamously, maintained a secret "trial marriage" for fifteen years (her autobiography, *Anatomy of Me*, reads much like one of her eighteen melodramatic novels). But Hurst struggled mightily with the very problem she assigned Bea—career versus love—and also with a deeper question of identity similar to the one suffered by Delilah's mulatto daughter Peola. The light-skinned Peola is mistaken for a white woman; Hurst came from a German-Jewish family that most of her friends assumed was Protestant—a misunderstanding that led one of Hurst's suitors to withdraw his proposal of marriage.[28]

Bea and Delilah, both widowed with children, meet by chance. Bea has searched for a live-in servant in Atlantic City, but none of the black women she encounters is willing to give up her home. She asks a "scrubbed, starchy looking negress" if she knows of anyone who wants work. Delilah replies: "Honey chile, I'll work for anything you is willin' to pay, and not take more'n mah share of your time for my young un, ef I kin get her and me a good roof over our heads. Didn' your maw always tell you a nigger woman was mos' reliable when she had chillun taggin' at her aprun strings? I needs a home for us, honey, and ef you wants to know what kind of a worker I is, write down to Richmon' and ask Mrs. Osper Glasgow, wife of Cunnel Glasgow, whar I worked since I was married." The archetypal mammy has come north to aid the career woman, offering helpful advice on gender. Delilah might not have quite so pronounced a dialect as earlier literary mammies, but Hurst certainly is trying to give her one—we might assume that Hurst simply is not as talented as Chesnutt in this regard. As Delilah settles into Bea's household, we see that she is the effusive, superstitious conjure woman, and "there seemed no limit to the extraneous influences, tides, hog teeth, buzzard feathers, china-berries, red heads, black cats, spilled salt, white horses, voodoo, which could determine or prohibit her slightest action." She perpetually assures Bea that her own fate is in the hands of God, and all she really wants is the biggest funeral Harlem has ever seen. (She gets it.) When Bea first realizes financial success, she says, "Delilah, we're rich!" Delilah replies that "we're rich in the luv of the Heavenly Host, if that's what you mean."[29]

The combination of Bea's determination and Delilah's natural cooking and mothering genius builds a financial empire—first in candy, then in the B. Pullman waffle chain. Bea's drive to succeed causes her to neglect her daughter, Jessie, while Delilah is tortured by Peola's attempt to pass as white. Eventually, when Peola makes known her plan to go away with her white lover, who does not know Peola's ancestry, Delilah is devastated, crying, "No, no, no! Gawd don't want his rivers to mix!" Delilah expresses her concern for maintaining racial and gender order to the members of her white family as well. When more news of the waffle chain's success is reported in the *Wall Street Journal*, the earthy Delilah calls on Bea to turn her attention to her natural role as mother and wife: "Right kind of man-lovin' ain't vulgar, honey. It's de Lawd's patent for makin' enough babies to keep de world goin', wid enough left over for wars and cyclones and drownin' and fallin' off de tops of buildin's."[30]

Delilah wants to get her mistress back on track, to cease walking an unnatural path and follow the "Lawd's" plan for her—to make babies. She is an Old South mammy for the 1930s: seemingly simple but able to tell the emerging white career woman what she really needs to know. She is suspicious of material success and Wall Street because it seems to pervert the ordered relationships among her family, black and white. Delilah is Bea's surrogate mother, if not literal wet nurse; she constantly refers to Bea as "mah chile," while, like the slave woman, she appears unable to do anything to help her biological child.

No one listens to Delilah's advice. Bea continues her path, realizing too late that she is in love with a younger man, who, unnaturally, is her daughter's love interest as well: "Something not young was reaching out for youth . . . a woman who had been awakened deep down inside." Peola carries out her plan to pass as white, has herself sterilized (further defying God's order), and moves to South America. And in the end Delilah is Christ-like, suffering stigmata and dying for the sins of the whole family. The imagery is obvious, if clumsy, as Peola offers to wash Delilah's feet in return for forgiveness and silence. As Delilah copes with Peola's crime of "mixing the rivers," she anticipates her own trip down the river Jordan, taking solace in "the love of Him and the vision of traveling toward Him." She calls on God to forgive those who have trespassed against her. As the tortured scene with Peola and Delilah reaches its climax, Delilah's final words for her daughter are, "Dar's spikes through mah hands and dar's a spike through mah heart if ever dar was spikes in de hands and de heart of anybody besides our Lawd." While Delilah's symbolic stigmata might seem excessive, even for a Hurst story, one of the author's critics, Mary Rose Shaunessy, has noted that Delilah's sufferings are "typical of the Hurst economy: a heroine gives her life to reproach the one she has devoted all her life to in vain. By the same economy, Bea was punished for having become rich, famous, and powerful."[31]

Making mammy into Jesus does not make her more human. Whatever admirable human traits Delilah might have had—faith, love, and lack of concern for the material world—she is the black mammy, a spokeswoman for an old racial and gender order, particularly concerning the place of white womanhood. As the plot is structured, Bea would have been happy if she had followed Delilah's advice and sought "man-lovin'" and babies for herself instead of what she always thought she wanted. Peola would have spared herself much misery if she had recognized herself as black and followed God's edict to keep his rivers from mixing (although Delilah had mixed rivers herself). Ostensibly a story about a pair of interesting and independent women and the ups and downs they experienced in the business world, the written version of *Imitation of Life* (the two films are another subject) is really about what happens to women when they do not follow the natural order of race and gender, and the wise and humble mammy is actually a cartoonish oracle who knows the True Path for her sex and race, speaking for the preservation of the white patriarchal social order. Mammies give advice to white women—advice about love, God, and food, the kind of advice Aunt Jemima gave in advertisements.

The cartoonish oracle might not seem so unrealistic if Hurst had been interested in some of the other racial and gender questions that lie beneath the surface of her story. Delilah herself failed to keep God's rivers unmixed—why? Was she a Jezebel at heart, or was a white man unable to resist giving her some of his own "man-lovin'" regardless of whether she wanted it? Delilah reminds us that without a husband, her sole means of finding a home for herself and her child is in the service of a white household, circumstances that were not an "imitation of life" but a real dilemma faced by black domestics and obscured by Hurst's emphasis on the mammy as a deliverer of truth to white women. Perhaps a more realistic woman might have emerged from exploring the dilemma, a woman more like Clelia Brady, a black domestic born in 1909 Mobile, who said she "didn't love white people the way some people say they do": "I remarried, but it didn't work out. It was just horrible with him. I couldn't go nowhere. I was just like a prisoner. And to pay for a divorce, I went back to work again. A friend of mine lived around the corner, and I told her I wanted a job. She told this judge she had worked for about me. So I worked there to pay for a divorce. I worked until retirement out there."[32]

Keeping Bea on the True Path was a formidable task, but so was keeping Scarlett O'Hara in her corset. Lumping Margaret Mitchell's *Gone with the Wind* (1936) with *Imitation of Life* might not seem fair, given the former's enormous influence in shaping the popular memory of the South and the fact that Mitchell was a better writer than Hurst. Mitchell, however, uses her Mammy in much the same fashion Hurst used Delilah, as someone who understood the gender conventions of her mistress's society and struggled to keep Scarlett from breaking them. The difference, however, is that Mitchell turned Hurst's point on its head, critiquing the patriarchy rather than implicitly justifying it. *Gone with the Wind* also is often properly characterized as a racist novel, but just as often for the wrong reasons. The black characters are far removed from Dixon and Page; they are as attractive as Mitchell could make them, given what else she needed them to be. As Helen Dreiss Irvin has noted, the black males are nurturers, "Pork caring for Gerald, Uncle Peter guiding the childlike Aunt Pittypat, and Big Sam protecting Scarlett from attackers."[33] Mammy is similarly the "nurturer" of Scarlett and sister Ellen, but the real story of racism is in the nature of the nurture.

We first see and hear Mammy in chapter 2, when she "waddles" down the hallway to Scarlett's room at Tara. She is a "huge old woman with the small, shrewd eyes of an elephant"—a large animal with a long memory. "She was shining black, a pure African, devoted to her last drop of blood to the O'Haras. . . . Mammy was black but her code of conduct and her sense of pride were as high or higher than those of her owners. . . . Whom Mammy loved, she chastened. And, as her love for Scarlett and her pride in her were enormous, the chastening process was practically continuous." So are Mammy's worries about Scarlett's health, eating habits, dress, and ability to land a husband. When Scarlett pauses to admire her father's "vital and earthy nature," she does not realize that she possesses some of the same (male) qualities, "despite sixteen years on the part of Ellen and Mammy to obliterate them," to make her a southern lady, to make her the opposite of what Mammy is. What we know about Mammy we know through her efforts to make Scarlett a lady. When we hear her voice, she is speaking with authority on something she is not: "Young misses whut frowns an' pushes out dey chins an' says 'Ah will' an' 'Ah woan' mos' gener'ly doan ketch husbands. . . . Young misses should cas' down dey eyes an' say, 'Well, suh, An mout' an' 'Jes' as you say, suh.'" The mammy understands the rules as they apply to all men and women, not just Scarlett; she consistently reclaims her role as a controlling black mother who exists to raise white women to a higher degree of purity. While she could curse "w'ite trash" aloud, she knows it is "beneath the dignity of quality white folks to pay the slightest attention to what a darky said when she was grumbling to herself." Still, "Mammy had her own method of letting her owners know exactly where she stood on all matters." She told them what they needed to know, and they accepted it, even Scarlett. "What a young miss could do and what she could not do were as different as black and white in Mammy's mind; there was no middle ground of deportment between. . . . But it had always been a struggle to teach Scarlett that most of her natural impulses were unladylike. Mammy's victories over Scarlett were hard-won and represented guile unknown to the white mind."[34] Significantly, a black woman knows more about what it means to be a white woman than the white woman in question.

Mammy's meaning to the gender order is most clear when it and Tara are in ruins, the field hands departed, the livestock stolen by Union soldiers. Scarlett is looking for any sign that her old home and ways might remain, and when she hears Mammy's familiar footsteps again, she thinks, "Here was something of stability. . . . something of the old life that was unchanging." When Mammy finally appears, Mitchell tells us unflatteringly that her "kind black face [is] sad with the uncomprehending sadness of a monkey's face." With the fall of the Old South, Mammy was instantly demoted from sergeant-at-arms to as uncomprehending a child as any newly freed slave in Page's novels. Her first words dispel any illusions of security Scarlett might have: "Mammy's chile is home! Oh, Miss Scarlett, now dat Miss Ellen's in de grabe, what is we gwine ter do? Oh, Miss Scarlett, effen Ah wuz jes' daid longside Miss Ellen! Ah kain make out widout Miss Ellen. Ain't nuthin lef' now but mizry an' trouble. Jes' weery loads, honey, jes' weery loads." Mammy needs the old order far more than Scarlett and reverts to her irrelevant former role at the first opportunity:

> "Honey, y' han's!" Mammy took the small hands with their blisters and blood clots in hers and looked at them with horrified disapproval. "Miss Scarlett, Ah done tole you dat you kin allus tell a lady by her han's an'—yo' face sunbuhnt too!"
>
> Poor Mammy, still the martinet about such unimportant things even though war and death had just passed over her head! In another moment she would be saying that young Misses with blistered hands and freckles most generally didn't never catch husbands, and Scarlett forestalled the remark.[35]

The most prominent black character in *Gone with the Wind* has no real function beyond maintaining white southern ladyhood. This is not to say that

Gone with the Wind is not a great novel, nor does it negate Mitchell's critique of the Old South patriarchy. It also seems unfair to compare Mitchell too closely with Page, although some critics have done so, particularly in the realm of race relations. Mitchell clearly would have disappointed Page's white sentimental following—Page's version of Scarlett surely would have paid dearly for her rebelliousness (Dixon would have pushed her off a cliff). But just as clearly, her Mammy is a traditional one in the literary and historical sense, the noisy, bossy, fat, loving, authoritative black woman who is going to make ladies out of white women.[36]

Like Page, Lillian Smith was a novelist as well as a historian. Unlike Page, she also was a crusader for racial equality, and she did not see the things the mammy did, or the ideology she represented, as beneficial to both sexes of a biracially defined South. Smith was especially attentive to the complaints of white women, and her most powerful passages are those explaining the lies she believed white people of different sexes and classes told each other. In an essay titled "Two Men and a Bargain," for example, she described the class and racial alliance among rich white men and poor white men in a unique, if blunt, fashion. Mr. Poor White can sit in the front seat of the car, but not drive, as long, Mr. Rich White says, as he keeps Mr. Negro in the back seat, where both whites laugh at him. They both enjoy the ride for a time, but Mr. Poor White begins to have his doubts: "Mighty fine to sit in the front seat by Mr. Rich White, mighty fine to turn round now and then and see the nigger right there on the back seat where you shoved him. But still, you ain't driving. Mr. Rich White's driving, and you get restless, for it looks like he's driving down a road that goes nowhere, when you need to stop at the store to do some buying."[37]

Other authors of southern history, of course, have discussed the white class alliance that prevented poor whites from seeing their common interests with blacks. Smith's metaphorical approach is particularly interesting because of her emphasis on dissemblance by those involved; sometimes bluntly and coldly, sometimes as if she were half-awakened from a nightmare, she describes the ways people told and believed lies about themselves and, in the case of the mammy, the terrible consequences of doing so. Despite the wide-ranging effects of racism that Smith saw, she struggled to keep all of the forces in play in some of her arguments. For example, in the story of Mr. Rich White and Mr. Poor White, Mrs. Negro and Mrs. Poor/Rich White are not even in the car, reflecting a tendency on occasion to exclude women from discussions of class. In her evocative discussion of the mammy, she also omitted an important character.

In *Killers of the Dream*, published in 1949, Smith saw a psychic sickness born as a result of white motherhood vacated at an early age and filled by a black nurse. Speaking from her experience, she said of the mammy:

> They existed because there was rich psychological soil for them to grow in. In the old days, a white child who had loved his colored nurse, his "mammy," with that passionate devotion which only small children feel, who had grown used to that dark velvety skin, warm deep breast, rich soothing voice and the ease of a personality whose religion was centered in heaven not hell, who had felt when mind is tender the touch of a spirit almost free of sexual anxiety, found it natural to seek in adolescence and adulthood a return of this profoundly pleasing experience. His memory was full of echoes. . . . he could not rid himself of them. And he followed these echoes to back-yard cabins, to colored town.

The formative experience of being nursed by a mammy, Smith said, led sons of the planter class to commit their self-defined crime of miscegenation, to their ultimate discredit and to the disadvantage of the black men and women they in turn blamed for the supposed sins of "mongrelization." Smith's purpose was not simply to condemn race mixing but to identify cause and effect, to put the blame for the crime of miscegenation at the feet of the contemporary southern white male "politicians [who] plunge deep into men's minds and memories, and mixing the poison of these words with the guilt already there," produce the terror of lynching and votes for white supremacy and segregation.[38]

Smith's mammy was in some ways the same as Page's and Phillips's, but with an important departure once gender was introduced into the analysis. She outlines the tragic dimension for both the white mistress and the black servant, who are transformed by the adult white male into Madonna and whore and play the roles themselves in order to survive or to deny realities they are powerless to change. The point comes in every son's life in which he must recognize his white birth mother's primacy over the black wet nurse, Smith wrote. All his life, the mammy has met "his immediate needs as he hungers to have them met. She is easy, permissive, less afraid of simple earthly biological needs and manifestations." But, Smith said, departing from Page and Phillips, authority and punishment flow not from the mammy but from the mistress. "Sometimes, white child hates white mother after this ordeal, and clings desperately to his colored mother." The unresolved, unresolvable conflict continues as the boy grows into manhood:

> And now curious things happen. Strong bonds begin to grow as the most profound relationships of his life are formed, holding him to two women whose paths will take them far from each other. It is as if he were fastened to two umbilical cords which wrap themselves together in a terrifying tangle, and then suddenly, inexplicably, but with awful sureness, begin steadily to move, each in a different direction. . . .
>
> His white conscience, now, is hacking at his early love life, splitting it off more and more sharply into acceptable and unacceptable, what is done and what isn't, into "pure" and "impure"; Madonna and whore; Mother and nurse; wife and prostitute; white conscience and colored pleasures; marriage and lust; "right" and "wrong"; belief and act; segregation and brotherhood.[39]

The mother-son relationship between the man and the mammy is cheapened into sentimentality, but "the powerful drives of childhood will not stay in the little stream beds his culture gullied out for them." The white male denies the contradictions in his worldview through creating the oppositional categories of "pure" and "impure." The self-denial of his mammy is channeled into resentment toward his mother and wife and shameful visits to the other side of the tracks. The consequences of a divided motherhood are shared by everyone in the equation, Smith said, for "sometimes a sadistic feeling for all women overpowers him. He feels betrayed, cheated; and he despises himself and them for a treacherous partnership in which he seems always to have been the loser since childhood." James Baldwin hinted at a similar relationship between being raised by mammy and later seeking sex from Jezebel: "The youth, nursed and raised by the black Mammy whose arms had then held all that there was of warmth and love and desire, and still confounded by the dreadful taboos set up between himself and her progeny, must have wondered, after his first experiment with black flesh, where, under the blazing heavens, he could hide."[40]

At least one question remains regarding Smith's mammy. She wrote that the story of the mammy was really a tale of three "ghost relationships—white man and colored woman, white father and colored children, white child and his beloved colored nurse." Throughout Smith's scenario of psychological ferment, the little white girls are missing. They also were suckled by a black wet nurse; were they not torn between the "pure" and "impure" in some way? How were they to resolve the "powerful drives of childhood" with the racial and sexual order of their culture? By limiting her discussion to the irreconcilable urges of white men nursed by mammy and the ensuing misery of adult white women caused by the actions of white men, Smith seemed at least to ignore a painful area that she was particularly poised to explore.

For Smith, the "ghost relationship" between men and their mammies destroyed the possibility for healthy relationships between men and women, white and black. White men lived forever with an unnecessary, self-inflicted wound, and they in turn poisoned their relationships with mothers and wives, leaving black women with the role of prostitute, a role they played not only to survive white male appetites but to keep their families fed. Throughout *Killers of the Dream*, as well as in the discussion of the mammy, white women spin elaborate webs of denial in order to cope with the relationships between them and their husbands, their husbands and black women. Like Eileen McLean, a white woman interviewed by Tucker, they could value a loyal household servant while observing that "all they do between jobs is have illegitimate children. The Nigras all do that. That is just the way. They don't have the morals we do." Or like Helen Reed, another mistress with fond memories of "Mammy," the white woman might deny that children of mixed race existed.[41]

The mammy, regardless of her real affection for her charges, is an unwitting agent of destruction for families of both races, according to Smith. While everyone shared the painful consequences of divided motherhood, however, it is only fair to note that Smith was describing the long-standing grievances of white women—in discussing her mammy, she opposed the aspects of domination of black women that white men enjoyed at the expense of their wives. So she worked simultaneously to debunk Jezebel, not just mammy; the mammy was a peculiar tool created by white supremacists to nurture young white supremacists and run white supremacist households, and allow white men access to Jezebel's household, too. Smith saw the inner workings of a flawed system and found that the gears were grinding because of the unresolved relationships among race, class, and gender. Smith's mammy is different in important ways from Page's— her authority lessened, her sexuality emphasized instead of removed. Instead of representing living evidence of the legitimacy of the old white order, she, too, was a dissembler and an integral part of the white system of values, even though those values were contradictory and ultimately self-destructive.

Faulkner's Dilsey, Porter's Nannie

William Faulkner used the mammy to similar rhetorical ends, to describe a flawed set of racial, sexual, and class relationships, but with a different perspective from Smith's. In *The Sound and the Fury* (1929), Faulkner's Dilsey stands at the center of a disintegrating southern family, while somehow managing to rise above it herself. Like Delilah in *Imitation of Life*, she offers important observations about what the other characters are doing, and also like Delilah, she is ignored. But Dilsey, like Twain's Roxy, acts on behalf of herself and her family—her black family—and is not merely a reflection of the chaos in the white family surrounding her.

Faulkner is widely regarded to have, more than any white novelist, "shown an abiding interest in the life of black Americans, the historical and social forces conditioning that life, and the larger American destiny of which it is part."[42] He also, however, offered some confusing statements about states' rights and civil rights during the 1950s that muddy his reputation as a racial liberal. And we might not expect much of a departure from Faulkner when it comes to the mammy, given his dedication of *Go Down, Moses*, a collection of short stories published in 1942: "To Mammy, CAROLINE BARR , Mississippi, 1840-1940, Who was born in slavery and who gave to my family a fidelity without stint or calculation of recompense and to my childhood an immeasurable devotion and love." Faulkner did have a black nurse he called mammy, according to his memory and his brother John's.[43] Still, Faulkner's Dilsey Gibson, the maid in the Compson household, is simply someone caring and efficient, but not a superwoman, not merely a reflection of the white people around her, someone more real than the women we have previously seen.

If the Mississippi Compsons ever were a family, they were not one anymore by April 1928. The father drank himself to an early grave, the mother is a pitifully weak person. Son Jason is a sadistic embezzler; son Quentin a suicide. Son Benjamin is a castrated "idiot," and sister Caddy a fallen woman who leaves the family with a niece, who is in turn tortured by Jason and ultimately torments him. No one seems to know how to love his or her kin anymore, or even to express the smallest kindness. No one even knows what time it is: Quentin breaks his watch on his last day on Earth, Jason is forever losing track of the latest cotton-market reports, and Benjamin cannot read a clock. The greater meaning of the tumult surrounding the individual Compsons is the subject of numerous studies; more books have been written in the attempt to explain *The Sound and the Fury* than Faulkner wrote himself. But standing at the center of *The Sound and the Fury* is Dilsey, of whom Faulkner once said, "There was Dilsey to be the future, to stand above the fallen ruins of the family like a ruined chimney, gaunt, patient, and indomitable."[44] The traditional mammy still serves symbolic purposes, this time as the loving mother-survivor whose endurance is counterpoint to the disorder and hatred around her.

Dilsey is not the do-it-all mammy of the Old South. In fact, most things do not get done around the Compson household. In place of the sentimental mammy is a normal woman (arguably, being normal is a superhuman achievement in a Faulkner novel) who loves her savior but does not link her reward in heaven with servility toward whites on Earth. She awaits a trip to church as an opportunity to leave behind the small and large cruelties that the Compson men and women commit against each other and against her and her family. "I thank de Lawd I got mo heart dan dat, even ef hit is black," she tells Jason after he is cruel to Benjamin. Although Dilsey treats Benjamin with kindness—her kitchen is his refuge—she could do without hearing his whimpering and having to wipe off the food he spills on his clothes; she is, after all, only human and "cant do but one thing at a time."[45] One senses, too, that she could do without Mrs. Compson's incessant whining and self-pity, although she holds her tongue.

Sometimes Dilsey seems like a conventional mammy, the super–slave woman who against all reason clings to an unhappy white household as if it were her own. When Jason wonders why the family should provide for Caddy's abandoned niece, Dilsey says, "And whar' else do she belong? Who else gwine raise her 'cep me? Aint I raised ev'ry one of y'all?" Likewise, she performs the traditional mammy's task of keeping the other blacks in line when she lectures Luster for not bringing in wood early one morning or corrects Luster and Frony when they have worn their best Sunday clothes for a long walk to church on a rainy day. Also, she is the only member of the Compson household who knows what time it is, despite the fact that the kitchen clock only has one hand and constantly emits the wrong number of chimes. But she has no special power to nurture white ladyhood, or Caddy would not have become the mistress of a Nazi general, and the mammy cannot keep Mrs. Compson from toppling off her rickety perch of southern femininity. Likewise, Jason and the elder Quentin are not cavaliers with fond memories of their mammy's breast. Instead of waxing sentimental or seeking his lost black mother across the railroad tracks, Quentin dreams of incest with sister Caddy. Jason refers to Dilsey as a "damn old nigger," and when Dilsey reminds him that she raised all the Compson children, he only remarks, sarcastically, "And a damn fine job you made of it."[46] Who could argue with him? Not Jason, who rants about the black cook's absence from the kitchen but later boasts, upon discharging all the servants, that the Compsons are finally free of the "Niggers." Or perhaps the Compson children themselves are proof that Dilsey is wrong. Mammy did not raise them, or they would have turned out better. Then again, perhaps the family disasters are proof that Dilsey raised them, if we accept Smith's point of view.

The Compsons seek to disguise all the racial and gender disorder in their household, as well as their class fall, but Dilsey negotiates around it, alternately easing misery through participating in the lies the Compsons tell about themselves and sometimes letting disaster strike when there is nothing she can do about it. Dilsey, for reasons of her own, upsets the balance as the need arises. She endures misery when she must and seeks peace where she can find it. She is not a martyr; she keeps her own humanity intact despite the inhumanity around her. "I've seed de first en de last. Never you mind me," the Compson household survivor reminds the reader from time to time. Dilsey sounds a little like Estella, the maid described to Tucker by Ellen Owens. Estella always advised Owens, "Baby, you don't need to worry. You can only take one day at a time."[47]

Similarly, Katherine Anne Porter's Nannie in "The Old Order" and "The Last Leaf" (1934) is a black woman who emerges triumphantly toward the end of her life as a nursemaid to whites. She is the childhood playmate of her mistress, Sophia Jane, and as they reach adulthood and become mothers, Nannie nurses Sophia's children as well as her own. When Nannie is sick, Sophia nurses the black children and resolves that each mother should nurse her own children from then on. After emancipation Nannie chooses to stay with Sophia, but while they grow closer, they are never equals, because Nannie remains rooted in her old place in life. "It had been assigned to her before birth, and for her daily rule she had all her life obeyed the authority nearest her." She only discovers herself after Sophia dies and she leaves the white children to set up her own household. We last see her sitting "in the luxury of having at her disposal all of God's good time there was in the world." Nannie is a mammy that Page might have recognized as real except for her self-awareness of the role she once played, and still plays, in white men's minds. She turns her former servitude into an advantage in disputes with one of Sophia's children, reminding him that she deserves the same respect he would give his wife and mother: "He submitted, being of the latest generation of sons who acknowledged, however reluctantly, however bitterly, their mystical never to be forgotten debt to the womb that bore them, and the breast that suckled him." This is the other side of the relationship that Smith cursed in *Killers of the Dream*; in Porter's stories, dual motherhood allows the black woman to call on an old debt when the occasion arises. The power comes at an expense, for the mammy and Sophia both look back bitterly upon the circumstances they faced in life: "Who knows why they had loved their past? They wondered perpetually, with only a hint now and then to each other of the uneasiness of their hearts, how so much suffering and confusion could have been built up and maintained on such a foundation." Ambivalence of this sort, particularly between white women and their black servants, was suggested in the memory of Cynthia Berg, who grew up in a northern Alabama household in the 1950s: "Ruth sometimes was like an adult friend, and then sometimes she would hardly speak to me. You knew that was just the way she was. She would always say, 'I ain't studying you,' when she didn't want to bother with us. So we would bow out some way or other. That's when she didn't want us to do something, or she didn't want to do a certain thing we would ask her, or we were bothering her. And she would just say she wasn't studying us."[48]

As in Porter's fiction, a former servant could also maintain a measure of respect from a white male family member in real life. Gillian Kushner described to Tucker her grandmother's relationship with Mr. Lindsey, whose children she raised after his wife's death. "In the beginning, I guess, he didn't treat her as an equal," Kushner said. "But as the kids started growing up, he got used to the idea of her importance. Before, they had a good relationship, and if she needed something, she could ask him, and if they needed something, they could ask her, but it was still that she was black and they were white. Now they seem more equal. He'll talk to her more, and they'll go more places together."[49] It was not hard for Gillian Kushner to see give-and-take in the relationship between a black domestic and her white male boss, especially after the woman has literally raised the man's children. Why should it be so difficult for us to believe it? Sometimes, the lie being maintained might be that the woman is a servant, when she is really more like a mother.

For Faulkner and Porter, the mammy could be part of the dysfunctional society but also work independently for her own desires. In the novels of Mitchell and Hurst and the histories of Parkhurst and Woodson, the mammy carried (or thought she carried) intrinsically important information about how white and black men and women should behave lest society cease to function correctly. And for Smith, and, in a way, Chesnutt, the mammy image reflected the ways in which southern society was dysfunctional. During the first half of the twentieth century, in history books and in novels, the mammy was a very useful person. She could help explain the supposed truth or falsity of a number of assumptions about race, class, gender, and southern society.

But by the late 1960s, when she increasingly began to attract the attention of historians again, mammy underwent several important transformations. Her existence was affirmed and denied. She again became a leader of her class and a mother of her race. She also was described as a phantasm of antebellum days—someone southerners remembered because they wanted her to have existed, even though no one could prove she really lived. In the last two decades, arguments about the nature of American slavery have brought mammy into the spotlight, and she again has proved to be a most useful person to people with widely varying opinions.

How the Historians Undiscovered Mammy

There were two ways that historians could have dealt with mammy in the 1960s and 1970s. They might have worked to reinterpret the evidence about what she actually did in slavery and thereafter, or they might have written her off completely. They did both.

The mammy archetype of literature had already experienced a serious makeover during the Civil Rights and Black Power movements, as Trudier Harris described in *From Mammies to Militants*. The result in many cases is that the black domestic servant is no longer a mammy in the sense that she tells white people what they want to hear or symbolizes an acceptable ownership of motherhood; arguably, she is no longer a mammy in any way, but a militant. Aunt Jemima was depicted in some corners by this time as a sort of militant, particularly by artists. The militant maids who superficially resemble mammies in Douglas Ward's 1964 novel *Happy Ending* seek to steal as much as they can from their employers, which at least hints at a more complex relationship. But as the 1970s approached, fictional black women in domestic situations became more violent, hiding beneath the stereotype like Brer Rabbit but contemplating the deaths of their masters and mistresses. In Barbara Wood's story "The Final Supper" (1970) the slave Rose Lee poisons her Virginia master and guests at Thanksgiving dinner. Likewise, the seventy-six-year-old protagonist of Ted Shine's 1968 play *Contribution* secretly poisons a number of white citizens in a small southern town, singing happily to herself while she makes tainted cornbread. As Harris demonstrates, these characters are no longer people constructed to bolster white supremacy or southern ladyhood; they are seeking to overthrow it.[50] By this time, the mammy's value as an advertising icon became seriously compromised as well.

Once the old black maid is a revolutionary, she perhaps is no longer a mammy, in the sense that Dixon, Page, and Phillips might understand her. But by (murderously) opposing her racial oppression, she is singularly defined by it. Is there anything to say about her relationships with black men? Are all whites— men and women—worthy of murder, both masters and guests? Who does this person love? Must all of her relationships with the white race be severed in response to racial oppression? As more recent historians attempted to explain exactly what the lives of slave men and women were like, they needed to answer the question of what mammy and other slaves might have really been doing beneath a veneer of obedience.

Stanley Elkins could be said, in a way, to deserve much of the blame or credit for the mammy's further historical development. His 1959 book *Slavery: A Problem in American Institutional and Intellectual Life* theorized that American slaves were "infantilized" by the "adjustment to clear and omnipresent authority."[51] Elkins wrote broadly and generally about Sambo, but not about mammies. *Slavery's* philosophical companion was Daniel Patrick Moynihan's 1965 report *The Negro Family: The Case for National Action*, which found a "black matriarchy" to be the culprit behind the theft of black masculinity, imposing a "crushing burden upon the Negro male." In Moynihan's sometimes bizarre but (still today) popularly accepted analysis, the children of matriarchal black homes were deprived of "normal" —by which Moynihan implicitly meant "white" and "patriarchal"—gender relations and were destined for lives marked by welfare dependency, juvenile delinquency, poor education, crime, and general antisocial behavior.[52] For Moynihan, like Elkins, contemporary troubles could be traced to a disruption of black male identity under slavery, a dislocation that persisted beyond emancipation. The black male is the historical result and real source of concern; the black female is the culprit, her once-magical mothering ability somehow no longer restrained and somehow overwhelming the badly needed "fatherhood." In other words, if Aunt Jemima hadn't pushed Uncle Mose around so much, their children would not be killing time on street corners.

The importance of Elkins and Moynihan in shaping rather one-sided gendered arguments about mammy, however, is not so much what they wrote but what others wrote in response to them. The initial arguments that followed Elkins primarily were aimed at returning masculinity to the slave man, although their direct influence on the study of the underclass was considerable. One of the most significant examples, John W. Blassingame's *The Slave Community: Plantation Life in the Antebellum South*, hardly mentions slave women at all. He apparently saw no need to argue that slave women were not "infants." As for mammies, Blassingame said that "Samboes," to the extent they did exist, were "more ubiquitous" among house servants (although it is not clear whether mammy is a Sambo, or how ubiquity can be qualified) than any other slaves. The only paragraph specifically devoted to the mammy is an evaluation that, ironically, rings of U. B. Phillips's portrait of the mammy as the legendary surrogate mother of the Old South: "It was the black mammy who often ran the household, interceded with [the child's] parents to protect him, punished him for his misbehavior, nursed him, rocked him to sleep, told him fascinating stories, and in general served as his second, more attentive, more loving mother. Often the child formed a deep and abiding love for his mammy and as an adult deferred to her demands and wishes."[53]

Jessie Parkhurst's "prime minister" became Eugene Genovese's domestic forewoman with only a few variations. In *Roll, Jordan, Roll* Genovese captured the advantages and disadvantages of sharing a roof with the master and mistress, but he inevitably had to note that house slaves "became members of the family in a more literal sense" than other slaves. He emphasized the degree to which mammies and white mistresses worked together to raise each other's children— a point meant to serve Genovese's larger theme of an organic working relationship between master and slave. Likewise, he depicted white mistresses, mammies, and other female servants as sharing routine housework and romantic secrets. "The slaves needed masters and mistresses they could depend on; they did not need masters and mistresses to love them," Genovese wrote. "But the whites needed their servants' love and trust. The slaves had the upper hand, and many of them learned how to use it." House slaves in general did not emerge from Genovese's analysis as innately loyal and loving as they were in the myth of the Old South, although they somehow held the "upper hand," and some romantic aspects were retained. The masters, he said, needed the mammy's love as much as they need her housework. The housework itself became less significant in the bargain—the household is feminized and not an area of potential conflict, so class essentially is a masculine category.[54]

Genovese's description of the mammy, as opposed to house servants in general, changed when he attempted to answer the question, "Who were these Mammies? What did they actually do?" In response, he put a class-conscious coating on the mammy of the Old South legend, using terms that emphasized her rank in the household rather than sentimentalizing about motherhood: "Primarily, the Mammy raised the white children and ran the Big House either as the mistress's chief executive officer or her de facto superior. Her power extended over black and white so long as she exercised restraint, and she was not to be crossed."[55] The strong association of the mammy and mistress removes some other troubling questions that have surrounded mammy, such as Lillian Smith's speculations about the consequences of dual motherhood. *Roll, Jordan, Roll* is not about cavaliers suckling at mammy's breast.

The mammy might appear to have been a substitute mistress, but because the mistress was more forewoman than mother, the mammy was a kind of domestic slave forewoman, too. Genovese's analysis in many ways continued down the romantic road already traveled by turn-of-the-century racists: "In general, she gave the whites the perfect slave—a loyal, faithful, contented, efficient, conscientious member of the family who always knew her place; and she gave the slaves a white-approved standard of black behavior." She not only told masters and mistresses what they needed to know to justify slavery; she helped other slaves understand how masters wanted them to act. The different levels of subordination within the system of slavery, though, were still strictly class subordination in Genovese's formula, for class subordination "paradoxically meant not the subordination of one class en bloc to one another but the subordination of the individuals within one class to individuals within another."[56]

The final turn in Genovese's analysis was a Parkhurst-Woodson rehabilitation of the slavish person he had just described, a vision of a person who carried the rest of her class on her back in the years after emancipation. The mammy "put her power and influence" to the protection of her own family; "carried great weight when she championed the cause of some abused slave"; and "in her own way . . . defended black dignity." But, above all, the mammy and other house servants "carried Afro-American sensibility" into the southern culture and emerged as the "great integrationists in the black community, culturally as well as politically," carrying the seeds of black nationality if not black nationality itself. Genovese explained the apparent contradiction between describing house slaves first as integrationists and then as nationalists by arguing that the house slaves "remained suspended between two politics."[57] In seeing the house servants as a latent black bourgeoisie, Genovese emphasized his formula of class analysis, giving mammy a measure of dignity and humanity but setting aside questions of gender, or at least defining class as male.

In *Within the Plantation Household: Black and White Women of the Old South,* Elizabeth Fox-Genovese fashioned a similarly elegant and complicated model, but with considerable emphasis on southern households and the meaning of what went on within them. Fox-Genovese briefly but explicitly described a world of white motherhood vacated and then, significantly, filled by slave women. The mammy "signaled the wish [among masters] for organic harmony and projected a woman who suckled and reared white masters." The mammy also resolved the master class's inability to reconcile sexuality and motherhood; the mammy, as an asexual other, "displaced sexuality into nurture and transformed potential hostility in sustenance and love."[58]

In Fox-Genovese's description masters created the ideological construction of mammy to rob slave women of their autonomy in gender roles, particularly child rearing, but for a specific purpose. In being a mammy, a slave woman was telling the master that slaves bore total devotion to the master—why else would they rear the master's children as if they were their own? This is a key question: Why treat someone who is holding you in bondage with such kindness? Why raise their children as your own? Is it possible that someone—the master class, or at least Fox-Genovese—has mistaken a slave mask for the slave's actual self? *Within the Plantation Household* answers that slave masters valued the concept of "organic harmony," and in the mammy they created a figure to help prove it existed. The question left unresolved, however, is not whether masters wanted organic harmony in theory, but how well it worked in reality, particularly for white women but also for slave women. For example, in her ritual dismemberment of gendered interpretations of Mary Chesnut's diary, she argues that a comparison of versions of the diary demonstrates that Chesnut "was not arguing for women's rights but for the exceptional woman's opportunity to display excellence." But while Fox-Genovese exploits the contradictions in Chesnut's diary to deny gender an interpretative role, she leaves unchallenged one of the more famous passages in which Chesnut condemns the very unharmonious presence of mulatto children who look like their white master's kin.[59] The question is, Organic harmony for whom? White men were free to disregard their black children, while white women were forced to live with them. Meanwhile, black women were forced to conceive, bear, and raise those children. Beneath the organic harmony of a class analysis that unites masters and mistresses might lie an understanding of gender that cleaves them. If slave women breast-feeding white children can be taken as a contemporary, visible example of harmony, slave children of white fathers can be, and were, similarly interpreted as visible evidence of a disorderly society.

Perhaps no historian has offered a more sweeping explanation of how much the idea of the mammy might have meant to plantation masters and mistresses—while simultaneously denying the legendary mammy's existence—than Deborah Gray White in *Ar'n't I a Woman?* White recounted the evidence for the mammy as a historical figure, then argued that the smiling, omnipotently competent mammy was always more white self-delusion than slave reality. Looking at the "uglier and perverse" side of the legend, she noted that if the mammy did exist, "she must have been a very tired woman," given the enormous number of tasks she supposedly performed. More rational would be the belief, supported by the diaries of mistresses, that mammy could not possibly have done everything that needed to be done in the Big House, and that mistresses and house servants, working together, probably did not get it done, either. White gave further evidence of plantation mistresses who rejected the notion of turning over their children to a black servant, raising doubts about whether mammy was always the undisputed surrogate mother of the plantation.[60] The evidence led White to conclude that the picture plantation masters painted of loyal, loving mammies was a lie they told each other, a person who toiled largely in the imaginations of white plantation men and women.

If the mammy was perceived by her owners to be something more than just another servant, even during the antebellum period, what purpose could that perception have served? White answered that the mammy helped her white contemporaries maintain their understanding of Victorian womanhood—"virtuous, pious, tender, and understanding." Again, the controlling black mother is contrasted with supposedly saintly white womanhood. White emphasized the planter class's need for harmony and an "ideal slave" identified by Genovese but went further, linking mammy with white ideas about womanhood in general: "In the antebellum South . . . ideas about women went in hand with ideas about race. Women and blacks were the foundation on which southern white males built their patriarchal regime. . . . Mammy was, thus, the perfect image for antebellum Southerners. As the personification of the ideal slave, and the ideal woman, she was the ideal symbol of the patriarchal tradition."[61]

The mammy of legend, however, stood apart from the ideal of white womanhood in two important ways, White wrote. First, of course, she expended her energies on the "moral uplift" of a family not her own—supposedly freeing plantation mistresses to climb to their own lofty peak of southern womanhood. Second, the legendary mammy was, like Aunt Jemima, always old, even though household slave women themselves were not. White observed that "mammy's age might be a metaphor for the asexuality attributed to her," putting mammy above any "carnal taint." Mammy's impeccable service, loyalty, cheerfulness, and asexuality combined, in white minds, to bolster white planter values, just as Jezebel's wantonness excused miscegenation. As White concluded, "Mammy helped endorse the service of black women in southern households, as well as the close contact between whites and blacks that such service demanded. Together, Jezebel and Mammy did a lot of explaining and soothed a troubled conscience."[62] White brilliantly drew on all the things that Dixon, Phillips, and Page were thinking and writing about, and threw them back.

Ar'n't I a Woman? contributed two important observations to mammy historiography. First, the mammy was understood as a person who unwittingly transmits crucial values concerning sexuality from white men to white women—lifting southern white women to their unhappy pedestal. Second, White looked at the historical mammy and found her to be just as much of an ideological construct in her time as the mammy used by New South apologists. Despite whatever ground the mammy might have in historical reality, she was always more a white person's idea than reality. White's contribution was to argue that the mammy was not merely a legendary figure to those who looked back with longing on the plantation South; the legend was contemporaneous with the plantation South. The argument, however, still revolves around disproving and explaining the mammy myth; the debate, as much as it is informed by what slave women really did, for a change, is framed by a need to explain the "other."

White was not alone—or even first—in denying the mammy's existence. Other historians, following Blassingame's response to Elkins, studied the work slave women actually performed in both the Big House and the slave quarters.

Their findings explicitly challenged the idea that there was really any mammy who resembled the legend, that there really was any mammy at all. In *The Black Family in Slavery and Freedom* (1976), Herbert Gutman found little evidence for the typical mammy in the antebellum period. Catherine Clinton restated the doubts more forcefully in *The Plantation Mistress: Woman's World in the Old South* (1982). "In the primary records from before the Civil War," Clinton wrote, "hard evidence for her existence simply does not appear."[63] How could historians who doubted the typical mammy's existence, however, reconcile that conclusion with accounts by sentimental racists or, for that matter, by historians who acknowledged the mammy's existence while condemning slavery?

Mammies and Masks

There always have been possibilities other than accepting the mammy as a real historical figure or denying that anyone like her ever existed. Authors like Twain and Porter, at least, understood that their mammies purposefully concealed much of their true identities. Twain's Rachel masked her painful experiences in slavery beneath the good cheer that white people expected her to exhibit; Porter's Nannie concealed the ways in which she held the upper hand over her former white charges. It is possible that the sentimental accounts of the black slave mother and the seemingly authoritative historical accounts of her reflect the long-running act of masking described by Ralph Ellison. Not only the black woman but her so-called superiors, with "half-conscious awareness," toyed with identities such as slave/mother and black/white. "Here the 'darky' act makes brothers of us all," Ellison wrote. "America is a land of masking jokers. We wear the mask for purposes of aggression as well as for defense; when we are projecting the future and preserving the past. In short, the motives hidden beneath the mask are as numerous as the ambiguities the mask conceals."[64] Uncovering those motives seems an almost impossible task, at first. Mammy appeared to be a much easier person to understand when historians relied on all those sentimental white accounts of her simpleminded love and devotion, just as Twain's fictional Aunt Rachel seemed free of any worldly trouble—until "Mr. C——" asked. When historians ask the same type of question, they can determine why black women commonly termed "mammies" might have adopted parts of the persona so well remembered by whites, and what realities created the need for a mask.

Darlene Clark Hine, for instance, in an essay on rape and southern black women, described the move north by black domestics in the early twentieth century, who can be said to have "negotiated" new working relations in their kitchens. Certainly, she noted, we can understand the move as one born both of racial oppression and class oppression in the South, as an attempt to escape Jim Crow and to gain higher wages in a new locale. But Hine created a fuller picture of the experience of black domestics by putting the third factor—sexual exploitation—into play, rather than treating it as a subset of class or racial factors. "The fundamental tensions between black women and the rest of society—especially white men, white women, and, to a lesser extent, black men—involved a multifaceted struggle to determine who would control black women's productive and reproductive capacities and their sexuality." The conflicts that black domestics faced, Hine wrote, forced them to maintain a difficult balance in their relationships with white masters, white mistresses, and black husbands, and rather than explore any particular aspect of the balancing act, Hine sought to explain the balancing act itself. She said that far from having a racist, sexist persona thrust upon them, black domestics negotiated their own image as a means of survival, what Hine called "a culture of dissemblance." She argued that "a secret, undisclosed persona allowed the individual black woman to bear and rear children, endure the domestic violence of frequently un- or underemployed mates, to support churches, found institutions, and engage in social service activities—all while living within a clearly hostile, white, patriarchal, middle-class America.[65]

The self-imposed secrecy in everyday life, Hine argued, led to unintended results and misinterpretations inside and outside the kitchen door. Black women's dissemblance about rape by white men made possible histories in which the act was described primarily in ways that it robbed black men of "masculinity." It led the National Association of Colored Women's Clubs in 1896 to concentrate its efforts on downplaying, "even denying, sexual expression." There is a trade implied, a negotiation under uneven circumstances. While black women's efforts to better their lot meant operating in response to the mythical Jezebel, they also led to boardinghouses, training centers, and increased access to birth control. The mask of servility was not merely a tool used by whites to keep blacks within an ideological construct, supposedly elevating white women, displacing responsibility for rape of black women by white men, or simply keeping a black woman in the kitchen. Black women dissembled, too, doing the positive things that were within their grasp, unable to overturn a whole racist-sexist tradition that was not.

Hine did not talk about mammy, but the analytic approach could extend to her, too. For instance, one of mammy's apparently essential traits, her often fanatical religious devotion (as described by the historian Parkhurst and the novelist Hurst), might seem less an inherent characteristic than an exaggeration of a rather typical survival strategy for a black domestic. It is one thing to deny that the woman called mammy was any more religious than anyone else; it is entirely another to see the church as a safehouse, a place to escape from oppression as a black woman servant in everyday life. Louvenia Walker, another black domestic in Tucker's oral history, said of the church of her youth, "The older I get, the more I think those old people there knew the only way to get by in this world."[66]

Part of the difficulty of discovering mammy, Patricia Morton wrote, "resides in the fact that [she] seems most readily discoverable in the same sources that have endorsed this figure as an emblem of racial and sexual mythology."[67] But another part, Morton said, also resides in treating her only as myth and disregarding the ways in which lies and ideas about people play a significant role in their lives. Some sources treat only a part of her and make it her whole; others consider all aspects of her life, challenging the mythology but not denying its real power. While what Morton calls the "old faces of racism-sexism" are exposed and dismissed by contemporary scholars, the act of dismissing them, bit by bit, has too often framed the debate. Slaying the "old faces" of race, class, and gender, one by one, is important, but it also reveals what is seemingly undiscoverable about people. When overturning myths about mammy has also meant leaving unexamined the culture of dissemblance—once again, white, black, male, female, master, servant—in which she lived, the result is an unfinished portrait, not up to the task of replacing the stereotype.

There is a power in the naming of things and people like mammy, a power that comes from not only the name but the meanings inherently attached to it. The act of calling someone a mammy or the choice to deny that anyone was really a mammy reveals much of the argument that invariably follows. You may call someone a mammy to emphasize her place in an order, whether by race, gender, or class. You may call someone a mammy to emphasize her traditional qualities or to provide the unexpected, contrasting what is traditionally expected with what you really wish to explain. The power of naming, however, fosters its own kind of powerlessness, an inability to understand the true nature of things, as the American physicist Richard Feynman constantly pointed out to his colleagues and students, who were working to identify particles they could not even see. Feynman often retold a story from his youth in which a friend asked him to identify a bird as they hiked through the Catskill Mountains of New York:

I said, "I haven't the slightest idea what kind of bird that is."

He says, "It's a brown-throated thrush. Your father doesn't teach you anything."

But it was the opposite. He had already taught me. "See that bird?" he says. "It's a Spencer's warbler." (I knew he didn't know the real name.) "Well, in Italian, it's a Chutto Lapittida. In Portuguese, it's a Bom da Peida. In Chinese, it's a Chung long-tah, and in Japanese, it's a Katano Tekeda. You can know the name of that bird in all the languages of the world, but when you're finished, you'll know absolutely nothing whatever about the bird. You'll only know about humans in different places and what they call the bird. So let's look at the bird and see what it's doing—that's what counts."[68]

The difficulty with mammy, as the historian Morton and the physicist Feynman both show, comes at the very beginning of the analytical process, and not in the analysis itself. If historians acknowledge the mammy, they usually wind up describing her in a one-dimensional fashion—saying she was one thing, working tirelessly to deny that she was the "other" thing, and all the while playing against the stereotype the author often set out to debunk in the first place. If you wish to argue that mammy did not exist, you have a hell of a time talking about the lives of black women without acknowledging the presumably mythological evidence. If you argue that she did exist, you must attempt to find the truth to questions about motherhood and service and race in areas in which the evidence is contradictory and the witnesses sometimes deliberately evasive. The truth about mammy turns out not to have been one truth at all but a variety of truths and lies told by different people in different circumstances at different times for different reasons.

The task of saying what mammy was, if it means trying to bring all the contradictions together under one explanation, is at worst a fool's errand or at best an exercise in identifying what the contradictions were. The question is not whether she existed, but how she existed depending on those circumstances—

which are always identified and ordered by the person who sets out to answer the question. What mechanisms made her work in a particular case? What was the essence of the negotiation among race, class, and gender, both in the lives of domestics and the way people thought about them? It is different every time we examine it, depending upon the motives of the person doing the describing. In this sense, no single person named mammy ever existed; an idea about black female servants was negotiated among whites, blacks, men, women, historians, diarists, and novelists. *Mammy* is shorthand for a set of behaviors used to explain diverse concepts such as slavery, love, service, motherhood. When so much meaning can be bundled into a single term, the word itself is inherently imprecise, subject to new interpretations each time it is used, depending on who is using it. This is true for advertisers as well as historians and novelists. "As the advertising industry, which is dedicated to the creation of masks, makes clear, that which cannot gain authority from tradition may borrow it with a mask," Ellison observed.[69]

The chapters that follow demonstrate what those who introduced Aunt Jemima to the world wanted her to be. They relied upon imagery reminiscent of Page and Phillips, adding sentiment to Dixon's mammy, ignoring the complexity that was explored by Twain and, later, Smith, Faulkner, and a host of historians of slavery. They did so at their own peril—which did not amount to much in the first half of the twentieth century but forced them to make drastic changes during the second. The men behind Aunt Jemima pancake flour knew the power of the mammy image and gave it a lasting place in another venue, outside literature, history, and personal memory but drawing on all of them. Aunt Jemima's owners took the mammy through the looking glass of twentieth-century advertising to sell pancakes.

It all began with a lesser-known contemporary of Twain's, a newspaper writer who was an aspiring entrepreneur in the late 1880s. The mammy was Chris Rutt's inspiration, too, although he did not know it until he wandered inside the doors of a St. Joseph, Missouri, minstrel hall. What he saw next set the stage for the appearance of the most famous mammy ever, as her owners bragged, "the most famous colored woman in the world." Mammy Krenda and her ilk would be the inspiration for a multimillion-dollar enterprise.

We have seen the first of mammy, but we have not seen the last.

3 From Minstrel Shows to the World's Fair: The Birth of Aunt Jemima

Luck is the residue of design.
—Branch Rickey

Try a hot cake.
—Mammy in Margaret Mitchell's *Gone with the Wind*

In the autumn of 1889 Chris Rutt was a man with a problem. The former editorial writer for the *St. Joseph (Mo.) Gazette* had struck out on a new business venture in which he had no experience. In fact, no one could claim much experience at what Rutt was attempting to do: sell an amazing new self-rising pancake flour to the households of America. So far, everything had gone much better than one might expect. He and his partner Charles Underwood had acquired a bankrupt flour mill. Although neither of them had any experience in the culinary arts, or chemistry, or the infant industry of food processing—indeed, neither of them could even cook—they had by trial and error perfected their product. Now they were ready to market the self-rising flour, which was still known only by that unglamorous name. Nothing had come to Rutt yet as he walked the streets of St. Joe, but he was looking, according to the legend. He did not know it, but he was looking for Aunt Jemima.

Autumn of 1889 is as specific as anyone, even the authorized historian of the

Quaker Oats Company, can be in discussing the moment Chris Rutt met Aunt Jemima. No one seems to know the exact place, either, although St. Joseph was not a metropolis and probably had no more than three venues where minstrel shows were regularly staged. Rutt, mulling over his problem, walked into one of them, possibly Streckebein's Garden, Tootle's Opera House, or the Dime Eden Musee, or perhaps even the Grand Opera House, which carried minstrel shows less often. Once within, he encountered the blackface comedy team of Baker and Farrell. Again, this is only according to the legend, because newspaper advertisements do not confirm that Baker and Farrell were in town anytime in the fall of 1889, although an advertisement for an appearance by someone named Farrell in the spring at the Dime Eden Musee carried the simple tagline "You Know Him."[1]

The performers ended with a cakewalk, the traditional big finish for minstrel shows in which a variety of dance steps was performed in a circle. The rhythmic, circular dance was performed by slaves during harvest festivals in the American South and had been widely adopted by white men in blackface who practiced the stagecraft of mimicking black dances for the amusement of other whites.[2] One of the performers—no one remembers whether it was Baker or Farrell—was not only in blackface but in drag. He was wearing a dress, an apron, and a bandanna around his head, pretending to be a black cook. And then they began to sing:

I went to church the other day,
Old Aunt Jemima, oh! oh! oh!
To hear them white folks sing and pray,
Old Aunt Jemima, oh! oh! oh!
They prayed so long I couldn't stay,
Old Aunt Jemima, oh! oh! oh!
I knew the Lord would come that way,
Old Aunt Jemima, oh! oh! oh![3]

At that moment, Chris Rutt had found his trade name, and Aunt Jemima, as we know her today, had met her maker. Arthur Marquette's official company history of Quaker Oats, the source cited by nearly every account of Aunt Jemima's creation, describes the moment of serendipity simply: "Here was the image Rutt sought! Here was southern hospitality personified."[4] The number apparently was a huge hit with the audience as well as with Rutt; they supposedly whistled it in the streets in the following days that autumn, although none of the St. Joseph newspapers—not the *Gazette*, the *Daily News*, the *Catholic Tribune*, or the *Weekly Herald*—makes any mention of this performance or its effect. Despite the scant direct evidence that events unfolded this way, there is strong enough reason to believe the story, and no evidence of any alternative explanation. One thing about Aunt Jemima has always been clear: Her adoption as a popular trade name was at its inception a thing of chance. It was an unsuspecting visit to a minstrel show, a happy coincidence for a struggling businessman. Or was it?

Coincidence, Chance, and the Rise of the Self-rising Flour

A better question might be this: Do you believe in historical coincidences? If Chris Rutt had stepped in the path of a falling meteor on his way to the minstrel show, we could say a random event had occurred. When we look at a supposed coincidence such as Rutt's discovery of Aunt Jemima in context, considering its obvious links to other developments in the national culture, it looks less and less like a coincidence. Chris Rutt was not struck by a meteor; he instead tapped into major trends in the nation's popular culture and industry, and in doing so created Aunt Jemima pancake flour. It was not an unlikely coincidence that he did so, and it was no coincidence that it eventually worked.

Rutt and Underwood made their bid in the food-processing industry at the same time many other entrepreneurs were building similar businesses, thanks to advances in technology and transportation. National brands of all kinds of foods—crackers, soda pop, breakfast cereal—were made possible by the increasing urbanization of America toward the end of the nineteenth century, the growth of railroads into a system capable of moving both people and products from city to city, and the application of industrial practices not only to the production but the packaging of food, which in turn made feasible the transport of a variety of foodstuffs via rail to distant cities. We understand urbanization and railroads as familiar factors in the great changes experienced by Americans in the second half of the nineteenth century, but less celebrated are the industrial perfection of packaging and the possibilities that it offered. The development of the first practical mass-produced paper bags was spurred, like so many other things, by the Civil War, as northern mill operators sought a replacement for cotton sacks. In 1870 the mechanical process to stamp out today's familiar bag was patented, and the relationship between consumers and products began to change forever. Purchasers had been taking their own containers to grocers in order to carry products home and thus were constrained from buying more of an item than they had planned, on impulse; the arrival of cheap, mass-produced paper bags allowed buyers to carry home as much as they wanted of what they saw in the store. A simple paper bag eliminated longtime barriers to consumption and increased sales. One economist, writing in 1889, claimed that "nothing has had a greater influence in making possible the rapidity with which certain branches of the retail business are conducted as compared with 10 years ago . . . than the cheap and rapid production of paper bags."[5]

Paper bags, as an evolutionary ancestor of today's colorful, sophisticated, and often annoying packages, were an easily overlooked step toward a mass retail market for food, and they also were transitional in nature. Wholesalers of mass-produced food products eventually would have to overcome the system paper bags created, that of grocers buying in bulk and distributing differing amounts in retail according to the purchaser's desire. The relationship that existed before the paper bag—between local grocer and local purchaser—remained unchanged by improvements in package production. The mass market for name brands that were produced, packaged, priced, and sealed at a factory, transported by rail, and sold still unopened required further advances in the packaging process, specifically, the humble paper box. The perfection of a process by which factories could produce paper boxes was, as Thomas Hine has noted, the moment at which "packaging became a mass-market phenomenon." Although many early mass-produced products, including Aunt Jemima flour, were sold in paper bags, that is not how they typically arrived at local stores. Paper bags were too vulnerable to rupture, spillage, and vermin to travel long distances, so mass-produced food often required two layers of packaging: a paper box for transit and a paper bag for point of sale. In the eighteenth and early nineteenth centuries, box making was a craft, and the finished product was reserved for luxury goods such as jewelry and candy. In 1879 a Baltimore producer of bags altered a printing press to cut and shape paper. Cardboard—fluted paper between two sheets of thicker paper—had been invented five years earlier and seemed to be awaiting a reliable box-making process. Within a decade of the invention of box-making machines, the pioneers of the mass production of food, most notably Quaker Oats and the National Biscuit Company, were not only shipping in boxes but emphasizing to customers the sanitary benefits of doing so. The biscuit company eventually started putting the product itself in small, individual boxes meant for display at the point of sale after manufacturers discovered another benefit of cardboard: It was strong enough to allow brand names and symbols to be printed directly on it.[6] The ability to create a totally packaged product—sealed, branded, and only opened after it had arrived at the consumer's home—closed the circle of bulk retailing and changed the relationship between the product's owners and eventual purchasers by eliminating the middleman. Packages sold products, meaning greater efficiency and pricing reliability for entrepreneurs who adopted these innovations, and improved efficiency and power over price translated into greater potential for profit, assuming one had developed a product consumers recognized and wanted to buy in mass quantities.

This was the business world in which Chris Rutt and Charles Underwood attempted to make their mark in 1889 when they purchased a bankrupt flour mill in St. Joseph. That Missouri town is known mostly for its brief reign as the starting point for the Pony Express, but it also was an important milling center in the 1880s. By 1888, however, the amount of flour St. Joseph's mills produced far exceeded demand. When a mill fell into bankruptcy that year, Rutt, still writing editorials for the *St. Joseph Gazette*, and Underwood, a millworker, decided to try their hands at the business. They bought the property and set up shop as the Pearl Milling Company.[7] The mill's former operators had failed by marketing conventional products, selling flour in bulk to retailers, and Rutt and Underwood faced the same problem. They decided to create an entirely new product that in turn would create a new demand—a new use, really—for flour. Because pancake batter was difficult to make with any consistency, and because it used a relatively large amount of flour, Rutt and Underwood began experimenting with a self-rising flour that, when mixed with milk and cooked on a griddle, would produce pancakes. The product thus would be distinguished from competing flours by the fact that it was premixed and ready to use, an innovation only possible because the producer could package, brand, and ship it unopened and unchanged to the point of sale. After numerous tests on the kerosene stove in Rutt's home during the summer of 1889, they hit upon a mixture of wheat flour, corn flour, lime phosphate, and salt. They then conducted the first market test of a ready-mix product by inviting over the local librarian, Purd Wright, who told them it made good flapjacks.[8]

So when Rutt and Underwood sought to make their fortune in the food business, they followed major market trends, aiming to mass-produce something that would be packaged, shipped, and sold in the same form in which it left the factory. They were remarkably successful in assessing the market and developing a product to meet it and particularly insightful in creating a product that indeed could not have existed without advances in packaging and transportation. A further task remained: the naming of the world's first self-rising pancake flour. It needed to be something familiar, accepted, inviting. In drawing from popular culture, Rutt continued to follow market trends, but choosing the name of Aunt Jemima was indeed an innovation.

Old Aunt Jemima, Oh! Oh! Oh!

Thus we are back with Chris Rutt, settling into a seat at a St. Joseph minstrel show sometime in the fall of 1889. The mix has been created, the stuff is in the bags, but the partners are at a loss when it comes to a name—"Self-Rising Pancake Flour" is not catchy enough. What we should understand about Rutt's epiphany in the minstrel hall is that there is nothing out of the ordinary in his search for a brand name, and that the one he settled on is more interesting in the respect that it makes perfect sense, given the times, than in the manner in which he stumbled upon it. The second verse of the song Baker and Farrell performed on the stage in St. Joseph went like this:

> The monkey dressed in soldier clothes
> Old Aunt Jemima, oh! oh! oh!
> Went out in the woods to drill some crows
> Old Aunt Jemima, oh! oh! oh!
> The jay bird hung on the swinging limb
> Old Aunt Jemima, oh! oh! oh!
> I up with a stone and hit him on the shin
> Old Aunt Jemima, oh! oh! oh!
> Oh! Carline, oh, Carline
> Can't you dance the bee line,
> Old Aunt Jemima, oh! oh! oh!

It is no surprise that Rutt, looking for a diversion, strolled into a minstrel show that autumn day. Although the peak years of the blackface minstrel, which swept the nation in the 1840s, were long past, blackface performances were still common in American theaters throughout the second half of the nineteenth century and continued in some places even in the years following World War II. From the outset blackface minstrelsy balanced an envy of the supposedly pastoral, indolent lives of southern African Americans with an ostensibly realistic mocking of African-American mannerisms and speech—it was an act of both love and theft, as Eric Lott has written. It also was a reaffirmation of sorts for the white male working-class audience, which was invited to share in a preindustrial world of dancing, singing, fishing, and loafing while being reminded of its superiority to the silly, strutting coons depicted by white actors in burnt cork. The most familiar standard characters of early blackface minstrelsy were the country dullard Jim Crow, the subject of the most famous minstrel song (and supposedly inspired by the shuffling of a real crippled black man), and his city cousin Zip Coon, a posing dandy whose inbred stupidity unfolded in sketches. A confusing tangle of emotions, desires, loves, and hatreds was revealed during the interaction between a white interlocutor, the blackfaced sidemen, and the white men in the audience, an event that codified "the image of blacks as the prototypical Fool or Sambo," in the words of Mel Watkins. But this staging of the pejorative quality of blackness was really an act of creating whiteness, reminding white audiences that regardless of whatever trials they faced at work or home, they were uplifted by their race. It was the pay window for the "psychological wage" that W. E. B. Du Bois said white workers received in lieu of gains that might be realized through biracial solidarity.[9]

The cakewalk number Rutt saw was typical of the minstrel form, usually coming at the end of the show, which had three parts and may have been created by a black theatrical family headed by the performer John Luca in the early 1840s. Shows opened with a parade, or "walk-around," of all the blackface performers, who wore flashy clothes and took turns at singing popular songs. They arranged themselves in a semicircle, with the endmen—Mr. Tambo and Mr. Bones—at the end of the line, and the interlocutor, a white upper-class character, seated in the center. The interlocutor moderated the fast and ridiculous jokes and comic songs of Tambo and Bones, which often were at the interlocutor's expense, to the enjoyment of a working-class audience that watched a pair of silly black men outsmart a pompous white character. The second act was a variety segment called the "olio," in which the star attraction usually was a blackface stump speaker who ridiculed some topical issue, using numerous malaprops to make sport of emancipation or women's suffrage, for instance, and to show himself to be a fool as well.[10]

Rutt met Aunt Jemima in the third act. Typically, the final segment in a minstrel show was a plantation skit, heavy on slapstick, song, and dance, or, after the 1850s, farces based on Shakespearean drama. From the 1870s on, and especially in the 1890s, the final number was often a cakewalk, a dance in which the members of the troupe danced in a circle, with couples taking turns promenading in the center. Some scholars, such as Sterling Stuckey, argue that the circular cakewalk's origins are West African, while others maintain that it was from Europe. But all agree that the dance was maintained in America during harvest festivals on southern plantations, where slaves lampooned their masters' posturings instead of being lampooned themselves and competed for prizes, often a cake.[11] Thus the cakewalk that Rutt and the rest of the enthusiastic audience watched was the epitome of the minstrel show, at the same time both mocking and reveling in African-American culture, looking back longingly on an idyllic plantation South while nonetheless ridiculing its residents. The number wound up with this verse:

> The bullfrog married the tadpole's sister
> Old Aunt Jemima, oh! oh! oh!
> He smacked his lips and then he kissed her
> Old Aunt Jemima, oh! oh! oh!
> She says, if you love me as I love you
> Old Aunt Jemima, oh! oh! oh!
> No knife can cut our love in two
> Old Aunt Jemima, oh! oh! oh!
> Oh, Carline, oh, Carline
> Can't you dance the bee line,
> Old Aunt Jemima, oh! oh! oh!

The addition of the mammy—in this case, Old Aunt Jemima—in the pantheon of minstrel types appears to have been a postbellum event. Blackface transvestism is almost as old as the minstrel show, with, as Lott has observed, blackface "wenches" usually demonstrating the "profane and murderous power of women."[12] But by the 1880s, the standard mammy, a fat, cantankerous cook who, like her literary counterparts, slaved in the kitchens of the plantation South, was as well established and recognized as Sambo.[13] This was almost certainly due largely to the song Rutt heard performed by Baker and Farrell in 1889, which had been written fourteen years earlier by one of the greatest and most unlikely minstrel artists, a black musician named Billy Kersands.

Kersands, who was born around 1842, was perhaps best known for his comic routines. He not only was a songwriter, a 200-pound acrobat, and an innovative dancer (some historians credit him with the invention of the soft shoe), but he could, to an audience's amusement, stick several billiard balls in his mouth without interrupting his routine. One historian of nineteenth-century popular music wrote that Kersands's "massive mouth was as famous then as Jimmy Durante's prodigious proboscis is today." W. C. Handy once claimed that he saw Kersands put a coffee cup and saucer in his mouth.[14] But Kersands's most lasting contribution to the minstrel show was his music, which like the rest of its genre reinforced black stereotypes. One of his popular tunes, "Mary's Gone Home with a Coon," was the story of an old man whose daughter had run off with a black man:

> He's black, as black as he can be,
> Now I wouldn't care if he was only yaller,
> But he's black all o'er, he's a porter in a store,
> My heart is tore, when I think the matter o'er
> De chile dat I bore, should tink ob me no more,
> Den to run away wid a big black coon.[15]

His biggest hit was "Old Aunt Jemima." Kersands wrote it in 1875 and by 1877 had performed it onstage more than two thousand times, according to Robert Toll. He would continue to perform it until his death in 1915, and countless other minstrel performers copied it, bringing numerous Aunt Jemimas onstage into the 1890s. Eventually, other songwriters incorporated Aunt Jemima into their tunes in arrangements such as "Aunt Jemima's Picnic Day" and "Aunt Jemima Song."[16] There were at least three versions of Kersands's original song (and probably more) by the time Rutt saw it performed in 1889, some substituting "pea-vine" for "bee-line" in the refrain, and one version explaining how emancipation was offered to a slave:

My old missus promise me,
Old Aunt Jemima, oh! oh! oh!
When she died she-d set me free,
Old Aunt Jemima, oh! oh! oh!
She lived so long her head got bald,
Old Aunt Jemima, oh! oh! oh!
She swore she would not die at all,
Old Aunt Jemima, oh! oh! oh![17]

Despite what some might see today as the overt racism of some of his lyrics, Kersands's musical performances were hugely successful with the black audiences that occasionally saw them. Tom Fletcher, a black minstrel and contemporary of Kersands, said that "a minstrel show without Billy Kersands was like a circus without elephants." Toll offers an interesting explanation for Kersands's popularity among blacks: besides laughing at Kersands's exaggerated mannerisms, they read his lyrics very differently from white audiences. For example, in the version of "Old Aunt Jemima" that depicts crows, a symbol of blackness, escaping the "frog in soldiers clothes" who went out to "drill" them, Kersands might have been following black folk tradition of describing a black trickster, like Brer Rabbit, who escapes from a threatening authority figure. In the version in which a slave's mistress goes bald, black audiences "could endorse its protest against whites' broken promises while they laughed at the idea of a bald white woman." Toll notes that Kersands used the verse about the bald mistress long after white minstrels discarded it. Still, black minstrel troupes shared an important appeal with their white counterparts in the postwar era. Both races emphasized their characters' links to the plantation; even as white performers in blackface mugged and shuffled for their audiences, black minstrel troupes advertised themselves as "genuine plantation darkies from the South" and used names like Slave Troupe, Georgia Slave Brothers, and Georgia Slave Troupe Minstrels.[18] However, the difference in what black and white audiences heard at minstrel shows goes deeper than the obvious references to plantation life.

The most important reason that black audiences might have appreciated Billy Kersands's performance of "Old Aunt Jemima" is the fact that Kersands did not write the lyrics that inspired Chris Rutt, but instead, as many minstrel performers did, adapted them from a secular slave song, the work songs they sang as they sowed, planted, and carried bales. The songs helped break the tedium and coordinate work as slaves sweated under the sun and followed orders shouted by the overseer. As Sterling Stuckey and Sterling Brown have shown— and Frederick Douglass reported in his study of slave songs—slaves often performed songs whose lyrics commented on the irony of their situation: "We raise de wheat, dey gib us de corn; We sift de meal; de gib us de huss; We peel de meat, dey gib us de skin; An dat's de way dey take us in." Sometimes the songs focused on the broken promise of emancipation by a master or mistress, as in this example offered by Stuckey:

> My ole missus promise me
> W'en she died, sh'd set me free,
> She lived so long dat 'er head got bal'
> An' she give out'n de notion a-dyin' at all.[19]

It really was a slave song, after all. The very words Billy Kersands adapted to one of his versions of "Old Aunt Jemima"—the version, according to Toll, he used in front of black audiences, the one white minstrels were less likely to perform—had been first performed by slaves. Students of American blackface minstrelsy are familiar with ironies such as this; white men in blackface were grotesquely lampooning blacks by singing authentic black songs, unaware of the authenticity underlying their counterfeit. Meanwhile, Billy Kersands, in the same type of bizarre theatrical setting, was passing on pieces of that culture to black audiences.

One important difference remains, of course, between white and black performers who played Aunt Jemima: the white men were not only cross-dressing but blacking up as well. Aunt Jemima for much of her early career was a white man. The knowledge that the black woman was really a white man was an integral part of the pageant. Eric Lott and Natalie Davis both have observed that white men dress as black women at peculiar moments in history—"ritual and festive inversions" that might be in resistance to changing times or in support of tradition, depending on circumstances, paradoxically mocking and mimicking a culture for their own ends. It might be difficult for some to read black resistance into the lyrics of "Old Aunt Jemima," as Toll does. But it is also difficult to imagine the appeal of a white man, in drag and blackface, to an audience of his racial and gender peers without some reading between the lines. Lott speculates that the racial and sexual anarchy typified by the minstrel mammy allowed white men to relive "the forgotten liberties of infancy—the belly and sucking of breasts, a wallowing in shit." White male anxieties could be exorcised through a symbolic taking of a black female body.[20]

One does not have to accept Lott's complex interpretations of drag and blackface to recognize that the interplay between the white male Aunt Jemima and his/her audience was, like so much in the American minstrel theater, deeper than the "genuine Negro fun" that the posters for shows advertised. Drag and blackface lampooning also could have represented, for example, a safe way of expressing control over mothers, rather than wallowing in infancy. In any event, it is not too much of a stretch to imagine different singers delivering the song in different ways to different audiences in the decades after it was written; many different people performed it, bringing Aunt Jemima into minstrel halls in cities large and small across the United States. Eventually, of course, Aunt Jemima's largest and most important audience would be white women, and her claim to be an authentic black woman—not a white actor—would be the key to her success.

So when Chris Rutt picked up on Aunt Jemima's appeal—his blind coincidence, his moment of serendipity—he was merely awash in the popular culture of the time, when mammies were remembered fondly in novels and personal reminiscences and portrayed onstage. He did not invent this popular icon's appeal; he only adopted as a trade name and image something that was readily evident in the public domain. To use a more contemporary example, think of the hundreds of products aimed at children in the 1990s that incorporated a drawing or picture of a dinosaur. "Dinomania," as the biologist Stephen Jay Gould described the marketing phenomenon, had no logical explanation or starting point. It predated the release of the hit movie *Jurassic Park,* and the proliferation of dinosaur lunch boxes, bed sheets, and canned noodles can only be explained as a moment that numerous marketers, not acting in concert, accurately assessed the value of an existing interest that always had the potential for a craze.[21] Aunt Jemima was ready for some marketer to exploit, particularly because of the need for distinctive, simple, and popular trademarks to accompany the advent of national brands. Chris Rutt showed up at the minstrel show, perhaps on a whim, perhaps not, but by the time he got there, Aunt Jemima had been waiting for years.

A more entertaining way of looking at Rutt's "discovery" of Aunt Jemima might be to consider what else the pancake entrepreneur could have discovered as his trademark, had he wandered into a different show on a different night. The possibilities certainly exist, since St. Joseph newspaper advertisements for 1889 show a wide-ranging number of available characters. The competing theaters offered up different minstrel shows in late summer and early autumn; on 26 August 1889 a Boston company performed an outdoor version of *Uncle Tom's Cabin* featuring the renowned Sam Lucas, the first black man to play the title role in a serious production.[22] One might wish to argue that only by coincidence was the world spared "Uncle Tom's pancake mix" or "Little Eva pancake flour," but neither character lends itself to the product as obviously as Aunt Jemima in her kitchen. Most of the other acts Rutt could have seen in St. Joseph halls would have offered even less inspiration: the "Demon Man-Serpent" at the Dime Eden Musee, the "Semi-Human Acting Dog Trix" at the Grand Opera House, or "Spotted Ed, the Leopard Man," at the Musee.[23] None of these seems a likely candidate for immortality on the bag of ready-mix pancake batter.

By the fall of 1889, Chris Rutt seemed to have everything in place. The product was ready. The trademark's popular appeal was already demonstrated in the St. Joseph audience and in minstrel halls across the United States. One problem emerged in the months to come, however: Aunt Jemima pancake mix did not sell. It was not just bad luck that kept her from becoming a household name. Rutt and Underwood did not understand two further developments in the American economy that would become crucial to the product's eventual success: the evolution of marketing and distribution.

R. T. Davis Presents Aunt Jemima

Rutt and Underwood took the first two crucial steps in popularizing the Aunt Jemima brand, but they had no distribution network and little concept of the need to advertise a new product. By the end of 1889, they had no money, either. Rutt returned to writing editorials, and Underwood took a job with the R. T. Davis Milling Company, the largest flour miller in Buchanan County. Underwood's brother, Bert, registered the Aunt Jemima trademark and briefly attempted to market the mix himself. But in January 1890 the partners sold the company and recipe to Charles Underwood's new boss, R. T. Davis.[24]

By 1890 Davis had been in the flour business for about fifty years. His products were on grocery shelves throughout the Missouri Valley, and he had the necessary capital to launch a new product. Davis also was experienced in the area in which Rutt and Underwood were especially naive: the revolution in production and promotion of consumer goods that occurred during his years in the business, creating a mass market for consumer goods as the nation moved from rural to urban, production to consumption, and agricultural to industrial. Changes in law and technology in the 1880s and 1890s facilitated this process. From 1870, when Congress passed the first act protecting trademarks, to 1905, when trademark rights were affirmed to the point that they had no legal expiration date (unlike copyrights, for instance), the number of protected corporate names and emblems grew at a prodigious rate. Only about a hundred trademarks were registered with the federal government in 1870. By 1875, 1,138 were registered, 10,500 by 1906, and more than 50,000 by 1920. While the law protected the language that major firms used to communicate directly to consumers, advances in printing processes provided the means. Changes in printing costs and processes meant that publishers could depend on advertising instead of only literary content to make money, and a number of prominent magazines established in the 1880s—*Ladies' Home Journal, Cosmopolitan, McClure's*—set out to do so, directing content "toward the increasingly numerous and prosperous urban middle classes," who previously had shown little interest in literary monthlies. Changes in magazine content during the last decades of the nineteenth century created a demand for a new type of producer—the advertising agency. Before the 1890s advertising agents mostly brokered space, purchasing it from newspapers and magazines and selling it to manufacturers, who planned their own campaigns and wrote their own copy. In 1880 the Wanamaker clothing retail firm hired an agent to write its copy, and other large department stores began to adopt that approach. Likewise, producers of household products increasingly employed agents to write their copy, although in 1900 more than twenty-five hundred manufacturers still crafted their own ads. From the turn of the century to World War I, ad agencies were increasingly hired to promote new products.[25]

What companies could propose to consumers through advertising changed during the last two decades of the nineteenth century. After 1880 the extension of railroads helped create regional markets for products that could be produced uniformly and in greater quantities through centralized manufacturing. Still, most products were unbranded, and wholesale distributors, not the more distant producer, dominated the process of selling and controlled the way products were marketed. Manufacturers like Davis, however, sought greater control over the pricing and distribution of their products in order to assure maximum profit and predictability; "massive outputs demanded dependable markets." Firms such as Procter and Gamble worked to centralize the distribution process as well as manufacturing and thus took a greater stake in the promotion of their products, courting local merchants, creating in-store displays, and providing instructions on how the product should be used. New promotional strategies meant a new relationship had to be forged between the maker of a product and the person who eventually purchased it. Because the manufacturer's interest was not only in selling the product but in supporting a predictable price, the buyer needed to be convinced to accept no substitute for the manufacturer's product, and thus to distinguish among brand names.[26]

Davis put more than capital behind the Aunt Jemima brand; he brought a promotional strategy. He also possessed the insight to make three changes in Aunt Jemima. First, he added powdered milk to the mix, which meant that housewives needed only Aunt Jemima and water to make pancakes. Second, he added rice and corn sugar to improve the product's texture and flavor. The third change, however, was by far the most important: R. T. Davis decided to promote Aunt Jemima pancake mix by creating Aunt Jemima—in person. He mixed the mammy and the mass market, and the two have been inseparable since.

The image of Aunt Jemima as a legendary cook was the one upon which Davis attempted to capitalize in 1890 after buying the Pearl Milling Company, which he merged with the R. T. Davis Milling Company. He sent out requests to his large network of food brokers, asking them to keep an eye out for the personification of Aunt Jemima: a black woman with an outgoing personality, cooking skills, and the poise to demonstrate the pancake mix at fairs and festivals. In a time long before television and its myriad animated trademarks, Davis had decided to take product promotion a step further. His trademark not only would breathe and speak, but, in the tradition of traveling salesmen, its personality would sell the product, charming audiences into giving the mix a try.[27] This was a first, tentative step off the minstrel stage; Aunt Jemima needed to make personal appearances—live performances—before she gained a foothold in the world of trademarks. The purpose of a live appearance, however, was not to amuse with counterfeit of drag and blackface but to persuade with the presence of a "real" slave woman. As the trademark enabled producers to reach consumers directly—without the retail middleman's cracker barrel—the living trademark would enable Davis to talk to potential purchasers. A real living black woman, instead of a white man in blackface and drag, would reinforce the product's authenticity and origin as the creation of a real ex-slave.

Charles Jackson, a food wholesaler, found the first Aunt Jemima. She was Nancy Green, a fifty-nine-year-old servant for a Chicago judge. Born into slavery on a Montgomery County, Kentucky, plantation, she enjoyed sharing stories of her childhood in slavery. Davis, certain he had found the living Aunt Jemima, signed Nancy Green to an exclusive contract to play the role of her life. Her debut came at the World's Columbian Exposition of May–November 1893 in Chicago, within a booth designed to look like a giant flour barrel (fig. 1). She greeted guests and cooked pancakes, all the while singing and telling stories of life on the plantation, some real, some apocryphal. Purd Wright, the librarian who had taste-tested the first batch of pancakes and now served as Davis's advertising manager, distributed a souvenir button he had designed. On it was the likeness of Aunt Jemima; below her smiling face was the caption "I'se in town, honey." Aunt Jemima's debut was a smashing success. Crowds jammed the exhibit, waiting for a glimpse of her, and "I'se in town, honey," became a catchphrase. Fair officials awarded the "pancake queen" a medal, and Davis claimed that merchants who had attended the fair placed more than fifty thousand orders for his pancake mix. But more importantly, the persona of Aunt Jemima had proved to sell a lot of pancakes. Green, whose more pleasant face had replaced the hideous mammy on Rutt's original logo, began participating in sales promotions across the country. Aunt Jemima herself could not be everywhere; the legend, however, could.[28]

Purd Wright wrote the earliest version of Aunt Jemima's life story. Titled *The Life of Aunt Jemima, the Most Famous Colored Woman in the World,*

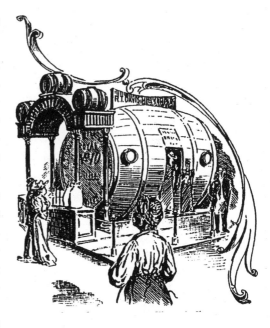

1. "Aunt Jemima at the World's Fair," *The Life of Aunt Jemima* (St. Joseph, Mo., 1895). (Courtesy of Burkett Collection, Hillsdale, Mich.)

the pamphlet blended fact and fiction—Nancy Green's slave stories with Wright's imagination—and served as the rough outline for more detailed stories in twentieth-century advertisements (fig. 2). Aunt Jemima was the loyal cook for Louisiana's Colonel Higbee, a prosperous planter on the Mississippi. Her pancakes were the envy of the region, but she would not share the secret recipe. During the Civil War, Union soldiers were threatening to rip Higbee's moustache off his face when Aunt Jemima interceded, offering the northerners pancakes, and the colonel was able to escape. According to the legend the northerners never forgot the taste of the most delicious pancakes in the world. After Higbee's death some of them persuaded Aunt Jemima to come upriver and share her secret with the world.[29] Themes that would dominate Aunt Jemima ads for years to come were introduced for the first time: Aunt Jemima rescues her owner or another man with pancakes; northerners discover a southern secret and return years later to bring it to the nation; Aunt Jemima demands to be paid in gold, not currency, for her recipe.

This is the essence of the myth that Davis used to promote the pancake mix until his death in 1900, a story maintained by the executives who followed him through one bankruptcy and a reorganization in 1903. Robert Clark, Davis's former general manager, assumed control of the company that year and renamed it Aunt Jemima Mills. He extended Aunt Jemima's visibility by beginning a rag-doll coupon promotion in 1906. Eventually, Aunt Jemima gained a husband, Uncle Mose, and "two cunning pickaninnies," Diana and Wade—all available to those who sent in three boxtops and sixteen cents or four boxtops and a dime.[30] The rag-doll campaign, even in bad times, was a consistent success for the milling company, as Clark recalled in a 1925 company memo; the first year, Clark found to his surprise that the company needed to hire extra help to process all the "bushel baskets" of requests "for this delightful southern mammy that could be cuddled, dropped, thrown and sat upon, and would

2. Inside cover, *The Life of Aunt Jemima.* (Courtesy of Burkett Collection)

still turn up, good as new. But it was impossible to deliver the dolls quickly enough." In late 1923 the company sought to measure interest in the rag-doll promotion and began offering consumers a choice: either six cents for a sample package of buckwheat flour, a sample package of regular flour, and a recipe folder, or, for thirty cents, all that plus the "jolly Aunt Jemima family" of rag dolls. When the reponses to the ads in *Good Housekeeping*, the *Ladies' Home Journal*, and the *Chicago Tribune* were tallied, 3,309 had chosen the six-cent offer and 4,853 the thirty-cent offer. In December 1923 the company placed a series of ads across the country, offering the samples for free and the rag-doll family for an additional dime. The ten-cent offer received 6,692 responses, outdrawing the free offer's 3,716 replies. The advertising memo only noted that it was "interesting" that the free offer was less attractive than the rag-doll offer, and that "the amount of money enclosed with the coupons has exceeded the cost of the space used to advertise the offer. It seems quite probable that this could continue to pull for some time."[31]

The personal appearance of Aunt Jemima at the 1893 World's Fair set in motion a promotional approach that persisted throughout most of the twentieth century, as real-life Aunt Jemimas—the descendants of the white and black men who played her on the minstrel stage—made thousands of personal appearances. The myth of Aunt Jemima and its trappings—rag dolls, salt and pepper shakers, and cookie jars—continued as the company prospered under Clark and again struggled during World War I. The story of the black mammy's pancakes was maintained by the Quaker Oats Company, which bought Aunt Jemima Mills in 1925 and applied its considerable marketing resources. The legend even survived the death of the original Aunt Jemima, Nancy Green, who was struck by a car in 1923. Other women eventually became the national Aunt Jemima in different media, and dozens of women played Aunt Jemima in smaller promotions as the personal appearances continued throughout the first half of the century. Throughout their careers, as with Nancy Green, the differences among the women who played Aunt Jemima and the character herself, as well as her origins, tended to blur. For example, the 15 November 1923 issue of *Missouri Farmer*, under the headline "Aunt Jemima Is Gone," mentioned that Green had been struck by a car and then blended the facts of Green's life with the fiction of Aunt Jemima's. It said that the boys in the home of the Chicago judge where Nancy Green worked loved the pancakes made by the ex-slave from Kentucky, and her pancakes became famous throughout the neighborhood. "In due time, a big St. Joseph mill heard about her, obtained her recipe and induced her to make pancakes at the Chicago World's Fair. . . . After the fair, the mill itself adopted her name and she was employed to go from one exposition to another to demonstrate her skill."[32] Nancy Green, of course, adopted Aunt Jemima's name, not the other way around. The idea that Aunt Jemima was a real person—or that Nancy Green and Aunt Jemima were the same person—has lasted a long time and can even be found in recent accounts. For example, a Gannett News Service report in 1989 said: "Aunt Jemima was a bubbly person and fun to talk to. Born in Montgomery County, Ky., she moved to Chicago shortly after the turn of the century and cooked for a judge's family, where her specialty was—get ready—pancakes. Aunt Jemima became famous at the World's Fair in Chicago in 1893 where, legend has it, she flipped more than a million pancakes by the time the fair was over. In 1923, Aunt Jemima, 89, and jolly as ever, died in a car accident."[33]

Nearly a hundred years after Davis's brainstorm at the Columbian Exposition, reporters still occasionally referred to Aunt Jemima as someone who actually lived, if not "the most famous colored woman in the world." R. T. Davis and Purd Wright built their legend to last. It was no coincidence that it did; rather, its lasting appeal reflects a century of hard work and a response to changes in marketing, advertising, popular culture, and technology.

But the legend would need caretakers during its long life—people with the vision to keep it alive and to expand upon it. Billy Kersands founded the character, based on the slave icon of southern reality and memory, and the dozens of black and white minstrels who performed the musical number kept her in the public eye. Chris Rutt capitalized on the image, and R. T. Davis understood how to use it. The people who really kept the image going, however, were those in the audience, the ones who applauded the original number, who responded to the mammy image in personal appearances. The aim of modern advertising, as it developed in the early twentieth century, was to give the audience what it wanted. And perhaps no one better understood that than the man who would do the most to shape the image of Aunt Jemima. James Webb Young was already a star adman by the time he met Aunt Jemima, but he would take that slave image, combine it with what he knew about the Old South and, more important, the contemporary market, and leave a permanent mark on American culture.

4 They Were What They Ate: James Webb Young and the Reconstruction of American Advertising

Oh see the little moron;
She doesn't give a damn.
I wish I were a moron!
My g—d, perhaps I am!

—James Webb Young, 1928

Perhaps there are historical coincidences, after all. How else would we explain the fact that when Aunt Jemima's owners decided the time had come for a new approach to their national advertising campaign, a man like James Webb Young was waiting to take it on? Young had, it seems in retrospect, all the traits that would be required to expand Aunt Jemima's legend: experience in how national advertising had developed and where it was going, an understanding of the mythological power of the plantation South, and a pronounced disrespect for the intelligence of his audience, in this case, female consumers. The story of Aunt Jemima and the story of an individual adman become intertwined at this point. She and James Webb Young reflect the way national advertising and the ad agency developed in the years after the turn of the century. They all rose together as advertising began to hold a mirror to American society, seeking to explore and exploit the innermost doubts, loves, hates, fears, and aspirations of the target audience—doing much the same as the performers in the minstrel show had, but on a much larger and more profitable scale.

Understanding Aunt Jemima means understanding a few more developments in the American economy that are much larger than her, however. She was most effective in a time when the advertising industry had developed the size and sophistication it required to exploit her image, and when the sort of servant she represented—a live-in black cook—was in relatively short supply, especially in the North. And she would await a meeting with someone in the advertising industry who realized how powerful an image she was—as an icon of Old South, white leisure—and who had the skills and insight to bring her possibilities to life in a way that pointedly spoke to her audience, in living color. First, I examine the changes in the American servant population that made Aunt Jemima's appeal possible, giving an important motive to the white housewives who were her target audience. Second, I demonstrate how American advertising, in the years just before and after World War I, developed as an industry that not only had the ability to capitalize on her image but was oriented toward doing so. And finally, I show how one advertising executive, James Young, was particularly equipped to take advantage of all these changes.

The "Servant Crisis" Dons Blackface

Advertising could be said, briefly if somewhat charitably, to be about proposing solutions to consumers' problems, if not creating the perception itself that the problems exist. Even the harshest critics of advertising would concede that it must to some degree draw its power from concerns that would fester whether or not advertising existed. Although modern advertising undoubtedly helped invent concerns about body odor and social status, it also addressed situations that are older than national magazines, processed foods, automobiles, and many other products that an individual ad might be touting. Advertisers do not invent every situation they exploit.

One example of this, especially important in the development of the twentieth-century Aunt Jemima ad campaigns, is America's nearly perpetual "servant crisis." As one economist put it in the 1940s, "It is a venerable Anglo-Saxon tradition to view the servant problem with alarm."[1] The "servant problem" in American history sometimes was a reflection not of a shortage of servants but of the regularity with which hired help came and went. In colonial times indentured servants sought to buy out their servitude before their time was up and rarely stayed on beyond that period, because of the availability of land. In the nineteenth century girls routinely worked in other homes up to the time of marriage, while boys sought apprenticeships and day labor for the purpose of setting out on their own. In more prosperous communities couples married earlier and reduced the time they spent in service. As Ruth Schwartz Cowan observed, complaints about a household servant problem before the twentieth century were related not so much to a shortage of help as to a shortage of "good help," which meant "someone who was (1) beyond adolescence, (2) experienced and skillful, and (3) subservient."[2] By 1825 the first society to promote the benefits of domestic service, and thereby attract more respectable women to the ranks, was formed in New York City. The nineteenth century marks the long retreat in the urban North from a more casual hiring of rural girls as "help." As middle-class employers increasingly recruited urban women, the servant problem was blamed on the Irish immigrants who filled the ranks or on the "intelligence agencies" who connected employer and employee. Domestic employment came to be more rational, disciplined, and demanding of an active supervisory role by the woman of the house. In the mid-nineteenth century domestic service was easily the most common occupation reported by women, and although census data before 1870 are fragmentary, up to 30 percent of American households had some kind of servant.[3]

From the 1890s on, the participation of white women in the workforce outside the home began its long rate of increase, from 18.9 percent in 1890, to 20.6 percent in 1900, to 25.4 percent in 1910. Single women, who typically filled the ranks of live-in domestic servants, naturally continued to dominate the ranks of women working outside households, rising from 40.5 percent in 1890 to 51.1 percent in 1910. (The figures are distorted because agricultural laborers were counted among women in the labor force, and additionally, the data for 1890 to 1930 overcounted all laborers by including anyone who had been counted in the labor force the previous year.) Moreover, the domestic labor numbers overwhelmingly demonstrated that white women only accounted for a small number of married domestic workers; while 2.5 percent of white domestic workers had a husband in 1890, 59.5 percent of "nonwhite" domestic women had a husband.[4] Still, in absolute numbers from the 1900 census, only 522,751 black women worked as servants, mostly in the South. Throughout much of the nineteenth century in the North, from at least the famine migrations of the late 1840s and early 1850s, the Irish "biddy" was the symbol of a servant problem, not the black washerwoman or maid; in 1855 alone, black women made up only a thousand of New York City's 31,000 domestics.[5] The major problem with Irish serving women was their Catholicism, but employers also "shuddered at 'Irish impulsiveness' and turbulence, and were disgusted and morally shocked at the Irish propensity for strong drink," according to one observer in the 1850s.[6]

The major development in the servant population in the early twentieth century reflected the mass migration of African Americans northward in the World War I era. By 1910, as increasing numbers of white women found work not only in factories but in waitressing and department stores, more of the women employed in domestic service in the North and the nation as a whole were black. By that year 795,236 African-American women were in domestic service, according to census figures. The 1920 census showed a large dip—down to 697,389—but that reflected a change in enumeration techniques rather than a decrease in black female domestics, when census takers abandoned a 1910 instruction to ascertain occupations as specifically as possible. George Stigler, an economist who studied the 1920 results, advised that the decline was at least "over-large" and probably "not entirely real." By 1930, after the census was changed back to 1910 standards, it reported slightly more than one million black women in household domestic service. All the while, the overall numbers of domestic servants continued to decline; by 1930 the total number of servants per 1,000 U.S. families had fallen to 67.7, from 94.3 in 1900 and 93.1 in 1910. (In 1920, the year the census undercounted domestic servants, the number was 61.3 per 1,000 families.) As domestic servants became rarer, more black women were becoming domestic servants.[7] Families seeking domestic help—with an increasing lack of success in the years after World War I—were increasingly trying to find black women to work for them.

The eventual replacement of white women with black women in the overall domestic force was disruptive in both the North and South. Employment agencies recruited black women from southern households, and newly arrived black domestics in the North used the only employment advantage available to them, movement from household to household and city to city within the North. Southern whites, of course, complained bitterly about northern agents' successes in recruiting black men and women and warned of the poor prospects they would face in the heartless cities above the Mason-Dixon Line. At the same time, because the most effective method of changing working conditions was to switch jobs, northern mistresses continued to complain about the difficulty of finding and keeping a servant, by now a black rather than Irish one. In addition, African-American servants newly arrived from the South were increasingly reluctant to accept live-in service, in which they would be on call at all hours of the day. In 1923 a group of Baltimore matrons complained that "Negro women demand to go home at night for one of two reasons. Either they really do go to their homes to do the work they must neglect during the day, or particularly the younger ones want to amuse themselves and spend much too large a portion of the nights at dances, or movies or festivals. . . . In either case, they are trying to burn their candles at both ends and their health suffers, while the employer suffers from a tired servant utterly unequal to the requirement of her day's work."[8] The black women in question saw the issue completely differently. At stake were personal dignity and privacy, not the right to "burn the candle at both ends." As Velma Davis, a Washington, D.C., domestic, remembered: "Living in you had nothing. The job was for them, not your life. [From the] time I could, I started to try to get something that let me have some rest. A rest at the end of the day. That's why you try to live out. You'd be willing to take any chance to live out to just have some time that was yours."[9]

Employment agencies heard other complaints about the black women recruited to work in northern homes. The servants tended to seek marriage and to have children, and thus were said to "find it difficult to sleep on employers' premises" and stole food to support their families. They refused to accept a week's trial employment, insisting (usually correctly) that they could find an immediate offer of permanent employment elsewhere. Some employers complained that they expressed a particular dislike for their work and the intention to get out of it. Statistical evidence of the extent to which they did so is fragmentary, but the numbers that exist suggest that the turnover rate must have been very high. A Washington, D.C., employment office tracked 1,000 black domestics in 1921-22 and found that 317 remained in their job one week or less, 582 from one to three months, and 101 four months or longer.[10]

Thus the servant problem both remained the same and changed in the early twentieth century, with long-standing concerns about the loyalty and efficiency of household working women continuing, but increasingly involving black women. As mistresses of households as far-flung from Dixie as Detroit and Milwaukee complained about the difficulties of keeping black serving women, the United Daughters of the Confederacy proposed, unsuccessfully in both cases, a training school for new mammies and eventually a commemorative monument to the mammy, as recognition of a long-lost standard of unstinting service, love, and loyalty. No one, North or South, owned Aunt Jemima anymore, and the problem only worsened during the First World War, as black women took whatever temporary opportunities were presented to leave the household and try their hands at factory work. The ratio of servants to families in America steadily declined from the turn of the century through the world war and the Great Depression, decreasing a third by 1940.[11] The drop is explained by two interlocking factors. The first is the reluctance of an increasingly black servant population to take and hold domestic positions—the early twentieth-century version of the servant problem—and the second complementary development was the rise and promotion of laborsaving devices for the American household.

The Irony of Laborsaving Household Goods

The evolution of household appliances reflected the long nineteenth-century industrial trend away from "housework," as crafts typically performed at home became rationalized, mechanized, and performed for wages at centralized factories. Before industrialization, most housework produced goods and services consumed within the home—food, soap, candles, clothing—still according to a sexual division of labor. By the middle of the nineteenth century, the distinction between household and nascent industry was blurry, because, as Susan Strasser has explained, even an increasingly urban society maintained much of its rural character, with households producing a significant amount of what they consumed even as men more regularly left home in the morning to slaughter beef, make shoes, or puddle iron. "Men left home to work; women's work remained intertwined with the rest of their lives, their time restructured by some products . . . but still fundamentally their own."[12]

From about the turn of the century to the 1920s, as gas and electricity, indoor plumbing, and improvements in mass production and distribution systems spread industrial progress beyond the homes of the very wealthy, middle-class urban households experienced their own industrial revolution. Standardized goods replaced a variety of homespun or makeshift objects, replacing the production of housewives during the latter part of the nineteenth century. Cowan, in *More Work for Mother*, demonstrated how changes in technology and distribution of a single product—the stove—changed American homes in a relatively short time. The Bessemer process of making steel not only increased the production of steam engines and steel rails, for the delivery of products, but made possible better and cheaper stoves, replacing the pig-iron models that were difficult to assemble and susceptible to cracking. More reliable and plentiful cook-stoves in turn meant that a greater array of foods could be prepared; the stew from the pot over the open hearth could give way to delicacies that could not have been prepared at home earlier.[13]

The cast-iron stove and its gas and electric successors, however, changed the equation of household labor. As Cowan noted, they were "labor-saving" devices, ostensibly aimed at female labor but really saving what had traditionally been male labor. Advances in stove making reduced the need to gather fuel by chopping and splintering wood, typically the responsibility of husbands rather than wives. In addition, improvements in stove technology did not reduce cooking time or difficulty of many items—bacon took as long to fry on a cast-iron stove as in a fireplace—and actually added to the work involved in cooking. A housewife needed to know how to regulate the dampers for different types of food, and "once she had conquered this art, it was possible for her to boil potatoes, simmer a soup, and bake an apple pie for dinner all at the same time; this combination would have been impossible on an open hearth."[14] Better stoves eliminated the necessity of single-pot cooking, increasing the variables faced and the time consumed by American women in the kitchen.

The problems presented by new possibilities in the home extended to a wide variety of products, not just the kitchen stove. Using a vacuum cleaner, for example, is easier than dragging rugs out to a line and beating them, or even sweeping with a broom, but the product—and similar ones aimed at easing household chores—also set a new standard of cleanliness for the household of the early twentieth century. Homes had to be cleaner and had to be cleaned more often, because they could be. As Cowan argued, the problem with saying that the vacuum cleaner made household work easier is the question, Easier for whom? Likewise, while improved systems for bringing running water inside a household eased what had been the woman's job of keeping the home clean, in a less obvious sense it made that work more difficult, by making it possible for women to keep homes cleaner, by making women more "productive" cleaners.[15] New ways of living and working inside the home were connected from household to household as newly strung electrical wires began to stretch across the horizon. In 1912, 12 percent of dwellings had electrical service; that number had risen to 35 percent by 1920 and 68 percent in 1930, with an accompanying reduction in cost as the service gained broader use.[16] New products for the household amounted to a technological imperative in the years between the turn of the century and the Great Depression; the argument for accomplishing some feat of cooking, cleaning, or even personal hygiene amounted to the fact that one could do so. And because modern appliances offered the promise—if not the reality—of removing the need for female labor rather than transferring it from domestics to housewives, the search for perfection was not perceived as putting middle-class women to work.

Why shouldn't the American household have strived for perfection, especially as long as someone else, preferably a hired servant, was doing all that work? But the household servant, once so common in middle-class and even lower-class American homes, was becoming less common, and the point of owning a toaster is that you can make your own toast, not tell Aunt Jemima to do so. However clear-cut any improvement in household technology might have seemed, regardless of how good any product ever was, no one would buy it if he or she was unaware of its existence or the argument in favor of purchasing one. Accompanying the explosion of household goods, increased industrialization, and distribution and transportation networks in America was the rise of another business that had existed in one form or another since about the time of the Civil War: the advertising agency. It sold more than vacuum cleaners and toasters to American families. It sold "modernity." And oddly enough, one of the ways it would do so was to employ that by then old standby, Aunt Jemima.

Selling a Way of Life

The American advertising agency grew up with the mass production and distribution of household items. The ad agency of the 1870s was as decentralized and small as some of the business enterprises it would serve, like Chris Rutt's Pearl Milling Company. There were no copywriters or art directors, or any market research; most ad agencies merely brokered space in newspapers, and the client provided the copy. The business was far from a profession in anybody's eyes; Stephen Fox has remarked that in the absence of any government rules or self-regulation, "the entire business was conducted in a half-light of bunkum and veiled appearances," still largely centered around the sale of patent medicines. When Francis Wayland Ayer founded what is generally considered the first ad agency in 1868, he named it N. W. Ayer and Son, after his father, to give the impression of longevity and respectability, to separate it from the fly-by-night reputation that space brokers had earned. J. Walter Thompson, a former

New York clerk, further standardized business practices and made them more reputable by putting members of the growing magazine trade under exclusive ad contracts, and by 1878 he had made enough money to operate an agency in his own name. As his firm grew in the 1880s, he created the position of account executive, further professionalizing and rationalizing the business and creative aspects of the ad agency. Still, as late as 1892 no agency had a regular employee who wrote copy full-time. Increasingly, as advertisers were attracted by the reach of the Curtis magazine group (*Century*, *Harper's*, the *Atlantic*), copywriting became less of a freelance occupation and more of a profession. From the Civil War to 1900, the total volume of paid advertising rose from $50 million to $500 million, and Ayer's agency employed 160 people.[17]

The big breakthrough for the ad agency was World War I. Through the first decade of the twentieth century, as ad agencies continued to grow, they nonetheless focused on the more straightforward merchandising of products rather than promoting a wider range of causes or seeking to divine the depths of consumer consciousness. As Roland Marchand has observed, "World War I provided American advertising with new opportunities to exhibit its power and flexibility." Industry leaders organized the National War Advisory Board, which helped the government sell bonds and recruit soldiers. Both efforts were an enormous success, and as one adman noted, the American propaganda campaign taught consumers and advertisers alike that "any surface and every surface, and all approaches through the senses" were the terrain of advertising. In addition, the wartime taxing of excess profits encouraged businesses to put more money into advertising, an exempt business expense, and led to an explosion of full-page ads in national magazines. National ad volume increased from $682 million in 1914 to $1.4 billion by 1919; it would reach nearly $3 billion by 1929. Two years after the war, the J. Walter Thompson Company, now the largest New York agency, had increased its employees from 177 to 283. New agencies sprang up in New York City, and older firms, like Chicago-based Lord and Thomas and Philadelphia's N. W. Ayer, had branch offices there. The term *Madison Avenue* to describe American advertising was in popular use by 1923.[18]

As American advertising became larger, more profitable, and more accustomed to dealing with issues weightier than the Uneeda biscuit, it grew more sophisticated at targeting consumers. One of the first steps toward understanding consumers better was the J. Walter Thompson Company's (hereafter JWT) commission of a demographic study, *Population and Its Distribution*, in 1912.

The book, which at first listed stores by category and by state, grew by the 1920s into a voluminous profile of the consumer population so valuable that more than two thousand companies used it. It provided the factual background for modern market research. But advertising changed in another, perhaps more important, fashion. Postwar ads were dominated by a "therapeutic ethos" that, in the words of T. J. Jackson Lears, "appropriated the prestige of science and played on intimate self-doubts while promising to restore or preserve the buyer's health and beauty."[19] While processed foods and household appliances had "liberated" women of the burden of supervising servants—or trying to find servants—its accompanying advertising burdened them with new fears: that their children were not well fed, their husbands were unhappy with their housekeeping, their friends had noted embarrassing lapses in their hygiene. Increasingly, ads relied on the "whisper" technique—displaying someone talking behind someone else's back about bad breath, body odor, or some other neglect atypical of civilized living. Cutex explained to women why the subject of an advertisement "failed to pass the test of critical eyes" and warned that "hangnails and coarse ragged cuticle make you ashamed of your hands." P. and G. White naphtha soap offered a moment of suspense when it asked, "Does she unfold her handkerchief in secret—or can its whiteness stand the light of day?"[20] Post's bran flakes told women, "To be slim and radiant, eat like a cave woman." Cannon towels asked women, "Would you like to have visitors go into your bathroom and see the towels that are there all the time?" A woman preparing for her first elegant dinner feared her upper-class companions would judge her by skin care; as she reached for the dinner silver, "She could feel every eye on her hesitating hand." Men were not spared, either, although much advertising for men's products was aimed at female readers. An ad for Williams shaving cream reminded gentlemen that "critical eyes are sizing you up right now," and Listerine said of a sad-looking fellow, "his mirror couldn't tell him" that he had the dreaded halitosis. Marchand termed these ads a series of "great parables," stories told to remind both men and women that judgment, class fall, and humiliation waited around every corner; all could be prevented by consumption. Americans lived in a "democracy of goods" that allowed the traits of elite life to be purchased by middle-class shoppers.[21]

To create a visual image of that elite life, illustrators increasingly included maids or other domestic servants. Marchand has called them "props" that provided the "visual index of class in a domestic scene." The maids in advertisements usually bore little resemblance to the decreasing number of women who actually were in domestic service by 1920: the maid depicted in ads was generally young, white, and probably Anglo-Saxon; the woman actually in domestic service was typically older and black.[22] There were some black faces in the fantasy homes of advertising, although they did not live in those homes. Unlike Aunt Jemima, they were mostly anonymous women and a few men who were not depicted as doing much labor themselves but often were watching white people easily solve a problem with the use of a laborsaving product. Most were like "Mandy," who was amazed at how quickly her mistress unclogged the sink with Drano, or the black chef who described Armour's Star ham as "The Ham What *AM.*"[23] Before the magazine age and well before the post–World War I boom in advertising revenues, black images, although not necessarily servants, were an integral part of many advertisements in both North America and Western Europe. Supposedly humorous soap advertisements played on the futility of attempting to "wash an Ethiopian white." Such ads were meant to remind white consumers of their standards of civilization and cleanliness through contrast with allegedly unkempt, ignorant savages. Black children were commonly depicted as enjoying the fruits of the South, especially watermelon but also peaches, pears, grapefruit, and even coconuts and bananas. The connection between produce and black images not only suggested the bounty of the American South and tropical climates but reminded audiences of the themes from minstrel shows. Black southerners loafed under shady trees, sustaining themselves effortlessly with fruits and vegetables that fell right off the vine or, especially in the case of watermelon, were stolen from another person's yard.[24]

An alternative approach to depicting either black or white servants, as Strasser has noted, was to eliminate the servant image altogether and depict women doing housework themselves, quickly, easily, efficiently. As Marchand's examples of the "French Maid" in many ads demonstrates, however, Strasser was not correct in stating that "after World War I, pictures of maids virtually disappeared from advertising for women."[25] What is clear is that advertisers worked at least two ways to address the servant problem. One was to attach their product visually to a household servant in order to give it a high-class identity; the second was to suggest their product made a servant unnecessary.

The J. Walter Thompson Company not only led the postwar advertising boom in terms of profits and size but also contributed significantly to the creative changes in ads directed toward women. From its early relationship with the

Curtis magazines, JWT had been dominant in advertising products aimed at women. When Stanley Resor took over the agency from its founder in 1916, his wife, Helen Landsdowne Resor, came into the corporate suites with him. "In advertising these [women's] products I supplied the feminine point of view," she said in an interview years later. "I watched the advertising to see that the idea, the word, and the illustrating were effective for women." By 1920 JWT's figures showed it as placing more lines in the major magazines aimed at women— *Ladies' Home Journal, Woman's Home Companion, Vogue*—than any other agency, while it trailed somewhat in advertising placed in magazines aimed primarily at men or mixed audiences. Under the management of Stanley Resor and the creative guidance of Helen Resor and James Webb Young, JWT made tremendous strides in developing ads primarily aimed at women, from Woodbury soap to Pond's cold cream to Odorono deodorant. As the advertising business boomed after the war, JWT moved past all other agencies in total billings, a position it would keep for fifty years. The Roaring Twenties were especially heady at JWT as billings grew from $10.7 million in 1922 to $20.7 million in 1926 and to $37.5 million by the end of the decade. The agency's lush offices in the Graybar Building next to Grand Central Station—complete with a two-story conference room and an executive dining room reconstructed from an eighteenth-century Massachusetts farmhouse — demonstrated how far the advertising profession, and JWT, had come from the patent medicine days.[26]

In the postwar years the advertising business had gained status in society and, not coincidentally, became a business that directed others on that path, or implied that products would impart status upon them. During this period advertising leaders saw themselves as making more than money; they were "claiming recognition as a preeminent civilizing and modernizing force," educating consumers on standards of health, beauty, and class. Accepting this role meant also accepting at least two inherent contradictions. Advertising, as a spokesman for modernity, also had to transcend its very nature, using mass communications to achieve a personal tone and strike a chord with the individual consumer. But the assumption that the economic citizenry needed moral uplift also meant that advertisers perceived that their audience was culturally and intellectually distant, and that appeals to popular taste, particularly of women, by necessity were shaped not to appeal to reason but to "rather raw and crude emotions."[27] The mostly male and all-white advertising elite considered the cultural gap to be pronounced not simply among different classes but between men and women and viewed the latter as weaker emotionally and mentally. Assumptions about women were not limited to the men who worked in advertising, either. In April 1917 a "Miss Waller" of JWT's Chicago office, in a training exercise typical of the agency, took a job behind the counter of Marshall Fields. The JWT office newsletter reported her findings to the male-dominated staff: "What impressed me most in my week's experience, was that all women, rich or poor, are fundamentally the same. They are on the whole, easily influenced."[28] It made targeting advertising much easier, of course, if the mass market of women was considered homogeneous by its (lack of) intelligence rather than diversified by its class. "It was both a comfort and a challenge," in Marchand's words, "to conclude that even 'The Colonel's Lady' must be addressed in a language different from that normally spoken among advertising men."[29]

Meet James Webb Young

It could be argued that no one worked harder to create "The Colonel's Lady," and that no one expressed more contempt for her, than James Webb Young, a mercurial adman who was the creative force behind not only the J. Walter Thompson Company's Aunt Jemima campaign but many of its other important ventures aimed toward female consumers (fig. 3). "Early in my career I sought a mate," he said in an address to his colleagues in 1928. "I realized that women were the great consumers, and that I must have a laboratory in which to study them. I advise all young men in advertising to marry early. This will give you time to find out whether you have picked a typical consumer, and if not to correct it before it is too late. By the time I was 30, I knew all there was

3. James Webb Young in 1927. (Courtesy of J. Walter Thompson Company Archives, John W. Hartman Center for Sales, Advertising, and Marketing History, Duke University Special Collections)

to know about women. This knowledge led to my greatest success, and made my fame secure."[30]

Young's meteoric rise through the ranks of advertising was a familiar story to JWT staffers. He was born in Covington, Kentucky, along the banks of the Ohio River, in 1886. His father, he reminded the JWT staffers in 1928, "was an Irishman. He had been a steamboat man on the Mississippi in Mark Twain's day. . . . From him I learned the picturesque language of steamboat men, and got the stories that later made Aunt Jemima famous." His mother, he said, "was a Southern belle. You could tell it by the way she hated niggers." He said his early years in the Covington boardinghouse his mother operated were a key to his later success in advertising, because he developed an understanding of "the common people":

I attribute all my success to the common people.

I love them because they are so easy to fool. My millions have been extracted from their pockets.

I acquired this love at a very early age. Fortunately for me, my mother ran a boarding house down by the railroad yards. A freight brakeman asleep in his underwear is one of my earliest recollections.

Once, a street fair came to town, and Little Eva, the dancing girl, stayed at our house. I learned that her charms were but paint, and her apparent viciousness the disguise of a kindly heart.

These early lessons I never forgot. Often as I wrote the copy that has made me famous, I have found before my mind's eye that sleeping brakeman—with his pants pocket gaping open over the back of a chair—and that rouged Eva, eating steak and onions at my mother's table.

Young went on to say that his mother tried to influence him against "poor white trash," but unsuccessfully, for "something instinctive in me rebelled. I seemed to know that my mastery of their minds would make my fortune."[31]

Young quit school in the sixth grade to find work in Cincinnati and wrote mail-order advertising for book publishers. In 1898 he was working in the mailing room of a Methodist book publisher and wrote ads aimed at ministers and Sunday school teachers. In 1909 he became advertising manager for the Ronald

Press in New York City, and sometime between then and 1912 he worked for the A. W. Shaw Company, a publisher of business books and magazines. Young had been a schoolmate of Helen Resor in Covington, and on her recommendation he asked Stanley Resor of JWT for a job in January 1912. "Much to my surprise, he offered me a job as a copy writer," which Young accepted after haggling long enough to get sixty dollars a week in salary. After a year and a half of arguing with the art department, which he believed sacrificed copy at the expense of illustration, he was appointed manager of JWT's Cincinnati office. He became the firm's vice president in charge of production in 1917 and moved to its New York headquarters.[32]

Young's greatest accomplishment before Aunt Jemima was the reinvention of the lady's deodorant ad. Odorono (odor-oh-no) had been invented in 1907 by a Cincinnati doctor who hoped he would perspire less during surgery. The physician's daughter began marketing the product to women (apparently men were expected to smell), but hygiene products posed a special problem to advertisers, who understandably wished to avoid offending the sensibilities of the targeted consumer. Young tried to avoid the problem by mentioning the scent while discreetly avoiding any explicit reference to the actual armpit. In his 1919 ad "Within the Curve of a Woman's Arm," the copy stated that "it is a physiological fact that persons troubled with perspiration odor seldom can detect it themselves." The objections raised to Young's implicit reference to the armpit and his forbidden discussion of female odors were considerable. Two hundred readers of the *Ladies' Home Journal* canceled their subscriptions, and the American Medical Association warned that applying Odorono to the armpit could be hazardous to one's health. Some of Young's female acquaintances complained personally, calling the ad an insult to women in general, and a few promised they would never speak to him again. But Odorono sales went up 112 percent in a year's time. Young had figured out a way to broach the subject, and however offensive it remained to some, the simple awareness of the product, plus the fear of not being able to detect personal odor that was plain to others, led women to purchase it. This was Young's greatest contribution to the "therapy" of advertising—what others in the business called "whisper campaigns"—and it was more or less copied by, among others, the Kotex sanitary napkin makers in the early 1920s, who faced a more serious illustrative challenge and solved it by depicting nurses attending to wounded soldiers.[33]

Young later claimed to have expected Odorono's success, and he again said that his early experiences in the boardinghouse, along with his detailed knowledge of women, were the key to shaping the campaign. "For the advertising of Odorono, I invented what I have often wittily called 'The sexaphone appeal,'" he told the gathering at his farewell dinner. "Others have written sex copy, but none has succeeded in blending with it, as I have, the emotional tug of the saxophone." He went on to joke that "this Odorono advertising was acclaimed as sheer genius. But this I deny. Anyone who had sat next to Little Eva after her dancing could have smelled out the reason for such copy as well as I."[34] In fact, Young always seemed to discount any credit for scientific methods of developing advertising, which were the rage at JWT, and constantly reflected on his experiences in the boardinghouse, in the South, and among the "common people." He said Stanley Resor had a "somewhat naive respect for the Ph.D." He scoffed at suggestions that John Watson, a Johns Hopkins psychologist hired by Resor, contributed much to campaigns, saying that "advertising absorbed John without absorbing much of his psychology."[35] Professionals and psychologists, Young believed, were no replacement for advertising men who knew the common people from experience; those who knew the lower classes and had risen out of them were the only ones qualified to express contempt for commoners, as Young so frequently did.

Young did sometimes emphasize the importance of market research, especially in his lectures to college students later in his career. But he also called for advertisers to absorb, instead of psychology or statistics, a knowledge of what he called "the types of factors which govern human behavior," that is, "the mores, the folkways, the customs, and the fashions." An example of the mores was "deep-seated racial ideas" such as "whites-blacks in our country." The folkways were subject to "change more rapidly," such as the notion that "women were scarce in this country—this tended to establish respect for women not found in other countries. Ziegfield knew his American folkways in glorifying the American girl. This could not have been done in England." The customs represented changes over decades, such as the "disappearance of the chaperon." Finally, he said, advertisers had to be knowledgeable of fashion: "backgammon came and went—even ideas" came and went, too.[36] Although imagination was important, the advertiser did not create ideas but responded to existing ones, according to Young. He called on the members of the trade to discover the folkways and learn the mores.

Discovering the Folkways: The South in Advertising

Young brought to the Aunt Jemima campaign, and others, what he understood to be the folkways of the South, at least the postbellum South he remembered from his father's stories about the Mississippi, his mother (the "southern belle"), and his own travels on the Bible-sales circuit for the religious publisher that gave him his first job. His story of the South was a postwar romance. Even the ads for Aunt Jemima that reflected on the days after the Civil War emphasized the leisure, food, and splendor that existed in the time leading up to the attack on Fort Sumter. Young was not unusual in making reference to southern ways in advertisements; what distinguished his campaigns was an attention to detail and to bringing a sense of reality to his story by reporting the development of his client's products as actual historical events.

That the South should have been an important image, particularly in food advertisements, is not surprising. The sociologist John Shelton Reed has pointed to the South's importance in American culture as a place of plenty, a "garden of eatin'" in which one folklorist allegedly uncovered more than a hundred words for cornbread in South Carolina alone.[37] Jackson Lears has offered the idea of southern agriculture and the implication of preindustrial abundance as an explanation for the popularity of Aunt Jemima and Rastus, the Cream of Wheat cook, that transcended racial stereotyping. "Part of the answer may be that the creators as well as the consumers of these images were recalling the nurturant world of warmth and plenty embodied in an older iconography of abundance." Still, why not appropriate the image of a white midwestern farmer as the wholesome symbol of an equally abundant region? Lears hinted at the answer when he noted that not only did the black cooks provide sustenance, but "they took care of (white) people," which brings the question of who is serving whom—the nature of the nurture—back into play. Interestingly, Lears also argued that "these sorts of desires remained largely subterranean in corporate advertising" until the depression.[38] However, regardless of the extent to which the depression spurred advertisers to adopt such a strategy to meet consumers' psychic and economic needs, Young's campaigns for Maxwell House coffee and Aunt Jemima, which reached their zenith in the 1920s, relied heavily on the legendary abundance of the South, and other advertisements referenced southernness in different ways.

The southernness Young worked to re-create in ads was a way of life for white people, something that had been peculiar to a certain region but now could be acquired elsewhere, thanks to the national market. That way of life emphasized less work for white people, with more time for activities associated with an upper-class lifestyle: long, sumptuous dinners, fine clothing, balls, and extended visits, for example. Sometimes an ad that emphasized a southern way of life did not need any black servants in it to imply the benefits of black labor; the evidence of white leisure was enough to do the job. In other cases, black servants were everywhere, explicitly performing the tasks that allowed white people to relax. And in other ads, southernness meant a sheer abundance of a product—grown and hauled by unmentioned blacks—that created a way of life enjoyed by white people.

The early 1920s campaign for Baker's coconut developed by JWT offers a prime example. In 1922 the Franklin Baker Coconut Company offered four brands of coconut: premium shred, Brazil, fresh-grated, and "southern style," which was, according to JWT memoranda, "a new and radically different type of shredded coconut packed moist but without the milk in sealed air-tight cans," and which had only slight distribution. JWT advised Baker that the variety of coconut offered under the trade name confused consumers, who also particularly disliked the fresh-grated, which was packed with milk. The ad agency told Baker to take fresh-grated off the market and focus on an expansion of its southern-style offering, even though in 1922 the former accounted for more than half of the company's sales, and the latter only 22.5 percent. JWT took the southern style national in a series of ads beginning in 1922-23.[39]

JWT noted that Baker's ads would have to mention the special advantages of "coconut for the first time put up in air-tight cans" by the "new Vitapack process." But the advertising, in what would become a trademark of Young's work, combined modern convenience with old-style southernness, for it emphasized the fact that new packing processes allowed consumers to buy the same coconut that southerners once purchased from "the old reliable Coconut Man." A 1923 ad is typical:

If you have ever lived in the South, you will surely remember the Coconut Man.

He stood in the market place in every town, and while you waited he opened fresh coconuts—newly arrived from the West Indies—and shredded for you their juicy meat.

The Coconut Man taught the people of the South to love coconut because he gave it to them the way it should be eaten—moist with its own juices, rich with its own delicious flavor—not dried out.

And now housewives everywhere can have coconut that has every quality of the fresh grated coconut that the Old Coconut Man gave to the South. Now for the first time coconut is being put up moist with its own juices in air-tight cans.

Baker's Coconut, Southern Style, gives you all the rich flavor of fresh coconut, moist and tender, so different from the dried kind.

The ad was illustrated with a large picture of a coconut cake and a smaller one of a woman in a bonnet buying coconut from an elderly white man standing behind a cart labeled "The Old Reliable Coconut Man." All of this was under a headline that said, "Startling new way of packing coconut."[40]

On JWT's advice, Baker emphasized the southern style in its print campaigns through most of the 1920s, adding "southern style" to the "Baker's Coconut" nameplate at the bottom of the ad. It kept the "Coconut Man" prominently in its ads at least until 1926, sometimes describing him with increased specificity. A 1925 ad titled "As Tender As If Grated by the Coconut Man in a Southern Market," said he "stands in the famous Lexington market of Baltimore. While you wait, he opens coconuts newly arrived from the West Indies." The Coconut Man himself was not a big part of the ad's visual emphasis: he was always dwarfed by a larger drawing of a coconut cake. But the South's alleged stranglehold on coconut, newly broken by advances in packaging, was usually prominent; one ad titled "Until Today the South Alone Could Have It" connected coconut with all the supposed goodness of southern cuisine, including (anonymously, though) the woman who made it: "Candied sweet potatoes, hot biscuits, and fried chicken for dinner—hominy and broiled Virginia ham for supper—who has not learned to bless the South for the secrets of her famous dishes! Until today the moist, full-flavored coconut from which the Southern Mammy made her ambrosias, cakes, pies and a hundred other dainties could be obtained only from the Seaboard States, from the old coconut man." In reality, coconuts had been shipped from the tropics to Charleston and then to New York and other points north at least since the 1870s; they were probably as much of a luxury in the South as in the North.[41]

Baker kept the southern theme—sometimes with the Old Coconut Man, sometimes without—years after JWT lost the account. In 1936, for example, its advertising aimed at restaurateurs urged them to use coconut to make "Dixie Bars," an old southern confection; "It would be smart of some cracker baker to bring back Dixie Bars," the ad suggested.[42] The main reason the emphasis on southernness persisted, of course, was that as far as Baker and JWT could tell, it worked. A JWT memo noted that by the end of 1926, sales of Baker's southern style had increased 143 percent since the ad agency took over the campaign, far outstripping Baker's other two brands—premium and Brazil—still available for retail, even though these two brands which were distinctly not southern style realized 84 percent of their sales in the South during that same period. The ten states with the largest increases in sales of southern style were, in order, Pennsylvania, Illinois, New York, Connecticut, New Jersey, Maryland, Ohio, Massachusetts, the District of Columbia, and Rhode Island. "It will be noted," the JWT memo continued, "that the states in which Southern Style has gained are states where the national magazine circulation is high. . . . This shows real progress on Southern Style and indicates that even the Northern states, which are particularly important on account of their larger population, can be made large consumers of Southern Style Coconut through advertising in national magazines."[43]

Other advertisers called on southern images in less direct ways. The Pennsylvania Railroad ran a series of ads in 1927 that introduced individual trains and their routes as characters. For example, "The Yankee" was "A Freight Train with a New England Conscience" that "sets himself on the job of making consistent, dependable on time arrivals." The southern equivalent was a vehicle known as "The Colonel," but instead of Puritan conscience the ads described the vehicle's uncommon hospitality, a rather unusual characteristic for a freight train. The headline of the ad ran, "At Yo' Service, Suh!" and the text said, "American tradition boasts no more picturesque figure than the Kentucky colonel, exemplar of chivalry and hospitality and connoisseur of the devastating 'cuss' word. The colonel's native heath is the great 'blue grass' region of Kentucky, celebrated alike for its horses, the historic Derby, and the late lamented mint julep. So it is only fitting that a freight train traveling daily to Louisville should be known as 'The Colonel.' And that is the name of the big Pennsylvania carrier that takes a daily cargo of merchandise from Chicago to and through the Louisville gateway."[44]

A more accurate name, if not a more attractive one, for a carrier of heavy objects throughout the South might have been "The Slave," but JWT's ads for the railroad did describe a freight train named "Uncle Remus." The ad was titled, "Uncle Remus Highballs North," and the illustration featured an old black man telling a white child about his journeys: "Sho, chile! I'se a traveler. . . . Mebbe to jedge fum my name you thinks I limps roun' on a cane, bent over like I had ate rhumaticks. . . . But you oughter see me when I gits loaded up fer de Nawth'n markets. . . . I'se as spry an' chipper as Brer Rabbit." If you heard "Uncle Remus" the train rumble by, the ad said, you might be reminded of Joel Chandler Harris's storyteller, because in its cargo holds was the "wealth from the South—luscious ripening fruits and choicest cool green vegetables to garnish the tables of fastidious Northern housewives."[45] It is interesting to compare the "Colonel" with "Uncle Remus." When the engine is personified by the southern colonel, the emphasis is on the personality traits—hospitality, chivalry, and cussing—for which the train is named. The ad for the other train is introduced by Uncle Remus in his black dialect—his black personality—but focuses on the rich foods of the South, grown in abundance there and taken north on Remus's back. Once again, African Americans are useful in an ad because, as Lears noted, they bring food to white people. Uncle Remus is a much more useful image than the slave for a freight train not simply because of his familiarity to white audiences but because he can talk about his work and tell great stories about his travels.

A few other ad campaigns were notable for their links to the South, but the ties were less direct than Baker's, the Pennsylvania Railroad's, or those of Maxwell House and Aunt Jemima. Penick and Ford, a maker of molasses syrup, increased its sales by dropping its Velva brand and concentrating on its Brer Rabbit syrup. JWT, according to 1926 internal memos, helped Penick and Ford eliminate northern consumers' confusion over the usefulness of molasses by emphasizing its southern roots and quality. Calvert whiskey, a client of one of JWT's rival agencies, took the same approach in promoting Kentucky Pride whiskey, emphasizing not only Kentucky's prominence in the whiskey-making world but the leisurely life of the sporting southerners who drank it. And ads for the Piggly Wiggly grocery chain in 1930 reminded customers that Louisville's "aristocratic hostesses still go to market. . . . With Mammy in the back seat to 'mind' the packages, they motor themselves to Piggly Wiggly."[46]

The real exemplars, however, of the southern mode in advertising were Maxwell House and Aunt Jemima, and James Webb Young crafted both of them. Young made all the points suggested by other ads—food in abundance, leisure, gentility, and black service—much more evident, he sustained those basic themes for a longer time, and his success was demonstrated by increased sales. Young, like a postbellum diarist remembering his mammy, insisted that he drew from his personal experiences and memories in shaping these two campaigns. His South was a place where white people celebrated over good food, where North and South came together over coffee and pancakes, and where white labor was erased by the picture of black men and women bringing plates to tables.

Maxwell House: The Birth of a Coffee

In 1924, after a couple of years of solicitation, the Cheek-Neal Coffee Company of Nashville, Tennessee, moved its account from the firm of Cecil, Barreto and Cecil to JWT. Young remembered the Maxwell House hotel personally from his days of selling Bibles across the upper South, and he dispatched a copywriter named Ewing Webb to stay at the Nashville hotel, "soak up the atmosphere, and go through old newspaper files looking for anecdotes from the hotel's social history." Typically, Young disregarded the market data his firm offered and later stubbornly insisted the ads owed more to memories than to social science. "The only 'research' done was for copy material in the files of newspapers," he said. "The rest of it was 'intuitive,' growing out of a certain range of personal experience, out of advertising experience, out of editorial sense for what is interesting, out of people who had writing skills, and out of art and illustrative skills."[47] As the campaign made clear, Young drew from what he chose to remember about the South, just like many historians and diarists of his time. But he either forgot, chose to forget, or never knew other details about the Maxwell House.

The hotel and the coffee's histories are easy to forget now, since they are no longer part of the brand's advertising campaign, but Young and Webb had latched onto a good story. A prominent land speculator named John Overton began construction of the hotel in 1859 and planned to give it his wife's maiden name, Maxwell. Its projected size led some locals to doubt it would ever be finished, or if it were, that it would ever be filled with guests; they called it "Overton's Folly." The hotel's other nickname came during the Civil War, when Union troops using the still-unfinished building as a hospital and barracks called it "Zollerback's Barracks," after the general in command. The establishment finally opened as a hotel in 1869. Although it would gain its reputation as the site of elaborate dinners and the place where presidents and other luminaries stayed, the first major gathering at the Maxwell House was a Ku Klux Klan meeting in April 1867, at which the newly formed group out of Pulaski, Tennessee, made former Confederate general Nathan Bedford Forrest its "Grand Wizard of the Empire" and established the rest of its organizational structure.[48]

Joel Cheek, the founder of the Cheek-Neal Company, taught school and worked as a food wholesaler in and around Burkesville, Tennessee, during the 1880s. By 1887 he had developed his own blend of coffee and was attempting to sell it to eating establishments, including the Maxwell House. When the manager refused to buy any, Cheek left twenty pounds without charge, and according to JWT's account histories, guests began to notice and approve of the change in coffee. After trying it for six months, the hotel management decided to use the coffee exclusively and agreed to lend the name Maxwell House to the brand. Cheek's new brand name was particularly successful in the South—through the turn of the century he established production plants in Houston, Jacksonville, and Richmond—but the company also sought to expand its share of the national market and later added plants in Brooklyn and Los Angeles. By the time the account came to JWT, the problem with Maxwell House was still a national one; a JWT evaluation in 1925 said that "Maxwell House had to meet the aggressive sales and advertising attacks of competitors who in most cases had the advantage of working in their own home territory."[49]

JWT and Young offered an interesting approach for taking a southern-based brand to greater national prominence: They told the coffee maker they planned to emphasize its regional character. The ad agency's market research (which Young pretended to disregard) demonstrated that the variety of national and regional brands of coffee had housewives confused, with "no single brand of coffee standing out in [their] mind." The proposal to Maxwell House said that its campaign would position the coffee as a high-class product—which was certainly no innovation—and would do so by borrowing from the "prestige" and "romance" of the Old South: "We considered at this point, judgment of a product being difficult on a comparative basis, a person takes more pleasure in it if he knows that it comes, say, from the private stock of a distinguished person. The same principle appeared to apply to women's views on coffee. The majority enjoy one brand more than another largely because of the ideas with which it is associated."[50]

JWT's official description of the campaign went on to catalog the ideas it would associate with coffee in the minds of women:

We knew from experience that beauty, romance and social prestige mean more than almost anything else to a woman, even when applied to foods. Consequently, we decided that the most effective copy appeal would be the romantic history of the old southern Maxwell House, after which the coffee was named and where it first became renowned.

This appeal gave us a background against which Maxwell House Coffee today could be effectively dramatized: the fashionable, gay social life of the old Maxwell House and the place our coffee played in the aristocratic functions of the Old South. The story of the Maxwell House, and of the many notable people who have stopped there, furnishes abundant material for a spirited picture in words and illustration. And this picture centers definitely on the one point most important in selling coffee—on flavor. Famous for its wonderful food in a land where good food was an art, the Maxwell House is the very symbol of fine flavor.[51]

The ad campaign begun in newspapers and national magazines during 1924–25 did just that, reflecting back on the Maxwell House as the apogee, not just the epitome, of southern dining delights and as the place where the famous, wellborn, and rich gathered. The approach eventually brought the North and South to reconciliation at the Maxwell House—with aged generals from both sides shaking hands—but also decreed a sort of national agreement concerning coffee, as Joel Cheek's blend of many coffees became one that the entire United States could swallow, a commercial translation of *E Pluribus Unum*.

The ads presented a variety of themes extolling the hotel's splendor. One was celebrity: "There I Met the Famous Men of the Day," "How a President-elect Was Welcomed to Dixie Years Ago," and "A Breakfast Feast for the First Lady of the Land" all were titles of Maxwell House ads. Some were much more specific than others, amounting to endorsements by historical (dead) celebrities and embellished descriptions of visits that actually occurred. For example, one ad was titled, "He Had Been President—Yet Here He Won the Honor Which He Wanted Most of All," and described a banquet for former president Andrew Johnson as he prepared to return to Washington as a senator. "And now in the dining room of the old Maxwell House, the distinguished men of his state had gathered to do him honor. There they feasted him. And there, over their coffee, they cheered and applauded him as he rose to speak." Another, "Breakfast for Mr. Roosevelt!" depicted Theodore Roosevelt working on his book *Winning of the West,* which the ad said "is generally considered by critics to be his master-piece." The ad claimed to explain "how T. R. wrote the book" and pointed out that the future president's close friends knew him to be "a great coffee drinker." How Maxwell House coffee helped Roosevelt write better than any other coffee would have was not specified. Maxwell House also claimed that Roosevelt coined the coffee's slogan, "Good to the Last Drop."[52]

Other ads focused less on specific persons and more on the social pageantry of southern life, stressing the company rather than the food. One ad claimed that "over this coffee many a southern gallant pledged his love." Another said that "here the notables of old Dixie came to dine." Yet others described "the famous Jackson Day Balls" at which "the distinguished men and women of Dixie gathered" in "rich and beautiful costumes."[53] There was a testimonial from one "southern belle" who said, "We came in for the great balls and always stopped there for several days." This ad went on to describe:

> Silver haired ladies with a look of eternal youth in their eyes, the beauties of long ago. It is they who can best tell you of the Maxwell House and of its glories.
>
> For years its stately ball-room brought together all that was loveliest and most gallant in old Dixie. From the great estates of Tennessee, from all parts of the South, the notable men and women of the time came to this fine, old hotel.
>
> "When I was a young girl, the Maxwell House played a part in my life that I shall never forget," are the words of one southern lady. "We used to drive in by carriage for each of the balls and stop there for several days. To me and to all my friends it was always a place full of enchantment."[54]

The hotel was so fancy, one ad noted, that the menus were printed on satin. An ad about the opening of the Maxwell House summed up what the copy-writer was trying to evoke. It was simply titled, "A Carnival of Southern Hospitality."[55]

The series did devote some thought to the food served at all the balls and dinners populated by famous politicians, gallant men, and beautiful ladies. One of the initial ads of the campaign made up a story about the origins of Maxwell House coffee—a strategy Young also used with the Aunt Jemima campaign. "How Seven Words Saved the Reputation of the Most Famous Hotel in the Old South" picks up sometime after the hotel had run out of Joel Cheek's free twenty pounds. A chef named Antoine tells the manager, Mr. Black, that, in the narrator's words, "complaints had come from the dining-room—actual complaints from patrons of long standing. Such an event was unheard of!" When Mr. Black asked Antoine what the problem was, the chef replied: "Ze ozer coffee you bought was better," the "seven words" referred to in the headline. The ad also called it "a reply that has made history," because it supposedly spurred the hotel to put its name on Cheek's blend of coffee.[56] Other ads referred to "Food worth traveling a thousand miles for," a testimonial supposedly from O. Henry, the short-story writer, and "When supper was brought to the belles of the ball in old Tennessee"; the latter ad claimed "it was the food at the Maxwell House, and above all else the coffee, that was always talked of most widely in that land of 'mammy' cooks and beaten biscuits." One ad claimed an old Maxwell House menu featured "twenty-four courses of game and fowl alone!"[57]

One consistent design element persisted in Maxwell House ads, regardless of whether they were dead celebrity testimonials, history lessons, or picturesque depictions of southern leisure or food. There are always black waiters, sometimes one and sometimes many, hauling around huge portions of food and waiting on the white people at the table. Almost every ad depicts an elderly black waiter, complete with huge gray or white sideburns and a bald crown, either bringing something in on a platter, taking it away, or simply standing by, observing the spectacular bounty of the white folks' meal. The Maxwell House, of course, as a high-class establishment would not have Aunt Jemima cooking in its kitchen— she was waiting at home when the guests ended their stay—because it had Antoine, the French chef who uttered the seven famous words that saved the hotel. But the hotel was populated, even teeming, with black porters and waiters; this was the source of white leisure, this was how the food got to the table, and that is why no Maxwell House ad was complete without black servants.

The black servant is prominently serving coffee in "The Carnival of Southern Hospitality" ad. In "Bringing in the Boar's Head at the Old Maxwell House," it is he who performs this act described as a traditional beginning of a feast. He serves coffee to Teddy Roosevelt, brings trays to the "belles of the ball in old Tennessee," and presumably handled O. Henry's luggage. He carries away empty cups as men enjoy "coffee and cigars at the old Maxwell House," and he even appears to be eavesdropping on Antoine as the chef pronounces those seven famous words to Mr. Black. Black servants are never the center of attention— certainly not the way Aunt Jemima would be in ads—but they are rarely absent in Maxwell House ads because they make a white world of leisure possible by making white labor disappear. At a time when some advertisers were making labor disappear by making servants disappear in ads, and others were populating households with "French maids," James Webb Young was making white labor disappear by making sure black male labor was always readily apparent. Powerful or famous white men were always served by humble black men in very public acts of subservience.

As Jan Vedereen Piertese has noted, advertisements in South and Central America traditionally equated black male labor with the delivery of coffee, tobacco, and chocolate. Usually, black men were depicted as harvesting or transporting the product, although some tobacco manufacturers showed black men smoking cigars in advertisements. But plenty of ads for goods that required harvest and transport never depicted black men delivering them; coffee, tobacco, and chocolate were more similar in that they were luxury goods.[58] James Young, of course, did not have to be aware of South American coffee ads to understand the connection between luxuries and black labor. In his South that link was obvious, as slaves and later servants, with little distinction between the two, not only explictly brought wonderful food to the table but implicitly did all the other things—planting, harvesting, butchering, cooking, cleaning—that made it possible for whites to enjoy the bounty. Young put black waiters—rather than waitresses—into his campaign for Maxwell House because, first, it fit the elite image he was attempting to create. Manservants, like valets or butlers, suggested a higher-class establishment than a mammy cook like Aunt Jemima or even more anonymous black maids would have. Second, Young's depiction of older black men hunched over silver trays amid postbellum white revelry suggested a place, after slavery, where everything was put right again. No uppity black men were demanding their places at the table; black women were doing work somewhere, invisibly. This state of affairs, while distinctly southern, was appreciated even by visitors from the North, like Theodore Roosevelt.

The reunion between North and South, and agreement on the proper role of black labor, became more pointed in later ads. While black servants in Maxwell House ads carried away food or refilled glasses, while the belles of the ball were socializing (often on the periphery), sometimes the white men at the tables were sharing cigars and talking. As the ad campaign progressed into 1926-27, they were talking about bringing North and South together. A 1925 ad titled "How the Red Rose Fought the White in Nashville Years Ago" depicted the struggle between Democrats and Republicans in the 1886 gubernatorial race, contested by a pair of brothers. Bob Taylor, the Democrat, chose a white rose as his symbol, while Alfred's was the red rose; Bob won.[59] Naturally, the ad depicted Bob as being feted at the Maxwell House. In 1926 an ad took on post-bellum reconciliation in a more direct way by depicting a meeting between "the distinguished generals of the South and North" at the hotel "nearly 30 years ago." Old men in uniforms sat around a table smoking and drinking coffee carried by the ubiquitous black waiter, and the ad, which was titled "Over This Coffee the North and South Pledged the New Brotherhood Years Ago," read:

"We greet you, not with bayonets but with blessings; not with cold steel but with hot biscuits and Southern hospitality," so the Governor of Tennessee long ago welcomed the veterans of the North to the battlefield of Nashville.

Nearly thirty years ago the distinguished generals of the South and North were brought together by the Tennessee Centennial at the old Maxwell House. Here the South could most fittingly do them honor. Here, at the Maxwell House, they could be offered the marvelous dishes and the coffee that were celebrated throughout old Dixie.

"We gathered at the Maxwell House," says one noted Confederate general, "and for the first time clasped in friendship the hands of our former enemies."

The ad said that Maxwell House coffee was "a gift to the nation from the old South," and that "gradually in all parts of the country, North and South, East and West, the families who most enjoy good living have heard of Maxwell House Coffee and have taken steps to secure it."[60] That theme, minus the old generals, persisted through advertising in 1927 and 1928. Maxwell House was advertised as "the first coffee ever to please the critical people of the entire country" in an ad that emphasized that Maxwell House was not a blend of coffee but a blend of different blends, made to please people of different regions. Another ad said that Maxwell House was "a new luxury that has won America." Later in 1928 the ads focused on Joel Cheek's job as a traveling salesman for the coffee, depicting him as a kind of Johnny Appleseed ("through the South he rode, spreading news of his discovery") who carried the "first samples of that special blend which has now captured America." Another ad described Cheek as "a southerner with an inborn genius for flavor, living in a land of critical tastes" who "created a blend which is today changing the habits of a nation."[61]

Eventually a Maxwell House ad would show midwesterners, ranchers, city folks, and southern colonels offering testimonials to the national coffee in the bottom half of the ad, while the upper half contained a typical illustration of the splendor of the old hotel in Nashville, where white women danced in finery and black men carried trays.[62] Maxwell House, in JWT's ads, was a blend of coffees from everywhere; it was a gift from the epicurean South, once reserved for the elite but now shared in the "democracy of goods." The democracy was whole again, its markets filled with the goods of the South, which were packed and transported thanks to the genius of the North. Whites were free to pursue a higher standard of living because the nation had settled troublesome questions about the proper role of blacks. Maxwell House became the nation's best-selling brand of coffee by becoming the coffee of national reconciliation. A bargain had been struck, one that erased the reasons why the Maxwell House itself was once a Union army barracks, or why its first gathering was a Klan organizational meeting. Maxwell House ads, like the movie *Birth of a Nation*, distorted the meaning of war and Reconstruction. In "dramas of reunion," as Nina Silber has termed many novels and plays of the 1880s and 1890s, black men and women were cast as servants "committed to their own social caste."[63] The depiction of blacks exclusively as servants not only redeemed southern society but eased northern concerns about maintaining peaceful class relations, particularly relations between black servants and white employers.

The proprietors of the Cheek-Neal Company expressed their praise for the campaign in writing to JWT, but the real test, of course, was sales. JWT was able to report that sales in a four-month period of 1925 increased over 1924 by 60 percent in April, 108 percent in May, 129 percent in June, and 87 percent in July. A JWT memo in 1928 noted that "letters praising the copy in the Maxwell House campaign are so frequent that Mr. Cheek is not filing them." In its advertising in grocery trade magazines, Maxwell House further drove home the notion that it had become the nation's consensus choice, advising store owners that they could save on their coffee inventory by stocking the "single coffee [that] has taken the country by storm."[64] To be sure, some consumers were unmoved, but JWT usually chalked that up to ignorance. A 1927 JWT newsletter reported the firm's advertising blitz to announce the opening of a Cheek-Neal plant in Chicago but noted that "Negro workers returning on the elevated from the stockyards were observed examining the [advertising] page with an air of complete mystification over the importance Chicago was placing on this old familiar Southern product." And, ironically, a JWT study showed that Maxwell House had failed by 1925 to gain a foothold in the New Orleans market because of "a belief which has been expressed that Maxwell House Coffee is too weak." A JWT newsletter speculated that New Orleans housewives were preparing the coffee incorrectly, observed that New Orleans grocers were "less progressive than the average Northern grocer," and predicted that "the younger generation whose habits and tastes are not so definitely set will be important factors" in the future market.[65] The problems with selling Maxwell House in some southern markets demonstrated how clearly southernness was sometimes not really southern but an idea about the South designed to appeal to a national audience. Southern grocers, the study seems to indicate, needed to become more like northern grocers. And southern housewives required a greater appreciation of a "southern" product before the product could attain higher sales revenues in the South.

Cheek-Neal kept the essential approach to advertising Maxwell House coffee well past World War II, even when the account moved to another agency in the early 1930s. When it moved into radio advertising, it sponsored the *Maxwell House Showboat* every Thursday night on NBC, a comedy and music review set on a southern paddle wheeler. It also featured two "black" male servants, Molasses and January, who poured coffee; the white radio actors who played them also appeared, in blackface, in Maxwell House print ads to promote the coffee and the show.[66] Advertising, it seems, not only could be inspired by minstrelsy, it could transform itself back into minstrelsy when popular entertainment on radio became a means to push a product. But perhaps advertising really was minstrelsy all the time.

Young left full-time advertising work when he was at his peak, quitting by the end of 1928 at age forty-two, and spent the rest of his days as a sort of advertising guru, serving as a business professor at the University of Chicago, chairman of the Advertising Council, and president of the American Association of Advertising Agencies. He occasionally turned up in temporary roles at JWT and served on its board of directors from 1928 to 1964. On the side, he sold Indian crafts from his ranch in New Mexico; he and his son ran a mail-order apple business for a while. He wrote fifteen books, most of them short and all of them about advertising, one way or another, and he had the good fortune to outlive his contemporaries in the ad world of the 1920s. By the time he died in 1973, at the age of eighty-seven, most of what he had done during his relatively brief career had been surpassed by other famous campaigns and by men who stayed in the business long enough to take the helm of an agency.[67] But he was famous within his profession for his imagination, particularly for those two campaigns in which he mined "popular ideas always in the background of the American mind," as he told his students at the University of Chicago:

> Mr. Mencken once said that one of the popular American illusions is that every male negro has a tenor voice, but of course they haven't. Another one is that all Southerners enjoy good cooking, although most of them don't. There is an enormous amount of southern sympathy in this country as evidenced by the fact that people throughout the nation are very responsive when the tune "Dixie" is struck up. . . . It was out of that background idea that the "South" was news for Maxwell House Coffee. . . . The same type of thing was done in building up the legend of Aunt Jemima as an old Southern cook.[68]

More famous than Young or any of his peers in the 1920s, of course, is the old southern cook herself. In a time when the household servant was disappearing, and when advertising was growing into an industry able to tell people that they were what they ate, drank, drove, wore, and applied to their armpits, James Young and the JWT staff applied their resources and proven methods to creating an image that would outlive them all: the slave in a box.

5 The Old South, the Absent Mistress, and the Slave in a Box

An idea is nothing more or less than a new combination of old elements. . . . I had something to do with creating a series of color pages which turned Aunt Jemima from a trade-mark into a real southern cook. This was done by telling a series of dramatic incidents which supposedly took place in the life of Aunt Jemima. . . . This particular idea grew out of material which I acquired as a boy. . . . It brought into new combinations the specific knowledge about the product.

—James Webb Young Lectures

When he had finished he took a certain twisted pleasure in himself; what he had done was certainly horrible, but he was bound to admit that he had done it extremely well.

—The advertising protagonist of Eric Hodgins's

 Mr. Blandings Builds His Dream House

In the Solomon Islands after World War II and in other islands across Melanesia, a strange following grew among the people who had seen U.S. military transports fly in, drop off a bewildering array of supplies and appliances, and then fly off. After the war ended there were no more American airbases, no more of the regular supply flights. In hope of bringing back the big planes and their loads of processed foods, ovens, and refrigerators, many of the natives began to form "Cargo Cults." They built airstrips for the planes that would never come and created supply houses to store the goods. They began to address each other as "sergeant," "paymaster," and "captain" and to assemble in military formations. They built "offices" and attempted to use flagpoles as transmission towers for wireless communication with the U.S. mainland. Some even adopted a hybrid version of Christianity, as the "Jesus Christ men" attempted to read Bibles and confessed sins—all an attempt to duplicate the rituals that apparently had brought the big planeloads of modern goods to the Americans stationed there a few months back. They had never seen the steel mills where raw materials were converted into the fabric for ovens and Jeeps or the food-processing plants where seemingly miraculous substances were produced, bagged, and stamped. They thought that approximating American culture was the key to acquiring the standard of living they associated with the occupying troops. If they acted like Americans, the big planes would come back.[1]

American advertising could be said to have developed a sort of Cargo Cult of its own, in that much of our advertising, in particular Aunt Jemima ads, made pointed references to an elite way of life, to rituals, and to a standard of living that could be purchased in the "democracy of goods." The target audiences of Aunt Jemima ads were no more concerned with revolutions in manufacturing and distribution than were the members of Cargo Cults; both were focused on how the products would change their lives. In both cases the products were indistinguishable from the behavior associated with them. Cargo Cults aimed to acquire American goods by acting American; Aunt Jemima was sold with the promise that the buyer could appropriate the leisure, beauty, and racial and class status of the plantation South by purchasing a box of pancake flour. For both, material circumstances drove perceptions—the sudden presence of American technology and affluence in the islands, the growing absence of servants and appearance of a mass market for household goods in America. But the perception of the consumers is the key to understanding both cases. The residents of the Solomon Islands believed an American lifestyle would deliver American products; American consumers believe American products will deliver an American lifestyle.

The business of American advertising, as it grew up in James Webb Young's day and as it exists today, is to create Cargo Cults, tying beliefs and behaviors to products. Like the inhabitants of the Solomon Islands, we see messages about ourselves and receive instructions about our behavior from the residents of the ads that now fill television screens, stadium signs, and interstate billboards. Men can be as suave as Billy Dee Williams if they drink Colt .45 malt liquor (and wear a tuxedo while doing so); women can approach the beauty of Cindy Crawford by purchasing the brand of cosmetics she is pitching. We all can unlock our potential as computer geniuses if we log on to the World Wide Web; we once were told we could share in the revelry of the southern elite by drinking Maxwell House coffee. The Aunt Jemima campaign, likewise, told white women they could approximate the lifestyle of hoop-skirted southern belles, complete with a complement of slaves, if they purchased Aunt Jemima brand pancake mix. The campaign also told white men they could be more rugged, dashing, and adventurous with a little help from their mammy. That is what being southern meant in the case of Aunt Jemima: appropriating a life of leisure with racial and sexual harmony, seemingly more free but inherently dependent on a black laborer. The mammy in Aunt Jemima ads served as a guide to that lost paradise where white men were gallant, women were unburdened by the kitchen, and children played happily around cheerful black servants who would never leave.

It was an absurd proposition—like the one the Cargo Cult members made to themselves in becoming "American"—but no more absurd than so much of ordinary American advertising. What helped the Aunt Jemima campaign avoid lapsing into absurdity as it rewrote history was its sense of reality. To tie the product to an era when an ideal white lifestyle seemed to have existed, its creators gave it roots in real times, places, and events. A veneer of reality was essential to selling a romantic South and keeping the dream world alive for decades. The Cargo Cults died off, and ad campaigns come and go. Only a few outlive their creators. Aunt Jemima was one of those.

Meet N. C. Wyeth

As Young said, he "turned Aunt Jemima from a trade-mark into a real Southern cook." One of the keys to doing so was the ad copy, and the other was the series of illustrations. From JWT's long list of freelance illustrators, Young selected N. C. Wyeth to reshape the Aunt Jemima image after World War I. Wyeth, the father of Andrew Wyeth and grandfather of James Wyeth, already was well established as a commercial artist by the time JWT hired him to replace the current image of Aunt Jemima (fig. 4). He had contributed illustrations for early Cream of Wheat ads and created the Santa Claus image that is still used by Coca-Cola today. In addition, he illustrated popular editions of famous novels such as *Treasure Island* and *The Last of the Mohicans*.

Wyeth is perhaps best remembered today as the patriarch of a great family of American painters, but his own story deserves retelling. Newell Convers Wyeth (his family addressed him by his middle name) was born in 1882 in the

4. "Aunt Jemima's Pancake Flour," *Good Housekeeping*, December 1916, 165

rural township of Needham, Massachusetts, and spent his youth working his father's farm and using his free moments to sketch. With his mother's approval but
against his father's wishes, he left the farm to study drafting at the Mechanic Arts
School in Boston, where he was graduated in 1899. After studying at another
Boston art school until 1902, he became a disciple of Howard Pyle in Wilmington, Delaware, and later Chadds Ford, Pennsylvania. Pyle was the most pro-
found influence in Wyeth's life, for the teacher insisted on a strict adherence to
realism among his students; their task was to capture reality without embellish-
ment, to bring it back faithfully for viewers. Thus, when a huge fire swept Baltimore in 1904, Pyle contracted with *Collier's* magazine to have his students contribute illustrations to accompany the text. After graduating from Pyle's
academy later that year, Wyeth went west to Denver, recording the exploits of
cowpunchers in his sketchbooks and scratching up cash as a mail carrier in Arizona. Most of his early illustrations throughout the first decade of the twentieth
century, including his Cream of Wheat ad, depicted scenes from the American
West. Later his insistence on precision and realism took him to the Adirondack
Mountains to research illustrations for *The Last of the Mohicans* and to the
Florida Everglades for *The Yearling*. His work for Scribner's printing of *Treasure
Island* allowed him to set up a studio on an eighteen-acre farm at Chadds Ford,
but he continued, unhappily, to rely on commercial illustration to finance his
more serious paintings. One of Wyeth's biographers wrote that the artist worked
quickly on his commercial projects, hoping to dispatch them, "yet he often had
grave doubts about the value of such paintings that he could produce so readily.
He longed to compose his own designs free from the pressures of adapting his
style to the public taste." Still, by the end of World War I and into the 1920s, he
was one of America's most prolific commercial illustrators and declined offers as
high as $20,000 a year to produce work exclusively for a sign advertising
agency.[2]

Wyeth came aboard the Aunt Jemima campaign in the spring of 1919, as
Young worked to revive the account through a new strategy. The veteran adman
had begun tentatively in 1917 to rewrite copy around the leisure of southern life
and rural nostalgia by focusing on such themes as "the ole swimmin' hole" and
to argue that the Aunt Jemima pancakes were economical and even patriotic
(American soldiers were depicted eating them), but the most dramatic innovation awaited Wyeth's arrival.[3] What he brought was verisimilitude for Young's
prose, rich and colorful illustrations depicting the plantation world described by

the copywriter. In an employee newsletter that spring, JWT boasted of a portfolio that would sweep the nation in the fall, after a trial in the New York market.[4] The campaign told stories that he learned from his father's days on the Mississippi, Young said, bringing back all the stock characters from a drama about the plantation South—the mammy, the colonel, the house slaves—save one, the southern belle. Like Maxwell House ads, they represented a vivid symbol of national reconciliation on the South's terms, roughly coinciding with Woodrow Wilson's tenure as president and the film *Birth of a Nation*.

The southern mammy represented by Aunt Jemima was the symbol of the harmony between North and South, men and women, and black and white. Her recipe bridged the Old South and the New, promising continuity between plantation days and the present. Her presence suggested the stable order typically associated with mammies in literature—black women in service to their families black and white; white women directing the social affairs of the household but free of the hard work associated with cooking and cleaning; white men atop the whole structure, protecting it but often aloof, worried about more important things. The mammy was the cornerstone of this construct in the pancake ads. She was not merely the product's namesake but, in a way, the product itself; she required the most prominent place in the advertisements. But ultimately, what the campaign left out, as well as all that it included, made it a resounding success.

"The Cook Whose Cabin Became More Famous than Uncle Tom's"

Young turned Aunt Jemima from a trademark into "a real southern cook" by creating a world that invited the consumer to enter and distinguished Aunt Jemima from the dozens of other figures whose names and faces were stamped on cans and boxes. The trademarks employed by the makers of such products as Cream of Wheat, Old Dutch cleanser, Gold Dust washing powder, Diamond Crystal shaker salt and Quaker Oats appear, at first glance, to be similar to Aunt Jemima in their depiction of racial or religious figures. It is important, however, to discuss how these trademarks were used, or rather, how they were not used. There was no attempt by the makers of Cream of Wheat to create a biography for Rastus, the chef depicted on the cereal's box, and Rastus himself never spoke or, in fact, did anything in Cream of Wheat ads. There was nothing magical about his cooking ability, and his personality was unknown to buyers. No one knew where he lived or what he did there.[5] Similarly, the Quaker on the Quaker Oats box acted only as a logo and did not engage the reader; indeed, he did not even appear in many of the company's ad campaigns.[6] Likewise, the presumably Dutch woman on Old Dutch cleanser lacked not only a face but also a name, and the advertiser made no attempt to link her ethnic identity with her ability to "chase away dirt."[7] The Quaker woman depicted on Diamond Crystal shaker salt appeared to be as much a play on words as anything; the word *shaker* related as much to the salt's intended use as it did the woman depicted upon the container.[8]

The Gold Dust twins, a pair of black children, were an example of a racialized image that connected "washing away blackness" with the product, as in the advertisements described by Anne McClintock and Jan Pietersen. But the Gold Dust twins were never connected with their audience as explicitly as Aunt Jemima was; unlike her, they had no personal histories and were not depicted as real people. Although the Gold Dust twins, like Aunt Jemima, appeared in person at the St. Louis World's Fair in 1904, that was the extent of the live performances promoting the product. The Gold Dust twins did appear on a radio program of the same name in the late 1920s, but the program and the product itself disappeared in the early 1930s.[9]

But most important, the Gold Dust twins could not have sold pancakes the way Aunt Jemima did. They were a pair of pickaninnies, the stereotypically dark, supposedly amusing children who in fact were featured in some Aunt Jemima ads and were a part of the product's promotional strategy. Aunt Jemima advertisements posed a series of allegedly historical situations in which, one way or another, the mammy whips up a batch of pancakes to save the day. That was not the role of the pickaninny in American advertising. Aunt Jemima, with one important exception, was never depicted as anything but an adult. On the one occasion that her childhood was mentioned, she was not a typical pickaninny but a "girl" slave who performed unexpectedly well as a servant. Aunt Jemima was different as well from all the other servants who were depicted in advertisements. Some of them were mammy types as well, but they were as anonymous as the black waiters who populated Young's Maxwell House ads.

The Aunt Jemima of Young and Wyeth was anything but anonymous. Their collaborations were filled with stories of her years on the plantation, reintroducing Colonel Higbee and Uncle Mose and adding a new specificity to their lives on the Mississippi. In an ad titled "Gray Morn," the advertisers reenacted an older story of Aunt Jemima's discovery by a fleeing Confederate general and his orderly (fig. 5). Subtitled "How Kind Fate Took a Hand in the Misfortunes of War Back in the Days of '64," the ad depicted the general and his orderly's flight behind Union lines:

> For two days the general and his orderly had been cut off from their troops; for two days, so the story goes, they had lain hidden in the bushes on the Mississippi's bank. Northern troops were everywhere, it seemed. No venture could be made by day, even for food. Only at night dared they move.
>
> And this was the second night already paling into day. Cautiously through the dark hours they had wormed their perilous way. Once a cracking twig had brought a sentry's bullet whizzing over their heads. Once a soldier's half-concealed cough had saved them from capture, perhaps death.

The ad went on to say that the two soldiers, fighting hunger as well as the Union army, finally passed through a gray fog and found a path to the river.

5. "Gray Morn," *Saturday Evening Post*, 20 November 1920, 112

"Who was in this place? Southerners—friends? A small detachment of lawless guerrillas? Or was it forsaken?" The soldiers crept forward cautiously, hid in the bushes, and waited for a sign of life as they watched smoke rise from the chimney. Then, the copy said, they heard the voice: "Lawzee! You chilluns pestah th' life out o' yo' po' ol' mammy with yo' evahlastin' appetite fo' pancakes!"

The dialect alone, we can presume, told the two men they had encountered a friend—their "po' ol' mammy," who would indeed look after them, just as she said, just as all mammies did. The mammy, by voice alone, was instantly recognized as an ally by the two white southern men. There was no reason to worry that a Union ambush awaited, or that some of Aunt Jemima's black kin, less sympathetic to the Confederate army, might turn the pair in. They ran into the cabin and found Aunt Jemima, who revived them with her pancakes, giving them the strength to make their way back to friendly lines. The ad explained that the general later told the story to a representative of a "northern milling company who traveled to the South after the war, and found her living in the same cabin along the banks of the Mississippi." The ad featured a Wyeth illustration of the famished general and his orderly being served by a gleeful Jemima. Thus were Aunt Jemima and her recipe discovered, and thus both came north—after giving life to two men removed from their male comrades.[10]

This story of Aunt Jemima's discovery was seconded by another ad, which depicted the anonymous general coming ashore at Higbee's Landing twenty years after the war to find the old mammy who had saved his life with her gift of pancakes. Titled "When the *Rob't E. Lee* Stopped at Aunt Jemima's Cabin," Wyeth's art depicted the general arriving with two other well-dressed men, his fellow travelers on the famous sidewheeler, and a smaller inset reproduced the art from the earlier ad, with Aunt Jemima serving the general and orderly (fig. 6). The general retold the story of his near-capture by the Union and said:

> The mammy seemed to guess ouah story and hahdly before we knew it she had us down at the table with big stacks o' pancakes in front of us. Just pancakes—that's all she had—but such pancakes they wuh! Nevah befoah had I tasted their equal—and nevah since.
>
> We learned afterward that the mammy was Aunt Jemima; befoah the wah cook in the family of one Cun'l Higbee, who owned a fine plantation heah, and that she was, in those old days, known all ovah the South fo' huh cookin' skill, specially fo' huh pancakes.

The ad said that the old general and his companion, who happened to work for a milling company up north, decided to see if the cabin still existed. It did, and so did Aunt Jemima, and, sure enough, she made them a batch of pancakes. The general expressed his gratitude with "bright pieces of gold," and later, "so the story goes," the representative of "a large Missouri mill" bought the recipe.[11] The ads reestablished several important and recurring facets of Aunt Jemima's story from Purd Wright's original pamphlet, making Chris Rutt's Pearl Milling Company part of the story, but anonymously, and establishing Aunt Jemima's pancakes as a sort of gift, something given freely out of love and later rewarded with gold, not cheapened by currency. Like Maxwell House, Aunt Jemima's pancakes were a gift from the South to the North, from a mother figure to distinguished men who used her talents with their technology. In all, the pancakes were a black creation, under the supervision of elites, from a land of plenty made available to all thanks to northern technology and distribution—a marriage of

6. "When the *Robert E. Lee* Stopped at Aunt Jemima's Cabin," *Ladies' Home Journal*, January 1920, 129

the feminine, black, and pastoral South to the masculine, white, and industrial North. It was similar to the gendered way the reconciliation between regions was depicted in novels and travel guides, as Nina Silber has described in *The Romance of Reunion*.[12]

Another ad displayed this marriage more clearly by showing Aunt Jemima making that trip to the North, where she would teach the milling company how to make her pancakes. Her trip bore little resemblance to the experiences of the thousands of former slaves and their descendants who traveled above the Mason-Dixon Line in search of a better life. In "Aunt Jemima Bids Goodbye to the Old Plantation," her departure was depicted as at best bittersweet, just as minstrel shows once featured nostalgia for the old plantation home.[13] She looked back on her beloved cabin and remembered her former master:

> Aunt Jemima turned. Through tear-dimmed eyes she saw what she was never to see again—her little cabin home.
>
> A thousand memories flashed across her mind. How happy she had been on that old Louisiana plantation! How kind, how noble, had been her "massa," Colonel Higbee!
>
> She thought of the morning she first took her mother's place in the big kitchen of her master's mansion; of his unconcealed pride in her as she grew into fame through her skill as a cook.
>
> Then, crowding out these bright memories, came those of the war—sad memories of the Colonel's going; of the manse so desolate, long crumbled in ruin.
>
> And she saw herself again—left alone with just her pickaninnies and a sheltering place, that sturdy little cabin.
>
> Now some twenty years had flown. She had raised her little family and it, too, had gone. Aunt Jemima was quite alone.
>
> But you remember, perhaps, that she had sold to a big milling company in the North the pancake recipe that had made her famous, the recipe that no other mammy could equal. Well, this was the day when she should carry out that stipulation of the sale which required her going to the mills and over seeing the preparation of a pancake flour to be made from her recipe and sold in a ready-mixed form.
>
> Grieved though she must have been to bid that last goodbye, she was happy, too. A new opportunity of service was open to her. If from her recipe a

ready-prepared flour could be made, thousands then could enjoy her pancakes as the Colonel's guests had done.[14]

Young's Aunt Jemima was like Thomas Nelson Page's Mammy Krenda, who looked fondly on her slave days and longed for the old plantation family, black and white, or like Margaret Mitchell's Mammy would be in *Gone with the Wind* more than a decade later—seemingly facing nothing but "weerie loads" after the war. But thanks to northern industry, when the "rather dazed old mammy" stepped off the train in St. Joseph, Missouri, the ad said, she found a new family to serve: the nation as a whole. "A way had to be found to mix by machinery the ingredients of Aunt Jemima's pancake batter, to mix them exactly according to her recipe! Equipment had to be built; it couldn't be bought. No one had ever made such a pancake flour before. At last the way was found." The ad also mentioned that it was Aunt Jemima's idea to add the dried milk to the flour mix, not R. T. Davis's. Finally, under the mammy's supervision the northern mill's pancakes and Aunt Jemima's originals were taste-tested side-by-side, and "no one could see or taste a difference between them. There was no difference!"[15] The large picture in the ad depicted Aunt Jemima taking one last look at the old

7. "Aunt Jemima Bids Goodbye to the Old Plantation," *Saturday Evening Post*, 15 January 1921, 66

cabin as she headed down the road; an inset showed her beaming at the box containing the finished product and bearing her likeness (fig. 7).

Jemima had to be loyal, too loyal to leave her family simply for the opportunity to make money up north. The tearful departure was an important part of the explanation of her journey, which could only take place after everyone else had died or left Higbee's Landing, for the archetypal mammy would never abandon her charges. The ads also emphasized that Aunt Jemima was rewarded in gold rather than, say, a cashier's check or a stake in the milling company. This ensured that her form of compensation reflected the intrinsic value of her Old South secret recipe, and by removing the stench of currency, that Aunt Jemima pancakes were a gift to the North made possible only by the giver's ultimate sacrifice of leaving her plantation world. Young repeated the themes he had explored in the Maxwell House ads, treating raw materials like coffee and flour less as commodities to be transported north and capitalized upon and more like gifts to the nation. The marriage of Yankee ingenuity and southern abundance, modernity and tradition, and male technology and female nature was similar to the picture of Union generals coming to the Maxwell House to reconcile over cups of coffee. The difference was that in the case of Aunt Jemima, the movement was from South to North, an old mammy cook coming up explicitly to help northern men show northern housewives how to take care of their husbands. The South gave not only Aunt Jemima pancakes but Aunt Jemima herself, and in the exchange she became famous. She came north with the recipe because the mix itself was not enough; she had to show the North how to make the pancakes, which presumably it could not do alone, even with the help of all its newfangled machinery. Aunt Jemima floated upriver to mammy the North, just as she had mammied the South.

Aunt Jemima's fame, according to the ads, was twofold. First, she was famous throughout the South "befo' de wah," again stressing the continuity between the Old South and the New South. Numerous ads make mention of how southerners traveled miles to sample the pancakes at Higbee's Landing, and a series of ads offered specific episodes. One titled "The Night the *Emily Dunstan* Burned" depicted a riverboat disaster sometime before 1861, complete with display type reminiscent of old newspaper accounts: "Pilot Jim's account—an affair of honor—the fire—Tom Maury, 'plucky devil'—in Aunt Jemima's cabin—the Aunt Jemima of pancake fame." The ad depicted Aunt Jemima looking out of her cabin door, horrified; the inset showed a huge riverboat sinking. In the copy the pilot remembers racing a rival boat, the *Skipper Queen,* on a run down the Mississippi. He suddenly felt the boat lurch and heard below deck something that "sounded like a cannon firin' down below an' the *Em'ly* shuddered, seemin' ter know her time had come." Tom Maury, the engineer, made sure all the passengers escaped, waiting until the last minute to swim to shore himself. The passengers, soaked and scared, waited for help along the banks of the Mississippi, "on the Louisiana side." And then:

> The women folks trudged into that cabin you see yonder, an' when us men went up we found 'em thar an' a nigger mammy was a-motherin' 'em all. Blast me, ef she didn't have 'em all calmed down! An angel could a' done no better.
>
> Well, it turned out that she was Colonel Higbee's "Aunt Jemima," the cook we'd heard tell about from Mizzou clear down ter N'Orleans.

Jemima, of course, welcomed the survivors with pancakes, and Colonel Higbee took them into his home. In comforting the women, Aunt Jemima was only doing what mammies do, according to the remembrances of the Old South in turn-of-the-century diaries, which Aunt Jemima ads were increasingly resembling in the 1920s.[16] In this ad we begin to see more concrete details about when and where Aunt Jemima lived, since the plantation is depicted as somewhere along the part of the river that runs between Louisiana and Mississippi. Another version of the *Robert E. Lee* riverboat ad said she lived at the confluence of the Red and Mississippi rivers, which means she lived in the vicinity of Simmesport, Louisiana, near the southwestern corner of Mississippi.[17]

Other specific episodes in Jemima's life on the plantation told readers more about the people in her life, especially her master, Colonel Higbee. One of the most interesting examples was titled, "How Aunt Jemima Saved the Colonel's Mustache and His Reputation as a Host." It also introduced Aunt Jemima's mother, Eliza, and offered an explanation of how Jemima came to cook for the colonel. The ad assured its readers that Higbee himself was a famous man in his day, although for what it does not say, and that he was always known for his mustache. "No doubt there was a day when Colonel Higbee had no mustache; yet, no picture of him as a boy having come down to us, it is impossible to state with absolute assurance this was the case." The ad says the colonel was receiving some important visitors—"the Carters, the Southwoods, and the Marshalls"— at "Rosemont, his big plantation manse." But something was wrong with "Eliza, the Colonel's old mammy cook," in the kitchen: "With her head wrapped in cold cloths, her bulky form bent far over on her folded arms, she sat—a picture of pain. Her daughter Jemima, first helper in the kitchen, hardly knew which way to turn." Then,

> All this Mose, the negro butler, had taken in at a glance, and he tarried just long enough to enlighten poor Aunt Eliza on the cause.
>
> "Didn't Ah tells yo' las' night as how some 'fliction was comin' when dat black debbil bird come flyin' into dis yeah kitchen? Ah jes knowed it."
>
> With that he disappeared around the corner of the house—to find the Colonel.
>
> "Good Lawd, massa. Aun' Liza's got a mis'ry!"

Colonel Higbee, the ad said, became so worried about the feeding of his guests that he began to pull the hair out of his face. The guests would be ready for breakfast soon, and the colonel thought, "If only Jemima . . . but she was just a girl; she couldn't get this breakfast." Mose interceded in the kitchen, and Aunt Eliza, heeding his warning that the colonel was about to pull out his mustache, put the girl Jemima to work. She planned the usual breakfast but added one dish: pancakes. The Carters and Southwoods and Marshalls were, of course, extremely impressed, and the colonel was grateful for her "unusual cooking skill." The ad declared: "The Colonel was in the height of his glory. His reputation was saved—and his mustache, too, though perhaps he himself never realized how near both of his prides came to ruin that morning."[18]

The colonel's mustache and masculine pride, it seems, were in perpetual danger, for in the original Aunt Jemima pamphlet, Purd Wright had depicted Union troops threatening to pull off the former, until Aunt Jemima came through with a batch of her miraculous pancakes. Eventually, the young Jemima (who is pictured in the ad's inset, below the larger art of the colonel yanking on his mustache as a worried Mose looks on and guests arrive) became a cook famous throughout the South, as dozens of later ads attested. The butler Uncle Mose, who is depicted as an older man in the advertisement, somehow lived long enough to work with the elderly Jemima and, some advertising suggests, marry her. A famous person, in any event, requires a biography, and a biography in turn requires the type of supporting cast this ad introduced, not only Mose and Eliza but Uncle Eben, who watched the colonel's chickens. They were a group of superstitious plantation darkies, fearful of the "debbil bird," as any novel of the antebellum South offered.

Aunt Jemima's greatest fame, the ads reminded readers, came when she ventured outside the South to advise that nameless "northern milling company," and Young and Wyeth persisted in placing an imaginary person in otherwise realistic places and events. One ad especially stands out, however, as an example of the blurring line between Aunt Jemima's reality and fiction. In March 1921 Young and Wyeth's "At the World's Fair in '93, Aunt Jemima Was a Sensation" took a real event, a real person, a fictional person, and the fictional person's background and melded them all (fig. 8). Although Nancy Green had been Aunt Jemima personified to thousands, Aunt Jemima became, in the ad, the real person who appeared at a famous exhibit at the 1893 World's Fair. The ad tells the story of what happened after the milling company representative brought Aunt Jemima north:

> There she was—at the World's Columbian Exposition, Chicago. And, up on a platform where all could see, she was making pancakes a new way—from ready

8. "At the World's Fair in '93, Aunt Jemima Was a Sensation," *Ladies' Home Journal*, March 1921, 86

prepared flour! You remember reading of how, some twenty years after the Civil War, a representative of a milling company in Missouri bought from Aunt Jemima her pancake recipe and persuaded her to direct its preparation in the great mills. Well, this pancake flour was the result. It had been made from Aunt Jemima's own recipe—the recipe that had made her famous through all the South even before the war, when she was cook in Col. Higbee's mansion down in Louisiana.[19]

The ad is an oddity in many ways. It picks up the Aunt Jemima legend but relates it to real events—past Colonel Higbee's mustache and into the World's Fair—moving her somewhere beyond mere puffery but nowhere near reality. It was not Aunt Jemima as portrayed by Nancy Green at the 1893 fair; the real Aunt Jemima was fresh off the fictional plantation created for her by Purd Wright after the exposition. The ad reminds readers that Aunt Jemima was mobbed by the masses and won a medal, things that actually happened, but the explanation for her popularity is rooted in fiction: "Those who knew her best, who knew her even from the time when she first came up from her little cabin home, they found her still the simple, earnest smiling mammy—it was all the same to her."[20] Nancy Green was not found in a little cabin on the Mississippi, of course, but in the kitchen of a Chicago judge's home. The ad also offers, once again, reference to the recipe's purchase by a "milling company in Missouri," meaning, of course, the real Pearl Milling Company, owned by a pair of bachelors (one of whom, the ad also neglects to mention, happened upon a minstrel show one night).

It does not matter that the ad was not factual, for no Aunt Jemima ad had ever been factual, but it is striking how much of the story of Aunt Jemima and her fame was intentionally rooted in reality. Aunt Jemima, who never existed, had become a real person through the imagination of the men who manipulated her image in personal appearances and in print. Perhaps sticking too close to reality in one detail, Young also made her deceased—two years before Nancy Green died in a car accident. "At that great World's Fair in '93, they saw Aunt Jemima in person; today we cannot," the ad said. "But what she did, lives on—that and her smile." (Future ads placed Aunt Jemima back among the living, with no explanation.)

To Young and Wyeth, Aunt Jemima became a real enough person to be included "among the famous cooks of history"—Sally Lunn, Alexandre Dumas,

Cardinal Richelieu, Carême, Queen Anne, and Vatel. She was real enough, according to a "distinguished writer on foods," to have left Mark Twain "hankering" for some famous Mississippi buckwheat pancakes during a trip to Europe. The ad writers eventually cited a source for all they knew about Aunt Jemima's life on the Mississippi and her discovery. The small-print note explaining the authenticity of their minstrelsy—their particular version of "genuine Negro fun"— appeared on numerous ads throughout the 1920s: "We are often asked, 'Are these stories of Aunt Jemima and her recipe really true?' They are based on documents found in the files of the earliest owners of the recipe. To what extent they are a mixture of truth, fiction and tradition, we do not know."[21] Young and Wyeth claimed that Aunt Jemima was "The Cook Whose Cabin Became More Famous than Uncle Tom's," refusing all offers for the recipe as long as the colonel was alive (including a "tidy sum" offered by "Henry Carter of Richmond") and until she came north (fig. 9). But there was no need, the ad said, to recount all the stories of her exploits on the plantation or her discovery by the northern mill; after all, "you've met Aunt Jemima herself" every morning at breakfast.[22]

But what were the housewives in JWT's target audience getting when they "met" Aunt Jemima? The answer lies in other ads that described life among the cast of characters at Higbee's Landing.

White Leisure in Aunt Jemima's South

Aunt Jemima and Uncle Mose and Uncle Eben and other slaves depicted in the ads toiled happily for a specific purpose, the comfort of Colonel Higbee's guests. Together they carried the luggage, prepared the cut flowers, made the beds, and in Jemima's case prepared the food that awaited the Carters and Southwoods and Marshalls who came to dance and relax at the Rosemont estate. Aunt Jemima's world was one of hard work performed so that white elites could pursue a life of greater fulfillment. In that way she was no different from the house slaves who worked at the relatively small number of real southern plantation homes. What distinguished her was the skill and joy with which she did so, according to the fantasy world of ads created by Young and Wyeth. Cooking for large groups was not depicted as an arduous feat performed in a hot, detached kitchen but as a magical gift made possible by the "sixth sense" possessed by a few select old-time mammy cooks—the same gift delivered to the North when Aunt Jemima was finally persuaded to sell her recipe. Food was not

9. "The Cook Whose Cabin Became More Famous than Uncle Tom's," *Ladies' Home Journal,* October 1919, 153

the result of labor but part of the joyful order of things, a critical part of the appeal to white women who not only increasingly took on more of the housework but were more likely to work outside the home as well. In fact, the ads demonstrate what Jeanne Boydston has termed the "pastoralization of housework," describing women's work as a "way of being rather than as a conscious form of labor."[23]

In one gloriously colorful, multifaceted ad, "When Guests Dropped In to Stay a Week or Two," the arrival of visitors to Rosemont was depicted in a series of sketches. In the large panel Uncle Mose unloaded luggage as hoop-skirted women and top-hatted men were greeted at the door, and he said, "Yas suh! yas suh—de Cun'l sho' do like lots of company." The themes of southern abundance and hospitality were present throughout, as Mose welcomed a surprise visitor attracted by Aunt Jemima's pancakes: "Is the Cun'l home? Marse John Henry happens in from Richmond to spend Thanksgiving." (He happened in from a distance of hundreds of miles.) The text is almost as colorful as Wyeth's illustrations:

> What a cheery bustle of coming and going there always was in the delightful Louisiana household where Aunt Jemima was cook! Such confusion in carrying all the carpet-bags and hat-boxes in and out! Such a pleasant flurry of excitement in greeting unexpected rituals—such cordial last-minute efforts to urge the parting guest to stay a bit longer!
>
> And yet there was never any commotion about caring for them all—though a whole family might "happen in" for a lengthy visit. There were plenty of extra rooms in the big pillared mansion—plenty of chickens and butter and eggs and rice and other good things to serve any number at any time! And always, at a moment's notice, Aunt Jemima could whisk up a batch of her famous pancakes—the like of which you'd never taste elsewhere in all the Old South!

The ad also depicted Mose as a pancake thief, as Aunt Jemima shooed him out of the kitchen: "Scat! yo' black rascal[.] Don't come hamperin' me when they's company waitin' fo' breakfast!" The ad said that "great piles" of those pancakes would disappear from in front of the waiting guests. One inset in the ad depicted a pair of women scurrying down the stairs (fig. 10). The caption reads: "Polkas till midnight—but the Colonel's guests were always prompt to breakfast!" This might be one of the few points at which Young's grasp of the details escaped him, since it is doubtful a real Colonel Higbee's guests would have been invited to perform the double-time dance developed in Bohemia in the early nineteenth century. At any rate, the picture of well-dressed white southerners packed around a large table, with the colonel by himself at the head would repeat itself in Aunt Jemima advertising throughout the 1920s and 1930s, usually accompanied with a caption that read something like: "The Colonel's guests at the Higbee plantation enjoyed these fragrant pancakes every morning. Aunt Jemima Legend."[24]

PolKas till midnight—
but the Colonel's guests
were always prompt
to breaKfast!

10. "When Guests Dropped In to Stay a Week or Two," *Ladies' Home Journal,* November 1919, 116

Another similar ad depicted such merriment and white leisure with a seasonal theme. In "The Last Christmas on the Old Plantation," guests came to visit Rosemont for the holidays in 1860. Again, Mose toted the luggage in while Higbee greeted the guests, and later, at breakfast, the butler exclaimed, "Lawzee, but dey sho' do Keep me humpin' fo' mo' pancakes!" Meanwhile, "the children, stuffed like little geese, delight in teasing Aunt Jemima" by forming a ring around her and dancing, to her obvious delight. The Big House could sleep and feed any number of guests: "All the cousins and aunts and uncles had flocked home for the merriest reunion ever! The rafters of the old mansion fairly rang, from the moment the avalanche of guests and luggage arrived, till the last carriage rattled down the driveway the day after New Year's. Never a shadow of the fast-approaching struggle between North and South that was to make this their last Christmas together."

That was the magical world lost. And again, Aunt Jemima serves all sorts of wonderful food, especially pancakes, "till her black face was all aglow with pride." Soon the war would interrupt all the revelry; the wonderful hospitality that came on the backs of Jemima and Mose had to end. But, the ad reminded housewives, "today every housewife has Aunt Jemima's secret at her command! Aunt Jemima Pancake Flour can be found in every grocery store, and with it the most inexperienced cook can make cakes with the same flavor that delighted these holiday guests on the old plantation!"[25] Aunt Jemima's pitchmen erased not only feminine labor but, in assuming that women were inexperienced, promised to eliminate the need for white feminine skill in the quest to please husbands.

That hospitality would even extend, eventually, to unwelcome guests at Higbee's plantation. In a later series of ads, done in cruder cartoon panels after both Young and Wyeth had left the account in the late 1920s, a highwayman was depicted as holding up Higbee and demanding $5,000 in gold from his safe. The two went to Rosemont, where the robber ordered Higbee to "dump it in mah carpet-bag," but at that moment Aunt Jemima came through the door to Higbee's study to call him to breakfast. The colonel responded, "Ah'll be there in a minute, Aunt Jemima." The robber declared: "Aunt Jemima? The cook ah've heard about all over the South? Ah've just got to taste her famous pancakes!" They sat down to breakfast, where the robber began to second-guess his intention to take the colonel's gold: "Colonel, Ah'm a sentimental fool. Ah can't abuse yo' hospitality. Take back yo' gold—just promise to say nothin' to the sheriff." The colonel answered: "Ah'll promise, suh. Yo' a gentleman in spite of yo'—ah—profession." Aunt Jemima's pancakes and southern hospitality could conquer anything, even the cold heart of a desperado.[26] The mammy has done her work well, bringing white men together through pancakes.

Aunt Jemima's revelation of her recipe to the northerners seems too much of a gift, until we consider what happened to "The Poor Little Bride of 1860," who came to Rosemont to take in the good times and later tried to replicate the magic in her new home (fig. 11). The 1920 ad depicted a newlywed couple visiting Higbee during their honeymoon. "What fun did they have, with everyone

11. "The Poor Little Bride of 1860," *Ladies' Home Journal*, January 1920, 143

making a fuss over them, and parties galore!" One morning the "little bride" strayed from the revelry to watch Aunt Jemima prepare pancakes ("What fun to watch Aunt Jemima at work"). She was "filled with a sudden new interest in housekeeping, [and] enjoyed nothing more than going out to the big kitchen." She watched Aunt Jemima prepare the pancakes that everyone in the region was talking about, "but it never occurred to her to ask Aunt Jemima just how she made those tender pancakes—it looked so easy!" Finally, the couple left to set up housekeeping in the North: "And then—a near tragedy! She could not make good pancakes—her husband's favorite breakfast. They would be tender—but tasteless. Or nicely browned—but leathery! Poor little bride! How she wished she had only had the foresight to get Aunt Jemima's recipe! But in the end they had to give up the idea of having pancakes." What then happened to the "poor little bride of 1860"—whether her husband shunned her, or they together found some meaning in a life devoid of pancakes—the ad did not say, but it reflected, "The bride of 1920 need never disappoint him" because "nowadays little brides have no such trouble! They can get the famous old recipe itself at any grocery store."[27] The woman who tries to replicate Aunt Jemima's labor—working without the ready-mix recipe—is headed for unnecessary trouble, however. "Little" brides—young, inexperienced—learn to love the kitchen and please their men through the aged mammy, whose presence removes the troubling problem of the work and expertise involved in meeting that end.

The actual recipe remained elusive. Dozens of ads hinting at its ingredients accompanied the stories of Aunt Jemima's days on the plantation, all suggesting that modern women could not possibly achieve the perfect pancake on their own, all showing Jemima's handwritten recipe, with one side of the page folded so that it obscured the amounts of different flours required to pull it off. Again, the mammy is essential in training inexperienced young white women to serve white male needs. A typical ad claimed "Once She Alone Knew It . . ." in the headline and went on to say, in the body copy, "From the very first everyone wanted to try it. The news of her closely guarded recipe travelled swiftly from plantation to plantation. Far and wide the women of those old-time southern estates heard the story of Aunt Jemima's secret." But Aunt Jemima never revealed that secret recipe of four flours—a "smacker of this and a pinch of that"—which in the 1920s still could "not be found in cook books," even though it was "America's most famous recipe."[28] While some ads boasted that never before was there "a recipe so many women had tried and liked," they also advised that Aunt

Jemima's ingredients were "special flours you cannot buy in stores today." The ingredients, as well as her way of measuring and mixing them, another ad said, are "known only to the millers of Aunt Jemima Pancake Flour"; in their test kitchen pancakes were made every five minutes to ensure that the mix adhered to the old-time recipe—the final marriage of mammy genius, southern hospitality, and northern know-how.[29] The sale of the recipe to northern millers kept Aunt Jemima's recipe safe forever, as male technology locked away black female knowledge.

Indeed, some ads in the series said, modern housewives were being inundated with recipes in their quest to manage households without servants. "Thousands of new recipes every week, yet this single recipe has won more users than any in history," one ad suggested. "Actually, it is one of the most striking features of the age we live in—this eager interest of our women in improved methods of cooking," the copy went on. "Where else in the whole world can we find the same sustained, organized effort to bring ever greater pleasure to the family at table?"[30] That old mammy cook, Aunt Jemima, could save modern women from confusion created by advances in the science of food preparation, and they should accept no imitations, the line of ads recommended. Despite the advance of the home economics movement in the late nineteenth and early twentieth century—or perhaps because of the movement's disregard for women's life experiences and judgment in favor of science, ledgers, lists, and recipes—Aunt Jemima ads urged women to ignore "sustained, organized" efforts and "improved methods in cooking" and look back to the antebellum South for answers. "When efficiency, expertise, and fidelity to the scientific method become the highest values," Glenna Mathews has noted, "the ability to resist a good offer from an advertiser is greatly undermined."[31] An especially irresistible offer might have combined tradition and science, as the Aunt Jemima ads did in making the recipe itself unattainable.

In fact, not only could no white housewife master Aunt Jemima's recipe, they warned, but no other mammy cook could, either. A 1927 ad, complete with the familiar folded-over recipe, advised that the pancake mix was "a recipe no other mammy cook could equal." Those few old-time mammy cooks who could master the work, another ad suggested, "had a sixth sense for flavor" which could not be replicated by others because "there is a special feeling for flavor in some people—a particular gift, like the talent of born musicians."[32] It was a talent that not even living black servants could be counted upon to demonstrate in the 1920s; a box of Aunt Jemima mix was thus advertised as superior, in a way, to that hard-to-find live-in maid. Sometimes the hyperbole became even more excessive; a 1926 ad quotes a French judge as saying that new recipes were so rare that they were "more important than the discovery of a new star." Why a "French judge" would be an authority on either pancakes or astronomy is not clear in the ad. A 1927 trade card in JWT's files puts the point more succinctly: "Make them with Aunt Jemima Pancake Flour and your family will ask where you got your wonderful southern cook."[33]

They could not have Aunt Jemima herself, or a substitute black housekeeper, or the recipe; what they got was a great deal of Aunt Jemima advertising. Indeed, JWT's campaign for Aunt Jemima flour was arguably successful not only because of Young and Wyeth's creative powers but because the agency persuaded Aunt Jemima Mills, and later Quaker Oats, to pursue a much broader campaign than either had previously considered. In the winter of 1923-24, the agency placed $5,000 worth of column space in the *Ladies' Home Journal;* by the 1926-27 season it was purchasing a full-color page every month, spending more than $70,000 to do so. JWT records throughout the 1920s show extensive placement of newspaper ads from October to February throughout the continental United States and Canada, from Amarillo, Texas, to Hamilton, Ontario, and from Norfolk, Virginia, to Tucson, Arizona. Ad schedules from 1926-27 show the agency aiming for specific markets such as Chicago with daily newspaper ads and also placing notices in country weeklies across the nation. It even branched out of the winter months to advertise pancakes in the summer of 1926, spending $26,000 on ads in the *Saturday Evening Post* and a total of $147,400 for mostly full-page, four-color advertisements in six other national magazines. The campaign for the winter of 1926-27 lists a schedule of ads, usually appearing every third day, in multiple newspapers in thirty-seven states and the District of Columbia, plus a separate schedule of newspaper advertising for Quebec, with special emphasis on Montreal.[34] In 1927 JWT exceeded all other agencies in placing ads in national magazines, especially in women's magazines. It bought 82,000 lines in *Good Housekeeping* alone—a margin of 25,000 lines more than its nearest competitor, N. W. Ayer. And JWT contributed to the six largest women's magazines nearly as many pages of advertising as the next four agencies combined, a total of 1,041 pages in *Woman's Home Companion,* the *Delineator, Good Housekeeping, McCall's,* the *Ladies' Home Journal,* and *Pictorial Review.* Lord and Thomas was second with only 390 pages; Ayer topped JWT slightly in the magazine ads aimed at men.[35] Aunt Jemima ads were in print virtually everywhere in the United States, increasingly in four colors and on full pages as the campaign reached the middle of the 1920s.

In addition, by 1930 JWT had begun creating Aunt Jemima ads for the slowly maturing medium of radio, a subject of much concern with some at the agency, as Stephen Fox's *Mirror Makers* and JWT's files indicate. One staff member wrote in a 1928 company newsletter, "Since JWT is going to nurse clients with radioitis, we are all for making the nursing beneficial. But let no one get the idea our honest fifteen per cent is coming easily."[36] In the minutes of an agency staff meeting of 15 October 1929, an account executive reported that Aunt Jemima would go on the NBC "red network" every day of the week at 8 A.M., with a New York performer named Phil Cook initially handling all the voices for the ads. The broadcasts of the 1930s predated taping, and no scripts or summaries of the program are extant in JWT's files. But the company newsletter did note that the radio campaign was following the plantation themes established in the print ads, in contrast to plans to advertise Cream of Wheat on radio, which proposed a completely new approach of telling stories to children and not exploiting the relatively anonymous Rastus. A JWT staffer in April 1930 told the agency's officers that he estimated Aunt Jemima sales had increased 5 percent since the start of the radio campaign.[37] One of the few records of radio ads extant in JWT's files shows that in a ten-week period from 26 September to 28 December 1931, Aunt Jemima spots ran fifteen minutes a day, five days a week on nineteen NBC affiliates, including Denver, Washington, D.C., Chicago, Baltimore, Boston, Kansas City, St. Louis, Minneapolis, Cincinnati, Cleveland, Pittsburgh, and New York.[38]

As the campaign increased in scope during the 1920s, it increased in variety of advertising approaches as well. One series of ads departed from Young and Wyeth's original plan in size, taking only a quarter page, and offered a strange twist in the copy, keeping Aunt Jemima at center stage while returning to her minstrel show roots.

"Aunt Jemima Says": The Return of the Interlocutor

Aunt Jemima was never much of a scientist, understandably, in Young and Wyeth's original scheme. Her recipe was more magic than anything. But the wonders of science in perfecting familiar dishes—making them more healthful and more easily prepared—was a major theme of the "fear" or "whisper" campaigns of the 1920s. Aunt Jemima, though, was meant to inspire love and warmth, at least to white consumers. She had no authority, as an antebellum southern cook, to expound on modern nutrition. However, Aunt Jemima ads did talk about new developments in homemaking and even current events by employing another voice in concert with hers, a distinctly white male voice in the advertising copy whose purpose was to explain or enlarge upon whatever "Aunt Jemima Says." This series of ads ran in *Good Housekeeping* and the *Ladies' Home Journal* in 1923 and 1924, in black and white, one-column or three-quarter-page format, as opposed to the full-page color ads that usually explained Aunt Jemima's legend. The largest image in the ad was a drawing of a smiling Aunt Jemima, and close by was a large caption that always began with the headline "Aunt Jemima Says" and featured a message in her black dialect: "Aunt Jemima Says: Pancakes is good fo' chillern—dependin' on de pancakes an' how dey's cooked[.]"[39] The purpose of this ad was to promote pancakes, and Aunt Jemima mix especially, as healthful food for growing children, provided adults knew how to prepare the food. In the smaller type below the Aunt Jemima caption, another voice advised housewives that "if you make pancakes as explained below you need never worry a particle about their being good for children." The authoritative voice did not just advertise the Aunt Jemima brand but offered advice such as, "To avoid smoke, bake them on an aluminum griddle which doesn't have to be greased."

Thus Aunt Jemima, the old-time authority on cooking, set the tone for each of the ads in this series in her broken-English captions that were supposed to amuse, the same voice that the lost Confederate soldiers instantly recognized in an earlier ad. The white voice expounded on the more serious details concerning nutrition, current events, and the need to keep husbands happy. For instance, an ad intended to emphasize the ease of preparing Aunt Jemima pancakes began with the mammy saying, "Makin' my breakfusts is like when yo' gets 'vited some place tuh dinnah en yo' helps by puttin' de watah on de table. Dat's jes how easy 'tis[.]"[40] Then the white male voice—the voice of the makers of Aunt Jemima pancake flour—spoke directly to white women, explaining just exactly what the humorous, if somewhat unintelligible, black mammy was talking about. The appeal is to busy housewives:

Breakfast is no trouble at all when Aunt Jemima Pancakes are on the bill-of-fare. You can even take an extra snooze—and have this breakfast on the table before your husband is ready, race as he will.

All the old-time measuring and mixing is done away with. You simply stir some water (or milk) into an equal amount of Aunt Jemima Pancake Flour— your batter is ready!

In another ad aimed at white housewives' eagerness to please their husbands, Aunt Jemima says, "My speriunce with men folks is—dey's mos' likeable when dey's set down to a pipin' hot plate o' my pancakes[.]" While the plantation mistress was still notably absent from the breakfast table, the ad recounted how much Colonel Higbee liked to set himself down before a plate of the cakes and suggested that the same tactic might work for the modern housewife: "And now, many a clever wife realizes that the best way to start the day right is to give her husband an Aunt Jemima breakfast, the satisfying sort of breakfast he craves."[41] Another advertisement dropped Aunt Jemima back into the realm of allegedly real events: "Aunt Jemima Says: Lawsy me now de Eskimo chillern want my pancakes so bad dey's got to have a aeroplane bring 'em." The white voice explained that "last March" there was a shortage of Aunt Jemima pancake flour at "Moose Factory, a Hudson's Bay post that's shut off from the rest of the world through the long winter months." The normal routes for shipping the product were cut off, so a single-prop plane, pictured in the ad, dropped off a shipment to "the Eskimos and Indians who traded there." The explanation concluded by saying, "And great was the joy of the Eskimo children when they learned what the strange big bird from the South was bringing them!"[42]

That last ad could be interpreted as offensive to multiple ethnic groups and seems to demonstrate that the voice in small type of the "Aunt Jemima Says" was indeed a white voice. All the copy in Aunt Jemima ads, with the exception of direct quotes from a plantation character, was written in proper English and from a white perspective. The legend of Aunt Jemima was explained from a white point of view, glorying in the joys of the Old South and portraying blacks as happy, simpleminded servants. The Aunt Jemima in "Aunt Jemima Says" is obviously jolly and not too bright, and as she became the primary voice of the display ads, she required some sort of translation—a need filled by the anonymous white voice.

That role was also filled in the stage shows that originally inspired the Aunt Jemima trademark, the show that Chris Rutt saw back in 1889, by the standard "interlocutor," a white actor who served as a sort of ambassador for the white audience, interacting with the silly men in blackface who flanked him on the stage.[43] The interlocutor reappeared in this sequence of Aunt Jemima ads, not as an intentional homage to minstrel shows but because the character of the mammy continued to require white interpretation. How could a black mammy be expected to explain what an "aeroplane" was or even have knowledge of Canadian geography? She would know how the right food pleased "men folk," but she could not be expected to speak to the pressures white housewives might experience in getting breakfast ready before husbands rushed off to work. That was not her role; a jolly mammy "befo' de wah" could not talk to white folks about these things.

So decades after she stepped off the minstrel stage, lost many of her more objectionable and foolish traits, and became a fixture in American commerce, Aunt Jemima still required an interlocutor to share her native wisdom. She was welcome in white homes—thanks to her gift of a miraculous secret recipe—but her blackness was indisputably central to her character, and some forms of wisdom were incomprehensible coming from a black voice. Anyway, the makers of Aunt Jemima pancake flour did not need her to be wise as much as they needed her to be the black slave of a wealthy southern gentleman, bringing a mythical world to life again. But, foreshadowing a problem Aunt Jemima's owners today face, advertisers in the 1920s found a limit to what a figure like Aunt Jemima could say to her audience. There was no need to worry about that in the bulk of the ads, which concentrated on her loyalty, her recipe, and most of all her genuine existence as a real-life figure in the Old South. All these things, combined with the skillful omission of a key element in the ads, amounted to JWT's strategy.

The Absent Mistress

One figure was always missing in Aunt Jemima ads: The southern belle never occupied Rosemont. No white woman of the house lived in Rosemont full-time; Colonel Higbee apparently had no wife, no daughter, to play the role of hostess, to supervise the slaves, to worry over Aunt Eliza's affliction or bask in the praise for Aunt Jemima's pancakes. No Mrs. Higbee welcomed the survivors of the *Emily Dunston* into her mansion, nor was there a woman of the house fretting about what sort of food the Carters, the Southwoods, or the Marshalls would find at their table. Given the southern lady's importance in the plantation lore mined so successfully by Young and Wyeth—a world in which men were courteous and gallant, slaves were loyal and happy, and children were well-be-haved—the absence of a mistress of Rosemont is conspicuous. Why wasn't she the one depicted in gorgeous color, dancing to the "polkas till midnight"? Shouldn't she have been the one supervising all of those house slaves? Her absence is as striking as the presence of all those black waiters in the Maxwell House ads.

The absent mistress, rather than a simple oversight, was a key part of the ads' appeal. The women whom JWT targeted in its ad campaign could not find or afford a household servant, let alone one as talented and loyal as Aunt Jemima. They certainly did not share the lifestyle they were invited to visit in Aunt Jemima ads—their laborsaving devices were vastly inferior to the slaves employed by Colonel Higbee and left little time for the Carters, Southwoods, and Marshalls, not to mention dancing until midnight. They could not even have the recipe itself, the advertisements reminded them constantly; their job was to add the water. Should they venture to do any more than that, they might wind up like "the bride of 1860," who, try as she might, could not duplicate the taste of Aunt Jemima's pancakes and suffered the consequences.

The southern mistress does not appear in the ads because they were de-signed to require white housewives to complete the thought themselves and place themselves in that role. They were the mistresses of their respective homes. Aunt Jemima, a real person, a real slave, with an actual Old South recipe, was working for them. In reality, they could not have Aunt Jemima, let alone a hired servant. But, the ads seem to be saying to white women, you can approximate the lifestyle once created for plantation mistresses by the efforts of female slaves through purchasing the creation of a former female slave. The ads urged white housewives to have Aunt Jemima, not to be Aunt Jemima. JWT was selling the idea of a slave, in a box. It was no different, in many respects, from the various beer ads that today invite white men to imagine themselves on a professional football field or in the presence of a long-legged model, or many other ads that invite us to visit some fantasy world that is connected with the purchase of a par-ticular brand.

But the campaign was distinct in some very important respects. As much as it encouraged role playing among white women, the universe it invited them to join came with a host of conditions concerning the proper roles of other people, white, black, man, woman. The white leisure of Aunt Jemima ads is inextrica-bly linked to the very real black labor of slaves—a clever pitch for a laborsaving device because it transferred the idea of doing any work to an imaginary person rather than the purchaser and ultimate user of the product. And beyond being simply removed from labor, white women were invited, through the use of Aunt Jemima, to trade their kitchen for a cotillion, joining a legendary world of fashion, social grace, and fine dining. It does not matter that southern white women—including plantation mistresses—in reality worked harder than James Webb Young ever imagined, as many historians of the South have demonstrated. Aunt Jemima ads were an idea about the South designed to speak to white women as they increasingly became household laborers instead of managers of household laborers, a drearier life than that imagined in the tableaux presented by Young and Wyeth. White women were to fill in the blanks in the ad and place themselves, as consumers, in a different context with the help of the product.

The advertisers reconstructed the South in their own fashion in an attempt to make white housewives similarly reconstruct their world. But the absent mistress is evidence of the ad makers' strategy—how they viewed their targets' intellect and emotional state—and not necessarily a guide to the only way the ads worked to build sales. White women, far from buying into a southern fable, also could identify with the mammy as a very successful server of males—just as so many advertisers of the time and today have tried to associate women and men with products. They also could have identified the product positively with a reaction against all those recipes foisted upon them by domestic science, all the options brought to them by advances in technology in the home. Aunt Jemima also could have represented an approving look to the past that diverged from the advertisers' vision, one that emphasized a woman's work as valuable, a woman as knowledgeable. All of this, admittedly, was wound up in racial, gender, and class nostalgia represented by the Old South images. The advertisers chose instead to use Old South imagery for all it was worth, emphasizing the black woman's work as worthwhile because it served white women and men and implying that white women needed to possess that black woman. They decided to appeal to whiteness rather than to demonstrate the competence of women in general, bringing white men and white women together through the labors of a black woman. As in the novels of Thomas Dixon and Thomas Nelson Page and the histories of U. B. Phillips, the mammy of Aunt Jemima ads was the symbol of a household in racial and gender order. That construct required not only a sense of racial supremacy but a dependency on a racial inferior, the mammy, in maintaining the order.

It was a Cargo Cult either way, because the product was presumed to be hand-in-hand with an American lifestyle, albeit in this case a very specific one, lost today but partially recoverable through the act of purchase. But these ads contain elements that make white men part of the Cargo Cult, too, since they are usually the narrators, and they are usually portrayed as dashing southern gentlemen—including the highwayman who trades Colonel Higbee's gold for a helping of pancakes. And they are not the ones cooking those pancakes, either. Aunt Jemima's advertisers did concoct a series of ads specifically designed to appeal to men and boys, and they indicate that as far as the men were concerned, dreams of the plantation South were not an advertising option. They had different fantasies to be mined. White men depicted in the ads, unlike white women, used the mix to do manly things, such as camping, hiking, exploring, and fishing. Because of this, they needed to have Aunt Jemima in a different way.

Aunt Jemima Goes Camping

At the same time that JWT was trying to persuade white women to enter the world of plantation leisure and whiteness, the agency was attempting to get white men and, in particular, Boy Scouts to take along a box the next time they went camping. Aunt Jemima pancake flour had some obvious advantages as campfire cuisine; it traveled well, was designed to be easy to prepare, and required only water. These were also the things that made it an attractive household product; but when Aunt Jemima pancake flour went camping, Aunt Jemima stayed on the box and out of the action. She did not personally help a distressed Boy Scout earn a merit badge, and no man roughing it in the woods was asked to imagine that he was a lost Confederate soldier. Instead, the ads focused on the practicality inherent in the product and, unlike the ads directed at women, depicted men using the mix themselves. Men did not need Aunt Jemima's personal assistance, but they needed Aunt Jemima mix—the results of the black woman's work rather than the black woman herself—to bond successfully over a campfire.

An ad from the June 1920 *Saturday Evening Post* is typical of Aunt Jemima's pitch to men. It shows a pair of outdoorsmen at their campground, one greeting another pair of men in a canoe, the other flipping pancakes in a skillet over an open flame. The headline reads, "Tender, Golden Pancakes—Right Off! No

Matter Who's the Cook," and the body copy claimed that "the 'greenest cook' that ever trailed off to camp can make 'em."[44] A newspaper ad from 1919 celebrated "the promise of trout and pancakes for supper" and said that "trout and coffee taste mighty good when you come in simply starved after a long day's fishin'—but when you have a stack of golden-brown Aunt Jemima Pancakes, too—oh, man!" Another 1919 fishing ad declared, "Here's the breakfast for you outdoor fellows!" and said the pancakes were "real nourishment that will bridge the gap from 4 A.M. until noon." It added, "Don't bother to wake 'the wife' so early—make 'em yourself. It doesn't take an expert to prepare an Aunt Jemima meal." A 1920 ad with art of some happy campers cooking pancakes summed up the approach: "This the old Guide calls a he-man's breakfast."[45]

Advertising aimed at boys, particularly Boy Scouts, was even more specific about how they could use Aunt Jemima pancake flour. In the late 1920s and early 1930s, JWT placed a series of ads in *Boy's Life* magazine that depicted resourceful Scouts using the Aunt Jemima brand to pass requirements and earn merit badges. Sometimes they took cartoon form, like "Jack Makes the Grade," in which Jack the Boy Scout passes "Requirement 7"—cooking—with a box of the mix, even though his scoutmaster advises him that he'd "better let me give you something easier," since pancakes are so notoriously difficult to make. Other ads in the series—produced after Young and Wyeth left the account—departed completely from the elaborate drawings and copy typically used in Aunt Jemima ads and instead showed photographs of Boy Scouts preparing pancakes. They had headlines such as "A Tip from Eagle Scout Hanson," "They Thought He Couldn't Cook," "The Last One Who Finished Washed the Dishes—But Who Cares!" and "Take a Tip from a Veteran Scoutmaster." As in the ads aimed at women, many of the appeals to Boy Scouts promised a free sample of Aunt Jemima, but these ads said it should be used "for your next hike." Scoutmasters were offered twenty-two free packages.[46]

In the ads for men and boys, the Old South—and its mansions, slaves, and balls—was dropped. They offered the mix, and not Aunt Jemima herself, as the solution to some specific, practical problems, such as filling up after a morning of trout fishing or earning merit badges. The target audience is shown using the product, not waiting for a slave to bring pancakes. They were serving themselves, really, even in the cases in which they served others. Aunt Jemima ads invited men to live in their own kind of fantasy world, but other than in the very important respect that the mix was a tool to please white men, it was in no way similar to the world women were invited to join. Passing Requirement 7 is considerably different from the challenge of feeding all those Carters and Southwoods and Marshalls who are showing up to dinner expecting the hospitality of the Old South. And preparing the food yourself is entirely different from imagining that it is being prepared for you. Aunt Jemima does not belong at a campsite, but Aunt Jemima pancake flour might. These ads never featured Aunt Jemima in any way, limiting her image to a usually small reproduction of the box. In the Boy Scout ads, the familiar tagline "I'se in town, honey," was dropped. Nonetheless, this was a variation on the gendered fantasies used in women's magazines: Aunt Jemima's product was needed to help men do manly things.

True to advertisers' predominant view of women at the time, Aunt Jemima's pitchmen assumed their main targets were intellectually inferior and thus easily manipulated, willing to pass into the plantation world where Aunt Jemima did all the work. In not so uncomplimentary a fashion, they viewed men as a different sell, requiring practical appeals to self-interest rather than service. The men Aunt Jemima reached might have been as likely to clean a fish or shoot a bear as their wives were to dance at Rosemont; eating a manly stack of pancakes before rushing off to work would be as close as they got to their fantasy countryside. Aunt Jemima inspired different fantasies in white men and boys than in white women, but in the end the product made women womanly, men manly, and turned boys into Eagle Scouts for good measure.

While the plantation theme continued after Young and Wyeth's exit throughout the 1930s, 1940s, and 1950s, other Aunt Jemima ads used more conventional themes in contemporary advertising, particularly fear. A series of ads in *True Story* magazine during the early 1930s mirrored the confessional magazine's content, portraying a housewife in danger of losing her happy home if she failed to please her man at the dinner table. The May 1931 issue of *True Story* featured an ad titled "Was My Fault Greater than His? Just at the Breaking Point the Unexpected Happened," a first-person account of a marriage on the rocks: "We were a happy couple at first. But some terrible change came over Harry when the children were a few years old. Worry . . . expense made him so irritable that he was like a different person." The narrator-wife said that "breakfasts were the worst time," as her husband usually stomped out the door without eating, angered by "the simple food on the table":

One morning, after a specially pleading look from me, he exploded. "I know, Marge, but I am not on a diet. After this, if you want to see me at breakfast, you'll have to give me something I'll relish . . . sausage and pancakes—"

"But darling, I don't have time for p-p-pancakes. You don't want me to neglect Betty and B-B-Bud, do you?" and I burst into tears.

"Of course not!" Harry's voice was a little softer. "But why don't you try that ready-mixed Aunt Jemima we used at camp last year?"

And they lived happily ever after. Other ads in the series had titles such as "In Danger. . . . But I Didn't Know It! Then My Salvation," "It Would Have Wrecked My Home! But This Discovery . . . Made in Time . . . Saved Me," and "I Almost Felt They Were My Enemies . . . Then—This Inspiration." Other ads, such as one titled "Wives Don't Know Everything," advised men to clue their women in on the Aunt Jemima brand, but these ads—typically a series of panels in which one man tells another about his wife's light, fluffy pancakes—seem aimed at women, since the body copy at the bottom said, "Have you, too, failed to serve Man's Favorite Food because you thought it was too heavy?"[47] A JWT staff member named Gerald Carson explained the approach in an article titled "Writing for the Tabloid Mind," noting that "an examination of the literature of the masses discloses a very narrow range of interests. They have extremely elemental interests, demand absolute directness, and no frills. . . . The readers of 'True Story' seem to dwell in a completely unreal and romantic world. They flop from one emotional crisis to another." He concluded that the masses sought "a secret formula for success and happiness, never looking within for wisdom and peace. The manufacturer who can offer the masses a better way of living in their own sort of a world . . . will have a rich and well deserved reward."[48] The prospect of advertising to the lower-class readers of *True Story* divided some JWT staffers; one wrote to the newsletter asking whether plans to use the magazine were "for the purpose of appealing to these morons?" Carson replied by lashing out at upper-class white women: "However pleasant it might be to advertise exclusively to 'nice' people—to the girls at Sweetbriar or Goucher or even, to take an extreme instance, Vassar—our success is too dependent upon the franchise of the common people for us to cherish a purpose so aristocratic."[49]

Still, throughout the 1930s the bulk of Aunt Jemima advertising continued to concentrate on the romantic world of "plantation flavor"—a phrase ubiquitous in newspaper and magazine ads—on Aunt Jemima, not on fear, or econ-

omy, or nutrition. The ads, created without the guidance of Young or the illustrations of Wyeth, reminded readers that the recipe was "Aunt Jemima's own,"
and they featured illustrations of Uncle Mose or Colonel Higbee or female
guests looking over the mammy's shoulder as she stacked up more of her creations.[50] Even an ad that tried to persuade housewives to make more pancakes
for supper declared that it was "an old southern custom."[51] The idea of buying
Aunt Jemima pancake flour to approximate the lifestyle of the Old South
seemed permanently entrenched in campaigns for the product, no matter who
was creating them.

Back to the World's Fair

"I decided," James Webb Young said years later, "to develop a series on what
you might call the Americana of the Deep South. I think I can say that the series was the first of what I could call 'the romantic school' [of advertising]. It was
a departure from nearly all the advertising of the day." Regardless of how one
might assess Young's effect on American advertising as a whole—it seems safe to
say that he was enormously influential—he did succeed in returning Aunt
Jemima to her roots and further mining the potential Chris Rutt saw on the
minstrel stage. Young and Wyeth personalized Aunt Jemima further, taking the
legend that Purd Wright created in a pamphlet and spreading it to every corner
of the United States (and parts of Canada). So it should be no surprise that
Quaker Oats resurrected Aunt Jemima in person for the 1933 Chicago Century
of Progress Exposition, returning her to the site of her initial tremendous success of 1893—forty years later, ten years after the death of Nancy Green. This
time, in the depths of the depression, another Chicago woman was recruited
from hundreds of applicants to play the pancake-flipping mammy, with the aid
of Lord and Thomas, Quaker Oats's new advertising agency. "Never was to be
forgotten," wrote Arthur Marquette in Quaker Oats's official company history,
"the day they loaded 350 pounds of Anna Robinson and sent her to New York
in the custody of Lord & Thomas advertising agency people to pose for pictures." In Manhattan, Robinson made personal appearances at El Morocco, the
Stork Club, the 21 Club, and the Waldorf-Astoria Hotel. Quaker Oats redesigned the package to make Aunt Jemima look like Anna Robinson, who continued the tradition of personal appearances on behalf of the company until her
death in 1951.[52]

Forty years later, after the death of minstrel shows, the rise of the ad agency, a world war, the advent of the depression, and one of the most extensive and innovative ad campaigns ever, Aunt Jemima had come full circle, back to Nancy Green's pancake-flipping and storytelling in Chicago. James Webb Young did not reinvent Aunt Jemima; he rehabilitated her earlier image, adapting it to the explosion of print advertising in the 1920s. As he told his University of Chicago students, "An idea is nothing more or less than a new combination of old elements." He kept the Old South and the slave in a box, and in the role of the southern mistress he cast the white American housewife.

And what was the harm in all this? In a "democracy of goods," after all, consumers cast their votes for the advertising campaigns they approve of and the products they wish to purchase. Arguably, this is the place to stop any discussion of the Aunt Jemima campaign: It traded on themes of racism and sexism, on a relentlessly sentimental and unrealistic portrait of slave life and Old South hospitality, and in doing so sold boxes and boxes of flour. Aunt Jemima, in the 1920s and continuing through the middle of the twentieth century, became an everyday part of American life, something to which people understandably gave little thought as they passed the ever-increasing numbers of products stacked on the ever-larger grocery stores frequented by increasingly affluent shoppers. But some potential consumers were disfranchised from the "democracy of goods" offered in Aunt Jemima ads by JWT in the 1920s and Lord and Thomas in the succeeding decades, and by the end of the 1950s they would be pushing for the vote. In the 1920s JWT analysts confidently cited illiteracy and low income among African Americans as factors overwhelmingly precluding consideration of this part of the population in the planning of any national advertising campaign. For example, a *JWT Newsletter* in 1927 noting the opening of a Piggly Wiggly store congratulated the grocery chain and said that the new facility was designed to appeal to high-class consumers. It added that "in five days 33,000 persons visited the plant, only three of whom were negroes. . . . At all the shows, the persons in attendance were people of the better classes, evidently people of purchasing power." Thus JWT pointedly conflated race with class in its official statements on marketing strategy. A 1928 memo even argued that the company should not attempt to appeal to literate African Americans through magazine advertising, suggesting that 90 percent of them would not be reached, regardless of which magazines ran the ads.[53]

On 1 July 1953 JWT reassumed the Aunt Jemima account after a long absence. It immediately announced a reemphasis on the plantation themes the agency had mined in the 1920s, "each page topped by an episode that harks back to the days in the Old South when Aunt Jemima was cook at the Colonel Higbee plantation." The agency also planned to promote the product by sponsoring a contest in which participants would describe "which pancake recipe you like best" and to feature it during the *Adventures of Ozzie and Harriet* television show.[54] Aunt Jemima print ads in women's magazines once again featured paintings of the belles trying, unsuccessfully, to pry the recipe out of Colonel Higbee's prized slave. The problem on the horizon was not apparent to Quaker Oats or the J. Walter Thompson Company. Aunt Jemima's owners had, over the years, taken her out of the minstrel show and maneuvered her through the rise of processed foods, household technology, and the servant crisis. After all that, she looked pretty much the same. They had tied the product to race and gender and expanded the scope of the campaign dramatically, and regardless of how many ways the strategy worked, it worked fabulously. But in the late 1950s the Aunt Jemima campaign was on a collision course with another great development in American history, the modern Civil Rights movement, and a product with such strong racial overtones faced even more significant changes and challenges if it was to keep its place in everyday life. Would white men and white women continue to bond over pancakes in such a time? Or could Aunt Jemima's owners set free the slave in a box?

6 The Secret of the Bandanna: The Mammy in Contemporary Society

I positively hate this illustration.
—Black respondent to survey by Paul K. Edwards, 1932

Change the Joke and Slip the Yoke.
—Ralph Ellison, *Shadow and Act*

In 1942 the Office of Strategic Services, a forerunner of the U.S. Central Intelligence Agency, created an elaborate series of devices for sabotage. Its scientists designed a candle that exploded when the wick burned down to a certain point, a barometric fuse that blew up enemy planes when they reached a certain altitude, and a device for destroying ships that detonated when it was eroded by saltwater. That year, an agent headed for the China-Burma theater carried a special OSS explosive known officially as Composition C, a powdered form of TNT resembling ordinary wheat flour and designed to escape enemy detection. The explosive could be kneaded into dough and baked into biscuits or bread and was even considered edible. Agents, however, were advised not to smoke a cigarette until the substance had passed through the body. The agency, instead of referring to the explosive by its suspicious-sounding official designation, used a code name that was easily understood by everyone who saw it mentioned in official documents. They called the ready-mix bomb "Aunt Jemima."[1]

Certainly, the name had fallen into popular usage; an eponymous product had become synonymous with a type of industrial design—the ready-mix. The greatest measure of the extent to which the southern mammy had become a part of popular culture, thanks in large part to the Aunt Jemima ad campaign, is perhaps not her depiction in movies, from *Gone with the Wind*, to *Mr. Blandings Builds His Dream House*, to both versions of *Imitation of Life*, or even the success of the ad campaign itself. What made Aunt Jemima special was how ordinary and uncontroversial she was, because the ultimate success of a brand name is dependent on the extent to which it can at the same time be instantly recognizable and not undesirable. At that point it has moved beyond the discrete sphere of advertising and into the vocabulary. For example, much to the Xerox Corporation's despair, the company has become so associated with copying machines that "Xerox"—not legally but practically—has become not only a noun but a verb; people commonly speak of "Xeroxing" a piece of paper. But there are dangers to creating a trademark so compelling that it falls into popular usage. The advertiser gains widespread product recognition but in the transaction loses control over what the name actually means. Xerox routinely places advertisements in journalism reviews to remind writers that not all photocopying machines are Xerox machines; as many newspaper reporters know, the best way to get a free Frisbee—accompanied by a stern reminder of the importance of laws against trademark infringement—is to write a story in which an off-brand flying disk is referred to as a "Frisbee."

Aunt Jemima pancake flour was in many ways a unique product. It was the first ready-mix, perhaps the first product promoted in person by a living trademark, and could be seen as paving the way for products that would have been impossible if not for advances in packaging—the "Aunt Jemima Effect," as Thomas Hine called it. It also was the subject of a uniquely long-running campaign that drew heavily on racial images and painted a cheerful picture of slave life throughout that long run. Thus the product also faced unique problems as its name became a part of the language. Aunt Jemima was designed by Young and Wyeth, and maintained by later advertisers, to evoke images of white leisure based on the perpetual servitude of blacks, a specific kind of nostalgia, all moonlight and magnolias, about race relations in America. Throughout the 1950s and part of the 1960s, Quaker Oats kept the nostalgia coming, not only in print ads but in the hundreds of personal appearances, the traditional approach to promoting Aunt Jemima and her recipe. The manufacturer even established a permanent presence at one of the shrines of American popular culture, Disneyland. But finally Aunt Jemima's reach had exceeded the grasp of Quaker Oats. Personal appearances by Aunt Jemima became opportunities for African Americans to voice long-standing grievances. As the "democracy of goods" slowly evolved to include more African Americans, the legend of the Old South and the image of a slave on the box had to be altered and then dropped. And Aunt Jemima, who talked so much in those legendary print campaigns, had to be silenced.

Today, Quaker Oats finds itself in a delicate position. In Aunt Jemima it still possesses one of the most recognizable and thus valuable trademarks in history. But it also markets a product whose name has become notorious. Far from accepting the smiling mammy on the box as insignificant, African-American observers criticized the advertising campaign at least from the moment that N. C. Wyeth and James Webb Young fashioned the romantic legend for the pages of women's magazines. They recognized her as a symbol of submissiveness, demanded that the trademark's owners quit using her, and called on black consumers to boycott the product. The trademark remained in use, however, and personal appearances by Aunt Jemimas continued into the 1960s, its owners unmoved by any real or potential black hostility toward the product. And in the 1930s through the 1950s, the archetypal mammy—sometimes slightly different from Aunt Jemima, sometimes a deliberate copy of her—became a film and radio archetype as well. The persistence of Aunt Jemima and the entry of the mammy into new media, however, created a climate in which African Americans not only succeeded in putting the Quaker Oats Company on the defensive, explaining and adjusting its famous black image over the 1960s, 1970s, and 1980s, but in creating a sort of language in which the words *Aunt Jemima* took on a political significance. Her trademark eagerness to please whites remained but in a totally different, disapproving context. Aunt Jemima means essentially the same thing she meant in 1919, but that instantly understood meaning encompasses a collection of traits no longer acceptable in the 1990s. In this sense Aunt Jemima is a guide to how the image of African Americans changed in popular culture over this century, and her own image remains politically charged today, makeovers and all. The OSS agents were more correct than they ever knew in borrowing her name for a time bomb.

The *Crusader*: Some Early Criticism

Almost certainly one of the earliest and still the most pointed of Aunt Jemima's critics among black journalists was Cyril V. Briggs, the editor and publisher of the New York–based *Crusader* magazine. Briggs was perhaps the most

radical of the "New Negro" editors who appeared in the years immediately following World War I, combining black nationalism with calls for a socialist revolution, and his *Crusader* is most notable for its strident opposition to Marcus
Garvey's Universal Negro Improvement Association. From August 1918 to its
final issue in 1922, the monthly *Crusader* reported on lynch riots, preached self-
determination for Africa, and discussed black cultural and sporting events. But
on occasion Briggs turned his attention and a pen, apparently warmed in hell,
to the advertising images he saw in both the white and the black press. He called
on the black press to refuse ads for products that promised lighter complexions
or straight hair:

> Many Negro publications have as just cause to complain of the paucity of
> race support as has the race in regards to their lack of loyalty and integrity dur-
> ing political campaigns and "carrying" of insulting Kink-no-More and Bleach-
> Your-Complexion advertisements as often and as steadily as they can induce the
> white manufacturers of these "aids" to a doubtful "beauty" to let them carry
> their race-insulting advertisements.
>
> During the past few months, The Crusader has been the recipient of sev-
> eral hundred letters congratulatory upon the absence of our columns of insult-
> ing advertisements and hotly condemnatory of the publications that carry
> them. This is a good sign of awakening pride. But does not the blame lie
> halfway between the grasping, race-selling editors and the Negro reader and
> business man whose scant support both in the circulation and advertisement
> departments drive the editors to the white man for support? It is simply a mat-
> ter of "who pays the fiddler calls the tune."[2]

Briggs argued that regardless of how poorly black readers supported their
press, editors could not accept such ads without bolstering "the Caucasian's assumption of superiority" and thus undermining the editorial columns on racial
pride. "By what inverted reasoning do certain Negro papers preach race pride on
one page while carrying on another page race advertisements that insult by their
brazen assumption that present-day members of the race that gave civilization to
the world would like to change their color and racial characteristics merely because white men, whose ancestors in centuries past wandered over Europe as
greasy, hairy savages, are now enjoying a little temporary power[?]"[3]

Briggs saw something even more sinister in Aunt Jemima ads. He first editorialized about them in September 1918, roughly the same time the Young and Wyeth version of the mammy began appearing on the pages of national magazines, billboards, and pancake boxes. Briggs never mentioned Jemima by name, but the references to her are unmistakable: "You have noticed them? Advertisements that caricature and insult the Race. Aunt Somebody or other with her midnight black, wrinkled face, thick red lips, and totally ugly and repulsive expression? And other advertisements that use the Race to represent ugliness, depravity and subservience. You have seen them in the subway and 'L' and have burned red hot with impotent rage, no doubt. They are part of the white man's propaganda to demean, ridicule and insult the Race. They are malicious targets aimed at what he considers a powerless people."[4] Briggs had never seen, he said, a figure like Aunt Jemima in real life, and he called on his readers to take action against her owners. One of his calls for a boycott is worth repeating in its entirety:

> One of the most widely advertised staple foods is given publicity through means that are decidedly insulting to the Negro.
>
> On its advertisements and on its containers it carries a most repulsive female face with thick red lips, coal black complexion, flat, face straddling nose, deep ugly lines and other tricks of the "artist" intended to make the picture as hideous as possible. This picture stares at you from every subway car and elevated station. It is supposed to represent a Negro "aunt," yet neither in America nor in any part of the so-called "Dark Continent" is to be found any human being of such repulsive features as this caucasian-created "aunt." No, not even the average red-nosed and choleric-looking white man can quite compare in absolute hideousness with this horrible nightmare of a demented artist's creation.
>
> This "aunt" is an insult to the Negro Race. An insult that should neither go unheeded nor unpunished. Thousands of our women are engaged as cooks in the homes of others and make the food purchases for these homes; millions more buy for their own homes. Both as housewife and domestic they can resent this insult to their race. They can make the money they spend TALK to remove this insult to their race![5]

It is difficult to assess the effectiveness of Briggs's call for a boycott of the pancake flour. If there are any records that might indicate a boycott by black consumers, or anybody else, during this period, they might be locked in the archives that Quaker Oats is reluctant to share. I have found no evidence of a boycott in the J. Walter Thompson Company's records. One also should be cautious in assessing the size of Briggs's audience. The editor claimed a circulation of 32,700 in October 1919, which would have possibly left the *Crusader* second only to the *Crisis* among the nation's black periodicals. It is likely that the magazine's readers, regardless of their number, were spread across the country; the editor said two thousand agents distributed the *Crusader* nationally, and a list of delinquent news agents printed in November 1919 included points as far away from New York City as Carthage, Missouri; Sterling, Kentucky; and Point Blank, Texas. A New York State senate committee, however, reported in 1920 that while the *Crisis* had a circulation of 104,000 and the *Messenger* and *Negro World* each more than 30,000, the *Crusader* had only 4,000. Briggs disputed this figure as late as 1958, when he claimed a "peak circulation of 36,000."[6]

Putting aside the possibly unanswerable question of whether any black consumers responded to the call for a boycott—and noting that the Aunt Jemima campaign persisted and its producers prospered long after the *Crusader* closed shop—it remains clear that Briggs's editorials foreshadowed two important developments in the pancake mammy's career. The first was assigning political importance to a seemingly mundane object and calling for action against its makers. It is important to remember that Briggs was writing at a time of peak racial violence across the nation, from the East St. Louis riot of 1917 to the "Red summer" of 1919. He also was at the center of intense disputes among "New Negro" leaders, eventually becoming identified as "one of the fellows that sent Marcus Garvey to prison." And his business had its own problems with postal regulators who looked askance at his affiliation with socialist organizations.[7] But Briggs's larger political battles did not blind him to the importance of everyday objects; he saw his political agenda reflected within them and demanded a boycott. The second tactic employed by the *Crusader* was offering positive images of the black woman, not merely denying "Aunt Somebody" but replacing her with real people. A continuing feature throughout the *Crusader*'s run was titled "Successful Business Women," and it congratulated women such as Dr. Julia P. H. Coleman, a "pioneer in the business world" who established the Hair Vim Manufacturing Company, "now famous throughout the world."[8] The magazine also included perhaps more traditional arguments promoting the importance of the black woman as mother. In "Negro Womanhood—An Appeal," Theodore Burrell asked, "Where is the wife who will shoulder the burden of motherhood and bring us sons on whose shoulders we may rest our 'crusade'?"[9] Whether the figure was a businesswoman or mother (or both), later generations would demonstrate the importance of fighting Aunt Jemima with alternative, positive images—eventually, even her owners would try to make her a businesswoman and mother. But because the *Crusader* was short-lived and limited in its distribution, it is not necessarily a guide to how larger numbers of African-American consumers reacted to Aunt Jemima ads. Arguably, they might not have cared and might have had bigger problems than a pancake campaign. So how did black consumers react to the slave in a box?

A Survey: "I Positively Hate This Illustration"

Significant evidence indicates that black consumers who saw Aunt Jemima ads during the 1920s and 1930s strongly disliked them for the very reasons that Young created them and for the very themes the ads emphasized. Neither JWT nor Quaker Oats, apparently, ever bothered to ask black consumers what they thought of Aunt Jemima or the plantation campaigns, but Paul K. Edwards, an economics professor at Fisk University, inquired into the attitudes of black consumers in southern cities regarding a number of different advertising approaches. Edwards published his results in a 1932 book titled *The Southern Urban Negro as a Consumer*, with a great deal of census and other data about what products African Americans bought, and why they bought them. He was particularly interested in brand loyalty among African Americans. His polling of consumers in major southern cities indicated they held strong national brand loyalties that in many ways seemed unrelated to specific approaches in advertising campaigns. For example, high percentages of African Americans preferred Maxwell House coffee, despite the fact that the brand's campaign in no way was designed to appeal to them; in Nashville, more than 70 percent of African Americans in the survey preferred the hometown brand. Edwards concluded that distribution, more than advertising or even price, was the major factor in understanding why African Americans purchased a particular brand; most urban southern blacks bought their goods at white-owned outlets, and their selections reflected the choices of the people who stocked the shelves.[10]

But Edwards also asked African-American consumers what they thought of different advertising approaches, particularly those that included black images. In each case he showed his subjects two different ads for the same product, one that in his judgment was relatively "race-neutral" (which usually meant, in reality, that it only included images of whites), and another that highlighted a black figure. He then gauged the subjects' responses in two categories: first, the extent to which the subjects simply recognized or remembered the ad, and second, their explicit reactions to the ad, either approval or disapproval, recorded in their own words. For example, Edwards showed his subjects two Rinso laundry soap ads. The first (advertisement A) showed two white women discussing the virtues of Rinso, and the second (advertisement B) showed a white woman and black laundress talking about the product. When the two ads were flashed simultaneously before their eyes, the second ad, including a black woman, gained the immediate attention of 183 of the 240 individuals surveyed, or 76 percent. Edwards reported that the ad attracted attention for three reasons: "(a) simply the presence in it of a Negro character; (b) the rather unusual association of a Negro woman with a white woman in the same illustration; and (c) the utilization in the copy of a neatly dressed Negro woman of intelligent appearance." When Edwards asked his subjects which ad, upon reflection, they preferred, a substantial majority—80 percent of men and women polled in Nashville, and 57 percent of those in Richmond—chose the ad with the African-American laundress. "One practical reason was given by a majority of these people for their choice," Edwards wrote. "They stated that if the experienced Negro laundress pictured in [the second ad] used Rinso and found it to be good as indicated by her testimony, it must have merit. . . . Others selected advertisement B, not through logical reasoning of this nature, but merely because of a favorable reaction toward the illustration which to them pictured a pleasant-appearing, attractively dressed Negro laundress who was permitted to use good English in conversation with her white employer."[11] Edwards found that African Americans did not object to members of their race being depicted in ads, but just the opposite; they even voiced approval of a laundrywoman, as long as she was depicted in a respectable fashion.

When Edwards turned to the Aunt Jemima campaign, he selected first an ad titled "Do You Know This Secret of Making Lighter, Fluffier Pancakes?" which used a very small image of Aunt Jemima and a very large picture of a plate of pancakes, although the copy played up the plantation legend. The second ad used a larger image of Aunt Jemima, with an inset illustration of her cabin, and the headline "She Mixed Four Different Flours in a Special Way." Edwards found that Aunt Jemima ads fared much more poorly in the "instant recognition" test than other ads with prominent images of African Americans; just more than half of the people he tested said the larger image of Aunt Jemima caught their eye before the big picture of pancakes. "It is quite clear, therefore, that the Aunt Jemima advertisement containing elements relating to the Negro race gained much less than a complete victory in the attention-value test" than the other ads sampled, Edwards wrote. The Aunt Jemima ads fared even worse in the specific evaluations by African Americans, with disapproval crossing all lines of class, sex, and geographic location. Edwards summarized the views of his subjects by saying that they objected either because of "their disapproval of the use of the 'mammy' type of Negro as pictured in [the] advertisement; because of the use in combination of this Negro mammy and the log cabin; or because of the use of the Negro mammy and the log cabin plus the reference to Aunt Jemima's master—all of which savored too much of slavery days." In other words, they objected to the very heart of James Webb Young's campaign—the plantation legend, the slave South, the loyal mammy. Men and women, unskilled and skilled laborers, and business and professional workers brought up the same issues. "Plays upon idea of Negro in slavery too much," said one of the male common laborers, and a female skilled laborer added, "I made my opinion about slave advertisements a long time ago, and the picture of Aunt Jemima would make me pass it by." A male professional said, "I positively hate this illustration."[12]

There was no way to misinterpret the results. They reflected deep resentment of the references to slavery and Aunt Jemima's master. Subjects disliked the log cabin and the idea that the magical mammy cook ever existed. They took specific exception to the handkerchief she wore on her head, seizing upon it as the symbol of servitude and ignorance. Edwards's work, in the absence of market research by JWT, is the best evidence of how black consumers responded, viscerally and unambiguously. An organized protest against Aunt Jemima was still years ahead, but something was simmering beneath the surface—something to which JWT and other ad agencies were apparently oblivious. African Americans wanted a different representation of their race in advertising, a better-spoken person, a free person, not an imaginary, rag-wearing, subservient piece of property happily flipping pancakes for the Carters, the Southwoods, and the Marshalls.

But throughout most of the twentieth century, the most popular image of black womanhood remained an Aunt Jemima–style mammy, particularly as portrayed in American films. The two versions of *Imitation of Life* (1934 and 1950) are actually very different movies. The earlier version, with Claudette Colbert, is truer to Fannie Hurst's storyline than the remake with Lana Turner, but both maintain Hurst's simple yet stigmatic mammy. The Aunt Delilah character, who helps the female lead build a pancake empire, is so clearly Aunt Jemima that *Imitation of Life* is really an imitation of an imitation of life. Although Donald Bogle, in his indispensable film history *Toms, Coons, Mulattoes, Mammies, and Bucks*, argues that Hattie McDaniel's portrayal of Mammy in *Gone with the Wind* was "free of the greatest burden that slavery—on screen and off—inflicted on blacks," meaning an innate sense of inferiority, he bases that judgment on the fact that McDaniel's Mammy "never bites her tongue."[13] This is a rather unpersuasive argument, given that McDaniel was portraying the outspoken Mammy just as Margaret Mitchell or, more to the point, Thomas Nelson Page and Thomas Dixon did. The archetypal mammy was always outspoken, particularly when it came to offering advice to white women, but that in no way compromised her place in the slave hierarchy or made her any less subservient, ultimately. And if McDaniel's Mammy was not as superstitious or silly as many popular mammies were (including not only the stock characters in Mae West films but *Imitation of Life*'s Delilah and Aunt Jemima herself in some ads), it should be noted that *Gone with the Wind* had Butterfly McQueen in the ridiculous role of the maid Prissy ("I don't know nothin' 'bout birthin' babies!") to complete that task. Mammy was a stock character in films as well as advertising because (white) people knew exactly what to expect from her—that's what stock characters are for. As Bogle has noted, a truly sympathetic portrayal of the mammy came not in *Gone with the Wind* but in the 1952 film version of Carson McCuller's *The Member of the Wedding*, a critically praised commercial failure that was carried by Ethel Waters's performance as the cook Berenice. Waters later portrayed Faulkner's Dilsey in a 1959 film version of *The Sound and the Fury*, which also flopped.[14] One should not look to mid-twentieth-century cinema, however, to find the real challenge to the Aunt Jemima image. Protests against Aunt Jemima were carried out at a local level, where activists, mostly in the Midwest, worked to put an end to personal appearances of Aunt Jemima, specifically. But before that happened, African Americans continued to redefine Aunt Jemima on their own terms, transforming the mammy of advertising and cinema into a base insult by practicing it on one another.

Playing the Dozens: "I Ain't No Aunt Jemima"

The folklorist Roger Abrahams moved into the Camingerly neighborhood of South Philadelphia, an area inhabited predominantly by African Americans, in 1958 with the intent of "following his nose" to collect evidence of the area's cultural life. His findings, documented in *Deep Down in the Jungle* and other books, include two facts important for a discussion of Aunt Jemima. The first was his general observation that "the greatest single distinguishing feature of Negro life in South Philadelphia is the importance of the mother in the family," because African-American women, often raising families without the help of fathers, assumed all the motherly roles of keeping house and tending children while also serving as breadwinners for their families. Abrahams's other revelation (among many) was his discussion of the practice of "playing the dozens," a series of quick-witted insults traded among black youths that focus intensely on defaming the opponent's mother. Abrahams concluded that the emphasis on insulting mothers was a "complete reversal of values" meant to signal a youth's transition from boy to man, from "mother-oriented to gang-oriented values."[15] Whether or not this interpretation is correct, what is important for the purposes of this discussion is the nature of the insults against mothers, what a young man might choose to say when he wished to smear another young man's mother.

Most of the taunts were sexual in nature, particularly among older adolescents, and alleged that the opponent's mother was a wanton woman. For example, one of the rhymes Abrahams reported went like this: "I fucked your mother on an electric wire. I made her pussy rise higher and higher." A response: "I fucked your mother between two cans. Up jumped a baby and hollered, 'Superman.'" Abrahams believed the harshness of the insults depended on the age of the combatants in the game. Younger boys were less likely to attack openly another boy's mother and thus open their own maternal authority figures to attack; but eventually they came to express resentment against their own mothers, because they were maternal authority figures who inherently posed limits on virility, by inviting attacks in verbal combat. "He must in some way exorcise her influence. He therefore creates a playground which enables him to attack some other person's mother, in full knowledge that that person must come back and insult his own." Thus, the young black men Abrahams observed invited their comrades to "do the work for them" and crafted insults in an aggressive fashion calculated to express their own virility, bonding by degrading women. "He has prepared a defense for himself against incest, homosexuality, or any other forbidden sexual motive. In this way the youths prepare themselves for the hypermasculine world of the gang."[16]

Oddly enough—it seems at first, anyway—Aunt Jemima, the asexual old mammy of the plantation in the white mind, figured into these ritual insults. Both Marilyn Kern-Foxworth and Karen Sue Jewell, in their studies of the mammy image and Aunt Jemima in particular, report that other common taunts launched by African-American youths included, "Hey man, ain't yo momma on a pancake box," and references to rag heads and handkerchief heads. Jewell argues that the use of Aunt Jemima in playing the dozens demonstrates how "images of African-American women have had a microcultural influence."[17] But what if we consider Abrahams's observations about the purpose of the game—to undermine maternal authority? It is not much of a reach to see Aunt Jemima, the obsequious servant, the woman who lived to serve her white master and make pancakes for his guests, the slave, as a deprecation useful in resisting maternal authority within the black male community. It represents a different interpretation of the meaning of Aunt Jemima, exposing gender conflict within the black community while using all the material that James Webb Young and N. C. Wyeth presented to create an image of black womanhood. It was another way to reinterpret Aunt Jemima as a strong insult rather than either a simple trademark or, as Young interpreted her, "a real southern cook." Paul Edwards polled southern urban blacks, men and women, upper and lower class, and found that they already considered Aunt Jemima an insult that they simply did not wish to see. Now a generation of young black men growing up in the urban North of the 1950s were dealing with Aunt Jemima in a different but still pejorative way: as an insult aimed by black men at other black men, but striking black women.

This method of insult was not limited to games among boys in the streets, because the African-American men who grew up to run for office in the 1950s and 1960s—some of them the most vocal proponents of civil rights legislation—learned to use the insult for political advantage, again against other African Americans rather than against whites. At this point the term *Aunt Jemima* began to cross sexual boundaries and became a way for black men to chastise other black men while adding an insult to virility as well as racial solidarity. They did not call their opponents' mothers Aunt Jemima, they called their opponents Aunt Jemima, as a sort of a substitute for the more traditional insult, "Uncle

Tom." When they did not use the term *Aunt Jemima*, they substituted related insults such as "handkerchief head." For example, in 1966 the Harlem congressman Adam Clayton Powell, under assault from members of his own race and party, insinuated that his critics were merely kowtowing to whites and said, "What I cannot abide are the black 'Aunt Jemimas' who snuggle up to the white power structure for approbation by denouncing 'black power' and telling Mr. Charlie what he wants to hear."[18]

As in minstrelsy, the lines between male and female, as well as black and white, were blurred in the game of insult. A black male resident of Washington, D.C., criticized black members of the city's school board in 1967 by saying that the board "is nothing but Aunt Jemimahs and Uncle Toms doing the white man's bidding." This method of insult was not limited to the 1960s or the Civil Rights movement but in fact can be found in accounts years earlier, suggesting that the resentment felt by African Americans had transformed itself into a common insult by the 1950s. In 1938 broadcaster and columnist Walter Winchell reported that the entertainer Bill "Bojangles" Robinson used the term to castigate other performers: "Bill Robinson's form of belittling when he gets angry with a performer at the Cotton Club: He groans 'You handkerchief head!'" A "colored service man" writing to the *Nation* in 1944 described a submissive black man who headed a Mississippi family by simply saying, "The father is a handkerchief head. The crook in his back would pain you." And Dr. William McKinley Thomas, a member of San Francisco's urban development agency, responded to his firing in April 1950 by noting, "If I had been an Uncle Tom or a handkerchief head, I could have remained in the position, but I am in violent opposition to discrimination."[19]

Decades after Briggs, the editor of the *Crusader*, had called for African Americans to recognize the "Negro aunt" as an insult, they were commonly using her as one. But the insult was not only a generalized slur in a game between boys. It implied that the target was subservient to whites; that he was playing along with them and undermining race solidarity; that he was a throwback to grinning, happy darkies laboring on the plantation. In other words, it said that he was behaving like Aunt Jemima, doing the very same things that Young and Wyeth depicted her doing, and doing them in the same way, with the same attitude, that she did. When black men called other men "Aunt Jemima," they meant that the person in question was a blockade to economic and social progress, to desegregation. When they called each other "handkerchief heads," they did so not only to belittle but to imply that someone in their midst was a race traitor as well as a person of suspect masculinity.

The insult was common trade among black separatists, as well, including the most famous one, Malcolm X. In his autobiography Malcolm X told Alex Haley that black professionals were betraying their race and said, mixing references to Aunt Jemima and Uncle Tom, "Today's Uncle Tom doesn't wear a handkerchief on his head. This modern, twentieth-century Uncle Thomas now often wears a top hat. He's often the personification of culture and refinement." And of lower-class blacks who affected white hairstyles by getting a "conk" (as he once did), Malcolm X was more direct: "It's generally among these fools that you'll see a black kerchief over the man's head, like Aunt Jemima."[20] Given Malcolm X's views about the importance of black manhood—and the importance that black women remain in submissive roles—he characteristically chose a street insult pointed directly at his targets' virility. He, too, was playing the dozens, except, like civil rights activists he opposed, in a more political sphere.

By appropriating Aunt Jemima as an insult, African-American men were "changing the joke" to "slip the yoke," in Ralph Ellison's terms.[21] But they were not challenging the definition of mammy or the image of Aunt Jemima; neither would have been a powerful insult if they had. In some ways black men were using Aunt Jemima the same way that white men had used her on the minstrel stage—to express masculinity and class status. So while the Aunt Jemima joke changed, particularly during the 1950s and 1960s, the difference was primarily in the joke teller's intent. The mammy had not changed. Black men might have been slipping the yoke themselves, but they were not removing it from the necks of black women. The rhetoric of racial solidarity, when bolstering the masculinity of black men, in this case offered black women little more than a traditional form of disrespect.

If African Americans considered it a supreme insult to be called an Aunt Jemima or "handkerchief head" by members of their own race—if boys considered it a supreme insult to call another boy's mother Aunt Jemima—how long could they have been expected to tolerate the use or depiction of Aunt Jemima by whites? An advertising trademark that had become a symbol of humiliation was becoming a problem for its owner. As Robert Weems has shown, major U.S. corporations slowly became aware from the mid-1950s through the 1960s that their marketing strategies were neglecting millions of potential customers. As African Americans continued to migrate northward into large U.S. cities, advertising trade journals began featuring advice on how to reach the "negro market" and how to persuade African Americans to "identify with your product." Advertisers began placing their messages on black-oriented radio stations, buying space in *Ebony* magazine, and hiring African-American consultants to help direct campaigns.[22] Marketers began, clumsily, to ask questions that had never seemed important before.

But in 1955 Quaker Oats instead forged ahead with its traditional marketing approach by initiating what was perhaps Aunt Jemima's most prominent personal appearance. It contracted with Disneyland to operate "Aunt Jemima's Pancake House" in the California theme park's Frontierland. Aylene Lewis, who had been Aunt Jemima in personal appearances and radio advertisements, played the role, apparently with great zest, flipping pancakes for luminaries ranging from bandleader Benny Goodman to Indian prime minister Nehru, and in its first eight years, the facility served 1.6 million guests. The placemats and menus at the restaurant replicated scenes from the old ad campaign, with text describing Aunt Jemima's legend. Lewis reportedly became good friends with Walt Disney and called herself "the happiest person in the world." Even Lewis's death in 1964 did not derail the operation, which had expanded in 1962 to serve more customers and was renamed "Aunt Jemima's Kitchen."[23] With the advent of television advertising, Quaker Oats recruited Edith Wilson, a blues singer and actress from Chicago whose film credits included *To Have and Have Not* with Humphrey Bogart, to play Aunt Jemima in spot ads. Wilson and Rosie Hall, a former employee of Quaker's advertising department, shared the role in personal appearances with Ethel Ernestine Harper, an actress and schoolteacher. In the 1950s and early 1960s, there were three national Aunt Jemimas on tour and one in permanent service at Disneyland. Other actresses continued to portray her at smaller events, such as trade shows and pancake breakfasts.[24]

No matter how many millions of white Americans were pleased with and entertained by Aunt Jemima's image, a decades-old animosity toward her remained among African Americans. That animosity was magnified in discussions that had nothing to do with Aunt Jemima's personal appearances or her product. Her name began to appear in political discussions, as a symbol of Uncle Tomism, and became a choice insult hurled by African Americans at each other. James Webb Young, in creating the Aunt Jemima campaign, had made a sort of political statement about the place of African-American labor and the virtues of the Old South order. But clearly no one at Quaker Oats or JWT ever anticipated the day when a product associated with black labor and white leisure would be a political liability. Instead, while African Americans were demanding to be seated at lunch counters and on buses, marching on Washington, and spending more money than ever before at the supermarket, Quaker Oats was sending actresses out to play the butter-tongued slave Jemima at schools and club meetings. The time-honored promotional approach that made her famous helped in the 1960s to make her infamous, too.

"Poor Aunt Jemima": The NAACP Works Locally

In 1956, two years after the Supreme Court's ruling against segregation in *Brown v. Board of Education*, and a year before Arkansas governor Orval Faubus's defiance of that decision led to the deployment of troops in Little Rock, the Aunt Jemima print campaigns and personal appearances were essentially unchanged from the 1920s. Ads still depicted the jolly plantation slave refusing to reveal her recipe to elite white women; Aunt Jemima still appeared personally at Lions Clubs and supermarket trade shows. Almost from its beginnings in 1909, the National Association for the Advancement of Colored People had sought to highlight black dissent against images in media, but it had concentrated its efforts largely on film, radio, and later television dramas and comedies and less on advertising. Probably one of its most successful campaigns was its earliest, against *Birth of a Nation*, the film version of Thomas Dixon's *The Clansman*, which W. E. B. Du Bois said did not kill the film but "succeeded in wounding it."[25]

The organization's official stance toward film mammies, however, reflected mixed feelings. For example, while many African Americans objected to the film version of Fannie Hurst's *Imitation of Life*, including Louise Beavers's role as Aunt Delilah, the *Crisis* reviewer praised the film, saying that Beavers's performance "was one of the most unprecedented triumphs for an obscure player in the annals of a crazy business."[26] The film version of *Gone with the Wind* and its servile blacks also earned a mixed reaction. The *Crisis* reviewer wrote, "God help us what 'Gone with the Wind' will bring us," and Walter White, NAACP executive secretary, felt the film hurt efforts to pass a federal antilynching law. Many members called on Hattie McDaniel to refuse the Academy Award she won for her portrayal of Mammy. But Roy Wilkins believed concerns expressed by the NAACP before the movie's release had moderated its images of slaves. And the

Crisis, sending further mixed signals, put McDaniel on its cover.[27] Even though she was barred from the film's premiere in Atlanta, McDaniel disagreed with her critics and continued to play the mammy not only in such movies as *Song of the South* and the TV and radio series *Beulah* but also in her own personal appearances to promote *Gone with the Wind* after its release. She and Walter White sparred frequently throughout the 1930s and 1940s over the consequences of "mammyism" in film. McDaniels defended herself by arguing that she was merely playing one of the few roles offered to black women, and that she was making good money doing it. She once responded to White's complaints about *Gone with the Wind* by asking him, "What do you want me to do? Play a glamour girl and sit on Clark Gable's knee? When you ask me not to play the parts, what do you offer me in return?" At least McDaniel was paid handsomely to perform a role that many black women played for little reward. She continued to play the role to the hilt, even dancing the cakewalk during some of her personal appearances, and she performed her own rendition of Al Jolson's "Swanee."[28]

The NAACP continued to organize protests against characterizations of blacks such as Jack Benny's assistant Rochester, Amos 'n' Andy, and Beulah and against blackface minstrel shows, which were springing up again in the 1950s, most notably in California and in community theaters across the rural South.[29] But the primary emphasis throughout most of the NAACP's campaigns was national, and its resolutions against media stereotypes focused on characterizations in national entertainment offerings, not advertisements.[30] The NAACP's efforts to persuade the entertainment industry sometimes led to even worse outcomes. For example, when CBS canceled the TV version of *Amos 'n' Andy* (because of ratings rather than the protests, Melvin Patrick Ely has shown), the program wound up being shown on more stations independently through syndication than it had on network television, and the logistical problems of mounting multiple protests rather than focusing on a single network hindered the NAACP.[31]

The NAACP had officially called for a boycott of Aunt Jemima in the early 1960s. However, protests against Aunt Jemima in the nascent civil rights era focused not on eliminating the national print campaign but on community-based efforts to cancel local appearances. Amos 'n' Andy, after all, traveled elusively over the airwaves to American homes, while Aunt Jemima visited communities in person, inviting more direct protest. According to the NAACP's files, these protests were especially successful in Massachusetts and in the Chicago and out-state Illinois areas, near the home base of Aunt Jemima's owner, Quaker Oats. In April 1956 the Florence Gas Range Company announced that Aunt Jemima would appear at a home and sport show in Springfield, Massachusetts. The company employed six women to play the role of an "expert cook" around the nation and claimed that the woman who would play Aunt Jemima at the show, to demonstrate the modern wonder of the gas range, was a member of the NAACP herself. According to Ruth Loving, the president of the Springfield NAACP, the organization did not object to the woman's presence at the trade show but was "firm in not having the young women to appear in the costume, but in other proper dress." Loving noted that a local newspaper had claimed that only the Springfield NAACP chapter, and not the national office, had lodged a protest against Aunt Jemima's personal appearances. She asked the national organization whether this claim could be disproved. The national office's records do not contain a reply to Loving, however.[32]

The local chapter was successful in pressuring Florence Gas Range to cancel Aunt Jemima's appearance at the show, where an estimated eight thousand people crowded to see displays sponsored by the Greater Springfield Home Builders Association. A local newspaper, the *Springfield Daily News*, noted the trade show's success despite what it sarcastically called the NAACP's "great triumph" against "Poor Aunt Jemima." It also warned that the organization was wasting its time making an "assault on a windmill," and that no one would take such an organization seriously in the future:

> By making this senseless objection, the Springfield NAACP has reduced the power of any future protest it might ever make, even if a future protest had some validity. The Springfield branch of NAACP will be remembered as the group which saw reason to use its influence to get Aunt Jemima benched.
>
> However foolish the Springfield branch's criticism may appear, and however it may weaken its case when it might have a valid reason to complain, still its ridiculous complaint is a great compliment to the people of Springfield. This silly objection tends to prove that the NAACP can find no valid reason to make complaints about racial relations in Greater Springfield. It is good for us to know that NAACP can find nothing more serious to complain about here than the appearance of a smiling (and very competent!) cook.[33]

The editorial writer made several assumptions that characterize a defense of the Aunt Jemima image even today. The first is that everybody—blacks and whites alike—understands that the image is at worst harmless and probably, by demonstrating competence in the kitchen, a positive picture of African Americans and particularly African-American women. That is, that in America a consensus exists over the meaning of the mammy image and the name Aunt Jemima. The second is that African Americans must have more pressing concerns than trying to blot out the image of "Poor Aunt Jemima," and attempts to do so would only forestall addressing those concerns. Indeed, the very act of protesting Aunt Jemima was taken as evidence that there must not be any more important problems; once again, the presence of a mammy was taken by some as proof of healthy race relations. It is worth mentioning, of course, that these two arguments are by their nature contradictory: a failure to concentrate on "valid reasons" to complain was rooted in a supposed fixation on Aunt Jemima, but the Aunt Jemima protest itself was supposedly evidence that there was in reality no basis for "valid" complaints in the Springfield area.

The distinction between valid and invalid complaints was not the concern of African-American employees of Western Electric in Kearney, New Jersey, who in addition to protesting injustices in pay and promotions at the Kearney plant—and noting that "there is not a single doctor or nurse in the plant"—asked the NAACP to register a complaint regarding a recent company "pancake party" featuring a "lone Negro woman dressed as Aunt Jemima." The pancake party was featured in a 1959 edition of a national company newsletter, *Pioneer Progress*.[34] John Morrell, the assistant to the executive secretary of the NAACP, registered the complaint with Henry Killingsworth, president of the Telephone Pioneers of America, which published the article. Choosing not to deal with pay or promotion, areas that were "not properly a part of this communication," Morrell told Killingsworth that he "may or may not know the extent to which the 'Aunt Jemima' figure has become one of distaste and humiliation to a great many colored people."[35]

Eventually, local efforts to block appearances by actresses portraying Aunt Jemima gained greater attention from the national NAACP office. Responding to complaints in 1960 against the Super Market Institute of Chicago lodged by the New England Regional Conference of the NAACP, Morrell began a correspondence with the institute. African Americans in Pittsfield, Massachusetts, had already persuaded a local grocery chain to stop personal appearances, and the owners of the chain, Jacob and Melvin Wineberg, suggested the NAACP also contact the supermarket trade organization. Don Parsons, executive director of the Super Market Institute, however, denied any connection between the organization and Aunt Jemima promotions, an explanation Morrell accepted. Frank Walker, the director of the New England NAACP conference, protested, insisting that the supermarket organization indeed was responsible, but congratulated the national office for making Parsons and his organization aware of the problem, as well as for putting the Super Market Institute on record as not supporting the personal appearances.[36]

The national NAACP had trouble pinning down the Super Market Institute, but local groups continued to fare better. The Racine, Wisconsin, branch reported in April 1963 that it had voiced strong disapproval of a planned personal appearance for Pancake Day at the local Kiwanis Club, which refused to cancel the appearance but promised to pass along the objections to representatives of Quaker Oats. The leader of the Racine NAACP, Sloan E. Williams, also said the branch had organized "local Negro storekeepers to write Quaker Oats Co. expressing their dissatisfaction with the promotional program of Aunt Jemima." Williams wrote Quaker Oats directly, saying that "the personal appearance of Aunt Jemima is objectionable to most Negroes in Racine. Such an appearance helps to perpetuate an undesirable and negative image of the Negro. It is a stereotype which depicts the Negro in a state and condition which no longer exists."[37]

The appeal apparently fell on deaf ears, as did a similar complaint about a Pancake Day by the Ypsilanti, Michigan, branch of the NAACP.[38] But the activists in Fort Madison, Iowa, were more successful. Virginia Harper, the local secretary, wrote to the national office to say that a planned Pancake Day in August 1964 had been canceled. The Jaycees in Fort Madison had planned to feature Aunt Jemima at a rodeo but, according to Harper, "voted *not* to bring Aunt Jemima to town, even though she wanted to come here and talk to us and explain why we shouldn't feel as we do." (There is no reference to which actress portraying Aunt Jemima wanted to do the explaining.) Harper added that "at this time the Jaycees in this community are still bitter."[39] Also in 1964, the Rock Falls, Illinois, NAACP chapter had forced the cancellation of an appearance by Edith Wilson as Aunt Jemima at a local high school. At first Forrest L. Tabor, the school superintendent, had been reluctant to cancel the event, sponsored by the city's Chamber of Commerce, asking the NAACP, "How do I explain to over 1,000 high school students and over 3,000 elementary students who remember Miss Wilson with deep admiration and affection and were looking forward with

great anticipation to her appearance this year?" But eventually the threat of pick-
eting forced the school to cancel the appearance after the NAACP rejected an
offer to have Wilson appear in street clothes "instead of her traditional kitchen
garb."[40]

By the time Edith Wilson's personal appearance was blocked in Rock Falls,
Raymond Harth, an attorney for the Illinois NAACP, was making sure that
Quaker Oats was aware of his organization's activities. He wrote to Robert Stuart, the company president, in October 1964, and his correspondence refers to
previous letters (apparently not extant in NAACP files) and telephone conversations with Quaker Oats. "Once again it becomes my duty to urge you to cancel an appearance of the character known as 'Aunt Jemima.' . . . So that there
will be no misunderstanding, we are opposed to appearance of the 'Aunt
Jemima' stereotyped character at any time or place, and in any costume." Harth
also referred to organizing in Rock Island, Moline, and East Moline against
Aunt Jemima and threatened Quaker Oats with continued embarrassment if the
personal appearances persisted. "It further appears," he said, "that it is the intention of Quaker Oats to continue this practice."[41] Quaker Oats was feeling the
heat and would respond to the changes in the "democracy of goods" by altering
Aunt Jemima's appearance and minimizing her presence. But there are many in-
dications that African Americans believe the company has not done enough.
The slave in the box would prove difficult even for her owners to emancipate.

Setting Free the Slave in a Box

It is not as easy to document the ways in which pressure from African Americans directly affected the changes in Aunt Jemima's image in the 1960s—especially since Quaker Oats and its archives are not forthcoming on the subject—
but the company appears to have adopted an increasingly defensive stance in the
mid-1960s which continues today. Protests and boycotts by black Americans led
Quaker Oats to drop the bandanna in 1968 and give Aunt Jemima a headband,
in addition to slimming her down and making her look somewhat younger.[42]

Two years later the company altered its relationship with Disneyland, which
changed the pancake house on its grounds from Aunt Jemima's Kitchen to a
more innocuous name, and an actress portraying Aunt Jemima no longer appeared personally after Edith Wilson was fired in 1966 and Rosie Hall died in

1967. Edith Wilson bitterly disagreed with those who said that her performances were "impeding racial progress," and years later argued, "The Aunt Jemima routine wasn't done for what a lot of people took it to be. There was a lot of that already going on in minstrel shows. I put my head in the sand to a lot of that. Otherwise you're always mad at people and situations. Prejudice is a feeling you have to tuck away. I've seen too many people spoil their lives by carrying that chip on their shoulder." In a 1979 interview, she defended her work for Quaker Oats by arguing that she was honoring the life of a real black woman: "I was fired because the NAACP asked why did they have to dress me in the old-fashioned costume like that? The people didn't like that, but they didn't realize that the people came to know this was historic. Aunt Jemima was the first person to bring a gold medal back from the Paris Exposition for her pancakes. She was from Mississippi and she came up to St. Joseph, Missouri. In the Civil War some of the soldiers from the North got lost and they wanted to get back to their regiment, but were afraid the South Soldiers might shoot them. They went up and knocked at Aunt Jemima's door."[43]

In retirement, Edith Wilson followed Purd Wright's basic story faithfully, although she swapped Chicago for Paris and had Aunt Jemima saving Union soldiers instead of Confederates. Other African Americans and white Americans, however, began to use Aunt Jemima as a lightning rod for their grievances after Wilson was fired. The counterculture musical *Hair* included a number titled "Colored Spade," whose lyrics were a stream of racial epithets including not only "Uncle Tom, Aunt Jemima, [and] Little Black Sambo" but also "Elevator Operator, Table cleaner at Horn & Hardart, Slave voodoo, Zombie, [and] Ubangi lipped."[44] In the late 1960s the artist Murray N. DePillars, in a commercial poster that sold four thousand copies, depicted an angry Aunt Jemima bursting through a series of boxes of the mix and waving a large spatula. On the ingredients side of all the boxes appears a black-gloved, clenched fist in a Black Power salute, and the text on the first box explains the protest by African-American athletes at the 1968 Olympics in Mexico City. The other boxes contain lists of places where racial conflicts had occurred. In the background are the Stars and Stripes, but the stars are really badges bearing the words "Chicago Police."[45] Another artist, John Onye Lockard, contributed a 1972 parody of the box depicting a scowling Aunt Jemima whose fist is bursting through the package; the artwork has the simple caption "No More." In both works the clear message was that Aunt Jemima was no longer a stereotype that African Americans would quietly tolerate.[46] The choice of action by both artists—Aunt Jemima breaking out of the box of pancake flour—is a revealing metaphor. The slave in the box was breaking free. No longer were black men merely "slipping the yoke" themselves by using Aunt Jemima as an insult; black men and women alike were challenging the mammy image and questioning whether it resembled any real black women. By 1983 the poet Sylvia Dunnavant put the mammy's escape into past tense in her verse titled "Aunt Jemima":

> She told me she got tired of wearing that rag wrapped
> around her head.
> And she got tired of making pancakes and waffles for other
> people to eat while she couldn't sit down at the table.
> She told me Lincoln emancipated the slaves.
> But she freed her own damn self.[47]

It might have been too early, still, to talk about Aunt Jemima being free. In 1983 the Aunt Jemima on the box was still the slave woman with the headband, the altered image from 1968. Kern-Foxworth, a journalism professor who has studied the image extensively, believes the 1968 change in appearance was crucial to the continued success of the trademark; she wrote in 1990 that "the physical attributes . . . became more positive and less stereotypical than the caricatures of the past." Noting changes in soft drink brand names such as Chinese Cherry and Injun Orange in the 1960s, Steven Dubin argued the rise of black consciousness and attention to black images in popular culture made some racial stereotypes in advertising less "grease" and more "grit" in the "smooth functioning of U.S. society," and that advertising agencies, interested in keeping the wheels turning, adjusted accordingly. In 1977, when *Washington Post* columnist William Raspberry was asked why he objected to the Sambo's restaurant chain but not Aunt Jemima, he similarly argued that the changes in Aunt Jemima's appearance, plus the fact that most people no longer connect titles like aunt and uncle to slavery, had made her an innocuous image. This is a conclusion, however, that many contemporary critics of racial stereotypes in advertising would challenge—after all, that is still Aunt Jemima on the box, "more positive" adjustments to her wardrobe and weight notwithstanding. The novelist Alice Walker in a 1994 essay argued that Aunt Jemima and the mammy she exemplifies, regardless of all attempts to refine her image, are too firmly rooted in the subconscious of white American culture to erase—even if the picture on the box has changed. Walker sees and hears the old version of Aunt Jemima everywhere, from the Dallas airport gift shops to the rantings of syndicated radio host Howard Stern.[48] Perhaps no matter how her owners dress her, Aunt Jemima is still a slave, something difficult to explain but too valuable to give up, considering the $300 million in sales annually by the 1990s—a dilemma not unlike that faced by antebellum slave owners who struggled to spin apologies for the peculiar institution itself.[49]

Eventually, Quaker Oats tried to free Aunt Jemima, once and for all, and escape the dilemma. The company had several choices. It could have dramatically dropped either the name, the image, or both. Keeping just the name or just the image, however, would have threatened brand recognition without freeing the company from criticism, since both the name Aunt Jemima and the drawing angered African Americans. Or, as the company had in the past, it could have altered the image and kept the brand name intact, which it did. In 1989 the company made its most extensive alterations to Aunt Jemima, removing her headgear, graying her hair, and giving her a pair of earrings. The attempt was, as a company spokeswoman said recently, "to make her look like a working mother," an image apparently supported by the company's extensive test-marketing of the new logo among blacks and whites. Making Aunt Jemima visibly older, the spokeswoman did not say, continued an old and historically inaccurate tradition of depicting mammies—removing them from carnal taint—and, we might assume, kept her distinct from young black mothers who presumably were not working to support their children. (Aunt Jemima must remain off welfare.) The change also reflected long-term changes in the workforce, as did General Mills's constant tinkering with Betty Crocker from the 1930s through the 1980s. The Betty Crocker figure, who also was depicted as a real person who wrote recipes and answered fan mail, has changed constantly to reflect the participation of white women in the workforce. That is, she was supposed to be an acceptable version of a white working mother. Of course, Aunt Jemima the mammy was always a working mother to her family, black and white, in the slave-day nostalgia of her previous advertising campaigns. The specific image of the mammy was outdated by real changes in race relations and the sexual composition of the American workforce, but the things the mammy did—providing nurture to white folks—and the notion that a cheerful, aged black woman performed that service had not changed with the revision of her physical image.

The slave link to the Old South specifically was not removed by the change in image; the spokeswoman also said that, bandanna or not, Aunt Jemima remains on the box because she is a southern character, and the South is known for good food and home cooking.[50]

The early returns were not positive, as a protest by Chicago-area African Americans against Quaker Oats demonstrated. While they demanded that Quaker Oats further integrate its management and invest more of its assets in the community, many of the protesters focused on Aunt Jemima—despite the makeover—in presenting their case. "We buy 70 percent of all the grits sold by Quaker," Nancy Jefferson, one of the protest leaders, told a newspaper reporter. "We also contribute very heavily to the sales of Aunt Jemima products—and its [the product division's] vice president is a white woman. If they're going to insult us, they could at least hire us to insult us."[51] Apparently, putting Aunt Jemima in a new dress, and even taking off her headband, was not enough to reduce the level of insult perceived by some African Americans, who saw the earlier Aunt Jemima every time they looked at the new version. In a 1989 letter to *Advertising Age*, Stanley L. Yorker wrote:

> Rather than the Quaker Oats Co. giving Aunt Jemima a "makeover," I and quite a few other African-Americans would prefer that they give her a well-deserved retirement.
>
> The Aunt Jemima brand was born 100 years ago, not exactly the most idyllic of times for race relations in this country. Americans of African descent had been freed and their bonds loosed, their political and, especially, economic manacles were still firmly secured, with the key to opening them as yet undiscovered.
>
> Barbara Allen of Quaker was quoted as saying that this "contemporary" Jemima would preserve ". . . good taste, heritage and reliability." I submit that it is actually in severe bad taste to continue perpetuating this stereotypical image of a people who've made significant contributions to America and the Quaker Oats Co. and that the "heritage" being preserved is one of callous racism.[52]

Yorker raised one of the more interesting questions concerning the madeover Aunt Jemima: Why not give her up? This and other questions were left unanswered by Quaker Oats: What makes a black woman a particularly southern character? Might it have something to do with slavery? And how many working mothers, white or black, identify with the name Aunt Jemima? Try to imagine a contemporary product aimed at men—cologne, for instance—using Uncle Mose as an emblem of masculinity or success. Clearly, though, the Quaker Oats Company believes, perhaps based on its own market studies, that yet again transforming Aunt Jemima into a working mother makes her even less "grit" and more "grease" in society. But Aunt Jemima, made over, remains grist for critiques of American racism. In 1990 the rap group Public Enemy blasted the American film industry for its reluctance to offer meaningful roles to black actors and especially black actresses. In the song "Burn Hollywood Burn," they complained:

> For what they play Aunt Jemima is the perfect term
> Even if now she got a perm.[53]

In 1993 "Aunt Jemima" was a weird sort of insult, even among white folks who claimed they did not realize the term had racial implications. In June of that year, the members of a Washington, D.C., high school rowing team gathered for their annual picnic along the Potomac River. Warren Hall, one of the few African Americans on the team, heard the coach call him forward to accept the "Aunt Jemima Award." According to a *Washington Post* reporter,

> "I was in shock," said Hall, 18, recalling the dead silence that greeted the initial announcement of the award, then the nervous laughter and applause of some students and parents. "I just wanted to throw it in the trash."
>
> Hall's coach later apologized, saying he gave the award in jest. When the team rowed, he said, its members all wore bandannas on their heads. Hall was the only one who wore his bandanna with the knot tied in front, reminding some rowers of the century-old Quaker Oats Co. pancake mix logo, Aunt Jemima, a stout black woman wearing a kerchief.
>
> But Hall's mother, Fatima McKamey, was infuriated that in this day and age, a high school coach would give her son an award rife with the ugly stereotype of a docile slave woman in the plantation kitchen.

The team's coaches apologized, saying that they did not understand that the name of the award was offensive. Fatima McKamey disagreed. "They're hiding behind their ignorance," McKamey said. "The cop-out is to say, 'Oh, I didn't know it was offensive. I didn't mean it.' Racism is so ingrained in some people's psyche that they don't know what's offensive." Interestingly, many of the white children on the team "didn't seem to understand what Aunt Jemima meant," according to the article. "I didn't know who she was until I asked my dad in the car on the way home," said Justine Wise, seventeen, a senior. "I just thought of her as the lady on the syrup bottle. He told me that she was a black slave woman who worked in the kitchen." The school asked McKamey to speak to the students and explain why Aunt Jemima was so offensive, but she said she was still too angry to tell them.[54]

One might argue that the reaction of white children is evidence that Aunt Jemima indeed has lost her original meaning, perhaps thanks to the fact that advertisements no longer play up her slave days. But the defenders of trade shows who were befuddled by black anger against "Poor Aunt Jemima" in the 1950s did not understand, either, and arguably, neither did James Webb Young, who apparently never gave the matter much thought, nor the J. Walter Thompson Company, which never asked. Somewhere, behind the image of Aunt Jemima, the working grandmother, lies that same old smiling plantation mammy; raw nerves are still waiting to be touched. And anyone—a food conglomerate or a high school rowing coach—who is ignorant enough to dare to play the dozens with African Americans today seems likely to elicit an unexpected reaction.

Making the White World Safe for Pancakes

Whether Aunt Jemima the working mother will have any special appeal to white or black consumers remains a question. Marketing experts today are still struggling with problems of ethnicity and language. For example, Gallo has attempted, unsuccessfully, to position Thunderbird wine in the marketing niche occupied by middle-class blacks, while Kentucky Fried Chicken, now renamed KFC, test-marketed the black consumers who make up 25 percent of its market, wanting to know if Colonel Sanders might somehow be offensive. They decided he was not, as long as he kept off the front porch of the plantation. The R. J. Reynolds Tobacco Company spent $10 million to target Uptown cigarettes to blacks, but the target audience instead protested, and the product was dropped. Budweiser was criticized for a series of British ads that showed Native Americans, whose rate of alcoholism is estimated to be five times higher than that of the general population, drinking beer. More amusingly, the Perdue chicken company's ad agency once accidentally translated its slogan "It Takes a Tough Man to Make a Tender Chicken" into Spanish as "It Takes a Sexually Stimulated Man to Make a Chicken Affectionate" in an attempt to reach a Latino audience. That appeal did not work, either.[55] And in 1996 General Mills adopted a novel approach in its plans to reintroduce the long-dormant image of Betty Crocker—a logo that, unlike Aunt Jemima, had been absent from its products since 1986. The company used digital technology to "morph" seventy-five women of different racial and ethnic groups into a single "super-Betty" and thus create an inoffensive image. For the first time Betty Crocker's owners are considering race as well as class in shaping her and risking a mother lode of criticism on both counts in doing so.[56] One wonders how an image of a single person—of any shade—can really be in and of itself a symbol of "ethnic diversity." Contemporary advertising is challenged by the need to appeal to previously unthinkable niche markets, as specialty magazines abound and cable television offers the prospect of five hundred channels. In the meantime, as global markets grow, American ad agencies must deal with areas in which very different racial and sexual sensibilities remain strong. For example, in Mexico, where a major department store recently boasted in TV ads that "We're working like niggers to bring you a white sale," Aunt Jemima, the supposedly deracinated working mother, is known simply as "La Negrita."[57] South of the border, it seems, they get right to the point.

Back in the United States, the problem is not what to call Aunt Jemima—since Quaker Oats is unwilling to drop the troublesome name—but how to use her image without angering anyone. What should she say? In the 1920s there was little doubt how she should sound; those "Aunt Jemima Says" ads depicted her mangling the English language and bragging about how all those Eskimos had to have her pancakes. Obviously, Quaker Oats could hardly have the modern Jemima opening her mouth and exclaiming "Lawzee! Mekkin' pancakes is th' mos' impawtines thing ah does, than which dere ain't no better, effen ah does say so!" as she did in a 1920 ad. They had to do something else. As Michael Omi and Howard Winant have described, America in the 1980s retreated from direct to more subtly articulated racial stereotyping, still drawing on the power of racial themes in an era of white resentment but not directly challenging racial equality. Kenneth Goings attributes the resurgence in sales of racist collectibles—lawn jockeys, trade cards, and postcards—to the same phenomenon, as deprecation of African Americans found a socially acceptable outlet in a kind of underground economy.[58]

So in September 1994 Aunt Jemima's advertisers trotted out the working grandmother image in their first national television campaign since 1990, but instead of having Aunt Jemima speak for the Aunt Jemima brand, they hired singer Gladys Knight and two of her grandchildren, which meant that a real black woman was speaking for an imaginary black woman. If the image and name of Aunt Jemima were still offensive, perhaps a real black woman could be counted on to ease hard feelings. Knight reminded reporters that she was not playing any role but herself—a working black grandmother (like Aunt Jemima)—and said, "I'm not Aunt Jemima, I'm only a spokesperson." She said the transformed image, sans bandanna, "helped in my decision" to endorse the brand. *Newsweek* magazine added, "Perhaps it's time to call her Ms. Jemima."[59] Perhaps it is, but her name remains Aunt Jemima; Cap'n Crunch does not require a real, apologetic white male sea captain to speak for him or the cereal that bears his name. Maybe her owners could have argued instead that the 100-year-old Aunt Jemima, by the late 1980s, was superannuated, released from servitude and allowed to wear her gray hair any way she pleased and to feed her own grandchildren instead of Colonel Higbee and the Carters, Southwoods, and Marshalls. But they did not make that argument, because that would have meant acknowledging what an Aunt Jemima or a mammy was and always has been—a slave. Maybe that is why she cannot speak for herself today; she might say something embarrassing.

Just the same, Quaker Oats cannot give up that name—it cannot call the product, for instance, Gladys Knight pancake mix, even though plenty of products today use a celebrity name and face as their trademark: (Paul) Newman's Own foods, Chicken by (Phyllis) George, and the grand champion, (Frank) Perdue chicken. Why not go ahead and have a real working black grandmother advertise the product, if that approach seems so persuasive, and use a person who is free of all of Aunt Jemima's historical baggage, especially the slave title Aunt? The answer is always that Quaker Oats has invested years and a huge amount of money in the product's brand recognition; consumers recognize the brand name, expect to see it, anticipate its presence at the supermarket, and thus buy it. At this point the argument that the remade Aunt Jemima is significantly different from the old version appears incorrect, because we cannot separate the elements that make Aunt Jemima, regardless of whether she herself is made over.

The (slave) name, the drawing, and the product are all bound together. The purpose of Chris Rutt's selection of the name Aunt Jemima, as well as James Webb Young's plantation advertising, was to build that brand recognition, in the latter case through making brand recognition and race and sex recognition the same thing. If Aunt Jemima is recognized as anything more today than Gladys Knight is, then it must owe more to Aunt Jemima's past than to her present—no one is buying the product because it is somehow connected with modern black working grandmothers, or Gladys Knight could do the job without Aunt Jemima.

Somehow, Aunt Jemima—the image, the name, and the product—is still effective among white people, and Quaker Oats will simply have to continue apologizing and explaining for as long as it wants the type of brand recognition that this particular product possesses. And all the while, Aunt Jemima maintains another source of brand recognition—the mere fact that she is black—which she seems unlikely to lose anytime soon, because Quaker Oats has not chosen to drop the image while keeping the name. "Whiteness is the norm. It's what advertisers expect and attempt to portray," noted Carleton University professor Eileen Saunders, who specializes in images in advertising. Saunders's opinion is seconded by the many black models and commercial actors seeking one of the rare spots for African Americans in national advertising.[60] Why does Aunt Jemima stand out among so many white faces on national products, if not that she remains an exception among modern black images: safe, subservient, still ready to whip up those famous pancakes. This is a type of racial nostalgia, not racial progress. The modern Aunt Jemima is a sanitized slave; she is to the issue of race what the insipid 1980s television comedy *Happy Days* was to the actual 1950s. Her blackness still reminds white consumers that they are white, and that whiteness is a good thing. Her sex reminds consumers that black women belong in the kitchen. In some respects Aunt Jemima has not changed a bit since 1889.

No matter how often African Americans—who are estimated to spend $300 billion annually—express distaste for Aunt Jemima, Quaker Oats will not stop using her. While African Americans periodically threaten boycotts and lodge protests against the product, white Americans apparently are not embarrassed enough to take such complaints seriously and stop buying the product. Lawn jockeys might no longer stand beside as many driveways as they used to, but Aunt Jemima sits comfortably in kitchen cupboards. Presumably part of the reason for her persistence must be Quaker Oats's tinkering with the image. Kern-Foxworth was right when she argued that changing Aunt Jemima's appearance has helped the product survive, but I believe she was wrong in arguing that the changes made the product less offensive to African Americans. Removing the bandanna and graying the hair might not have been enough for the black mass market, but it kept Aunt Jemima safe for the white market. If Aunt Jemima's image had not been altered, white consumers might have become uncomfortable with a product that so visibly and clearly articulated racism. But because the product articulates racism more subtly, white consumers can purchase it with little fear of appearing to be racists.

The black working grandmother is still working for her white family; the image keeps white consumers comfortable even as it and the name Aunt Jemima remind black consumers of the old slave image. The black working grandmother is as much a figure for feeding white imagination as Aunt Jemima ever was. Gladys Knight might be a real black working grandmother, but in her TV commercials she was playing a role. She depicted the black woman in her own kitchen, feeding her own grandchildren, in a campaign designed not merely to be less offensive to African Americans but to tell white Americans that the product was no longer considered racially offensive. In this sense Gladys Knight was as much of an imaginary figure as Aunt Jemima. In the words of Fatima McKamey, the black woman whose son won the Aunt Jemima award, "Racism is so ingrained in some people's psyche that they don't know what's offensive." Quaker Oats sought a black woman to play a role, explaining to white people that Aunt Jemima is not offensive, and Gladys Knight was available. (Hattie McDaniel has been dead for years.)

Years ago, Aunt Jemima helped advertisers and their audience answer all sorts of questions. The ads told whites that the South should be more like the North in accepting advances in production and marketing. The ads also said that the North should be more like the South in its view of antebellum life and black labor. They presented idealized images of white men as outdoor enthusiasts and of white women as managers of household labor. In addition, the campaigns married the past and the present, emphasizing the ways in which modern technology could give new birth to old-fashioned pleasures. The image of the mammy helped advertisers propose solutions for contemporary problems, assuring continuity between old and new, black and white, and men and women, no matter how the rest of the world changed.

White America still seems to need a mammy to answer its questions. The most recent changes to Aunt Jemima's image and the Gladys Knight ads are an attempt to answer the question, How do we notice race and gender? Quaker Oats and, presumably, other advertisers have a huge stake in the answer. The food company is betting that consumers will both notice and not notice Aunt Jemima. It hopes African-American consumers will approve of an attractive, well-spoken woman who cares for her children in a nice, bright kitchen. The company also wants whites to notice Gladys Knight's blackness, as an endorsement of the notion that blacks are no longer angered by the product. The promise of a color-free society exists within a scene of social harmony, just as James Webb Young's ads showed social harmony within a race-based society. Gladys Knight might have believed that she was not playing a mammy in the ads, but she, like the mammy, was someone whose very presence in the TV spot suggested a world of racial and sexual order.

The ad also constantly displayed the drawing of Aunt Jemima that adorns the box, sometimes filling up the whole TV screen. This was the link between past and present. Quaker Oats added Gladys Knight, but it did not subtract Aunt Jemima. She remained, redrawn in a way calculated to elicit minimal outcry but recognizable as the same woman, with the same name and slave title, who has always been on the box. Just as Gladys Knight reassured white Americans that today black women have enjoyed tremendous social progress—they can inhabit scenes in commercials that were once populated exclusively by whites—Aunt Jemima gave them that old-time brand recognition. There are comfortable things that white people do not have to give up, no matter how much the world changes, and one of them is familiar image of the smiling black female servant. The mammy continues to do for Quaker Oats what she has always done, marrying racial nostalgia with changing lifestyles. She helps white Americans to be comfortable with racial imagery as her employer ostensibly presents its product in a fashionably color-blind manner. Quaker Oats truly wants African-American consumers to buy its product, but it also wants to tell white consumers that they can have their pancakes and eat them, too.

Secrets of the Bandanna

Eldridge Cleaver remains a better source on Aunt Jemima than anybody at Quaker Oats. "The white man turned the white woman into a weak-minded, weak-bodied, delicate freak, a sex pot, and placed her on a pedestal," he wrote in 1968. "He turned the black woman into a strong self-reliant Amazon and deposited her in his kitchen—that's the secret of Aunt Jemima's bandanna."[61] While it might be enough to argue that the "secret of the bandanna" was simply taking a symbol of personal pride and making it a mark of servility, that does not explain how the symbol of servility worked. It does not explain the message Aunt Jemima carried from white men, or how it was interpreted by white women. Servility to whom? For what purpose?

The analysis might be overly harsh—especially given the fact that Cleaver again played the dozens by arguing that black women were partly responsible for the situation—but the author of *Soul on Ice* was on to something. It is true that the white woman who mixed Aunt Jemima pancakes was in no danger of becoming weak-bodied or more delicate, and the rise of processed foods did not bring any enhancement of her sexuality. But the mammy was a tool for white men to use in creating a fantasy in which white women could aspire to live, an alternative household in which they were the ultrafeminine, fragile mistresses who sat alongside Colonel Higbee as guests at his plantation. Race and gender, as Cleaver suggests, both are forces in explaining how the advertising campaign was designed. But class was a factor as well, for whatever vacuum cleaners might have done to enhance household work, they were not from Aunt Jemima's idealized plantation. They could not have made the white women an employer of labor, instead of the laborer herself. Aunt Jemima was designed to do that. It was an advertising fable tailored to address the realities of the drearier, work-filled days of white housewives, facilitating the transition from household manager to household laborer, just as the Old South myth also served as a balm for defeated white southerners.

But the campaign tells us as much about what was going on in the minds of the white male advertisers. Who really needed the Rosemont plantation to exist? Aunt Jemima could have been sold many different ways. It might have focused explicitly on the themes it mined implicitly: as a reaction against science, or at least a quick solution for women trying to put breakfast on the table. It was never necessary for the women to go to Rosemont. The men wanted to take them there because the trip emphasized subservience and service while de-emphasizing skill and independent thought. It was a reflection not only of what the white pitchmen thought women should be, and how women might be motivated to serve in that role, but what they believed white men should be as well.

The "Colonel's Lady" required a colonel to please with a fast, hearty breakfast before he rushed off to the campgrounds, or Appomattox, or, more prosaically but more likely, the workplace.

Aunt Jemima's race remains inseparable from the message white men expected white women to complete as the mammy again transmitted values from master to mistress. She could not have been white. A white Aunt Jemima, provided she did not quit domestic service for other work, ostensibly could have liberated white housewives from the kitchen, as Betty Crocker increasingly was redesigned to do, but she could not have accentuated their whiteness and femininity in the manner of the plantation mammy. Aunt Jemima was designed to be persuasive because she was a female black servant, in an age when perpetual human bondage existed, in a place legendary for its good food and white leisure. As such, she implicitly made white men and women what they should be—at least according to the white men who drew the ads and wrote the copy.

But there is another "secret of the bandanna," one that Cleaver could not have guessed, because he was part of the process that revealed it. The other secret is that the marriage of commerce, racism, and sexism that made James Webb Young's Aunt Jemima work—both as a product and as a symbol—for white men and women gave African Americans a tool to express their dissent, to say that the fantasy world of Aunt Jemima in no way represented who they were or what they aspired to be, while simultaneously exposing gender conflicts within the black community. This fact remained a secret for a long time, principally because no one who made or advertised Aunt Jemima felt any need to ask. When African Americans found a chance to share the secret—in Paul Edwards's marketing survey, at personal appearances, in art, music, and political speeches—they broadcast the secret loud and clear. They did not want it to remain a secret. The image of Aunt Jemima was always an insult to them. When they eventually received their opportunity, thanks to the commodification of racism and sexism, they made sure whites learned the secret, too. And today, anyone who claims he or she does not know the "secret of the bandanna"—who says that the woman on the box used to be offensive but now is race-neutral or even admirable, the "Ms. Jemima" argument in *Newsweek*—is either lying or ignorant. In this way Aunt Jemima remains a touchstone for social relations in the United States. Aunt Jemima will remain on the shelf only as long as she is an effective trademark; she will remain an effective trademark only as long as it is important for her to be a black woman; it will be important for her to be a black woman only as long as racism and sexism maintain their persuasive appeal among consumers. That is the consequence of her historical baggage. Her historical baggage is exactly what makes her effective.

No single person invented Aunt Jemima or her legend, not Billy Kersands, Chris Rutt, James Webb Young, or N. C. Wyeth—not even Nancy Green, Anna Robinson, Edith Wilson, or any of the other women who portrayed her. No single novelist or diarist invented the mammy, either. The idea of Aunt Jemima worked because of its appeal to existing white female needs in a time of revolutionary changes in the household, because of general white perceptions of self relative to blacks, and mostly because of white male power sufficient to define images of whiteness and femininity. As in Cleaver's explanation, white men are the manipulators, but white women, not African Americans, were the real target of white male manipulation. African Americans also proved to be adept manipulators of Aunt Jemima's image, turning her from trademark to epithet and turning the game on its head. That Aunt Jemima survives today, in whatever diluted form, only means the game has a long time to go before it is over. Attempts to adapt old racial stereotypes to meet contemporary reality, instead of simply removing them, are more than reminders of the foolish aspects of our past that we are unwilling to surrender. They demonstrate that some seemingly old-fashioned ideas about race and gender remain powerful in contemporary times.

Aunt Jemima lives on because white Americans like having a mammy. Quaker Oats can move her off the plantation, take off her bandanna, and tint her hair; it makes little difference. If times change, they might even be bold enough to put the bandanna back on her head. Aunt Jemima and mammy are tools used to interpret our legacy of racism, sexism, and slavery, either approvingly or disapprovingly. Keeping her around, spinning superficial explanations for her continued presence on that box, does not help us overcome that legacy. "And so we beat on," in the words of F. Scott Fitzgerald, "boats against the current, back ceaselessly into the past."[62]

Notes

Abbreviations

DU   John W. Hartman Center for Sales, Advertising, and Marketing History,
                    Special Collections, Duke University
JWT Newsletter   *J. Walter Thompson Company Newsletter,* J. Walter Thompson Company
                    Archives, DU

1. Cracking Jokes in the Confederate Supermarket

1. Hine, *The Total Package,* 1.

2. Oring, *Jokes and Their Relations,* 1–7.

3. Freud, *Jokes and Their Relation to the Unconscious;* Oring, *Jokes and Their Relations,* 1.

4. *Spy* 8:4 (Feb. 1994): 21–24, contains the only transcript I know of Danson's mostly unprintable remarks at the 1993 New York Friars' Club roast.

5. Oring, *Jokes and Their Relations,* 16–28.

6. Hine, *The Total Package,* 109, 213.

7. Ibid., 228–29.

8. Jack Hitt, "The Theory of Supermarkets," *New York Times Magazine,* 10 March 1996, 57, 60.

9. Foster, *Ghosts of the Confederacy,* 102–3, 120–21.

10. Thurber, "The Development of the Mammy Image," 94–95.

11. See White, *Ar'n't I a Woman?,* 44–47, 49, 55–58, 60–61; Clinton, *Plantation Mistress,* 202; Genovese, *Roll, Jordan, Roll,* 355; Blassingame, *The Slave Community,* 304–5.

12. Rotzoll et al., *Advertising in Contemporary Society,* 9.

13. Pieterse, *White on Black,* 195–98.

14. McClintock, *Imperial Leather,* 214–16.

15. Baldwin, *Notes of a Native Son,* 27.

16. Leeming, *James Baldwin,* 380–81.

2. Someone's in the Kitchen: Mammies, Mothers, and Others

1. Morton, *Disfigured Images,* 18.

2. Quoted in Gutman, *The Black Family in Slavery and Freedom,* 534–36. See also Morton, *Disfigured Images,* 28–29.

3. Rhodes, *History of the United States* 1:311, 335–36.

4. Cash, *The Mind of the South*, 95–97, 137.

5. Williamson, *A Rage for Order*, 39–42; Gaston, *The New South Creed*, 4–5.

6. Gaston, *The New South Creed*, 151–86; Woodward, *Origins of the New South*, 142–55, 158; Bailey, *Liberalism in the New South*, 120–21; Wiener, *Social Origins of the New South*, 215–21; White, "Old South under New Conditions," 161–62; Carter, "From the Old South to the New," 23–30; Foster, *Ghosts of the Confederacy*, 80–85; Taylor, *Cavalier and Yankee*, 177–201; Williamson, *A Rage for Order*, 247–54. The northern origins of the Old South are discussed by Gerster and Cords, "The Northern Origins of Southern Mythology," 43–58.

7. White, *Ar'n't I a Woman?* 44–47, 49, 55–58, 60–61; Morton, *Disfigured Images*, 5–13, 35; Christian, *Black Woman Novelists*, 8; Clinton, *Plantation Mistress*, 202.

8. Thurber, "The Development of the Mammy Image and Mythology," 96.

9. Page, *The Old South*, 156, 165–66; Phillips, *American Negro Slavery*, 313.

10. Ayers, *The Promise of the New South*, 362.

11. Page, *Red Rock*, 90–91; Gross, *Thomas Nelson Page*, 85.

12. Tucker, *Telling Memories among Southern Women*, 96–97.

13. Cook, *Thomas Dixon*, 73.

14. Dixon, *The Leopard's Spots*, 138–39; Bogle, *Toms, Coons*, 16–17; Dixon, *The Clansman*, 242–43.

15. Fishkin, *Was Huck Black?* 7–9, 96–99.

16. Twain, "A True Story," 406, 407; Fishkin, *Was Huck Black?* 97.

17. Twain, *Pudd'nhead Wilson*, 11–12.

18. An excellent exploration of Roxy's motives can be found in Viguerie, "My Dear Ol' Mammy," 290–308.

19. Woodson, "The Negro Washerwoman," 269–77.

20. Parkhurst, "The Black Mammy in the Plantation Household," 352–53.

21. Ibid., 357–58, 362.

22. Gaines, *Uplifting the Race*. In particular, see chap. 5, "The Woman and Labor Questions in Racial Uplift Ideology," 128–51, on the phallocentric nature of uplift ideology.

23. Render, *Charles W. Chesnutt*, 35–37; Andrews, Andrews, *The Literary Career of Charles W. Chesnutt*, 50–53; Ayers, *The Promise of the New South*, 368.

24. Gaines, *Uplifting the Race*, 435–49; Chesnutt, *The Marrow of Tradition*, 1–11.

25. Chesnutt, *The Marrow of Tradition*, 41.

26. Andrews, *The Literary Career of Charles W. Chesnutt*, 179; Chesnutt, *The Marrow of Tradition*, 296.

27. Harris, *From Mammies to Militants*, 37.

28. Bogle, *Toms, Coons*, 57–60; Hurst, *Anatomy of Me*, especially 16–19, 97–104 on Hurst's Jewish identity. See also Shaughnessy, *Myths about Love and Woman*, 7–44; Brandimarte, "Fannie Hurst and Her Fiction," 106–42.

29. Hurst, *Imitation of Life*, 76, 87, 145.

30. Ibid., 259, 186.

31. Ibid., 266, 271; Shaunessy, *Myths about Love and Woman*, 112.

32. Tucker, *Telling Memories among Southern Women*, 199.

33. Irvin, "Gea in Georgia," 67.

34. Mitchell, *Gone with the Wind*, 19, 25, 47, 53, 61.

35. Ibid., 329.

36. O'Brien, "Race, Romance," 153–55; Cripps, "Winds of Change," 137–52.

37. Smith, *Killers of the Dream*, 165.

38. Ibid., 126–28.

39. Ibid., 131–33.

40. Ibid., 134; Baldwin, *Nobody Knows My Name*, 94.

41. Tucker, *Telling Memories among Southern Women*, 230, 222.

42. Jenkins, *Faulkner and Black-White Relations*, 1. See also Davis, *Faulkner's "Negro."*

43. Faulkner, *Go Down, Moses*, frontispiece; John Faulkner, *My Brother Bill*, especially chap. 5; Williamson, *William Faulkner and Southern History*, 153. See also Blottner, *Faulkner: A Biography*.

44. Peters, *William Faulkner*, 152.

45. Faulkner, *The Sound and the Fury*, 167, 118. Others who have examined *The Sound and the Fury* often view Dilsey as a metaphor for Christ and Christian endurance, emphasizing the traits I have noted and the fact that "her" chapter is set on Easter Sunday. For a recent example, see Oates, *William Faulkner*, 74–77.

46. *The Sound and the Fury*, 149, 159, 216–17, 323.

47. Tucker, *Telling Memories among Southern Women*, 142.

48. Porter, *The Leaning Tower*, 35–36, 64–65; Tucker, *Telling Memories among Southern Women*, 245.

49. Tucker, *Telling Memories among Southern Women*, 44.

50. Harris, *From Mammies to Militants*, 155–79.

51. Elkins, *Slavery*, 88–89.

52. Moynihan, *The Negro Family*, 75. For a more recent example of Moynihan's continuing influence, see William Tucker, "All in the Family," 36–44, 76.

53. Blassingame, *The Slave Community*, 304–5, 266.

54. Genovese, *Roll, Jordan, Roll*, 332, 343, 344.

55. Ibid., 355.

56. Ibid., 356, 662.

57. Ibid., 358, 360, 364–65.

58. Fox-Genovese, *Within the Plantation Household*, 290–92.

59. Ibid., 352, 355.

60. White, *Ar'n't I a Woman?* 50–53.

61. Ibid., 56–58.

62 Ibid., 58–61.

63. Gutman, *The Black Family in Slavery and Freedom*, 443–44, 630; Clinton, *The Plantation Mistress*, 202.

64. Ellison, *Shadow and Act*, 54–55.

65. Hine, "Rape and the Inner Lives of Southern Black Women," 182–84.

66. Tucker, *Telling Memories among Southern Women*, 121.

67. Morton, *Disfigured Images*, 156.

68. Gleick, *Genius*, 28–29.

69. Ellison, *Shadow and Act*, 54.

3. From the Minstrel Stage to the World's Fair: The Birth of Aunt Jemima

1. *St. Joseph Gazette*, 25 May 1889, 5.

2. Watkins, *On the Real Side*, 143.

3. "Old Aunt Jemima," composed by James Grace, originally sung by Billy Kersands (Boston: John F. Perry and Co., 1875), Brown University Library.

4. Marquette, *Brands, Trademarks, and Good Will*, 143.

5. Hine, *The Total Package*, 24–25.

6. Ibid., 61–62.

7. Marquette, *Brands, Trademarks, and Good Will*, 139–40; Campbell, *Why Did They Name It . . .?* 40–41; Rutt, *History of Buchanan County*, 240–41; Levenstein, *Revolution at the Table*, 32; *Buchanan County History*, 374.

8. Marquette, *Brands, Trademarks, and Good Will*, 140–41.

9. Watkins, *On the Real Side*, 81–103; Toll, *Blacking Up*, 25–64; Lott, *Love and Theft*, 15–37; Roediger, *The Wages of Whiteness*, 11–15.

10. Watkins, *On the Real Side*, 89–93.

11. Ibid., 93, 143–45. The minstrel cakewalk is at least as old as the popular song "Walking for Dat Cake" (1877), but probably older. It become more popular, as Watkins explains, after its inclusion in the 1890 "Creole Show" and later in the acts of Bert Williams and George Walker, and by the turn of the century had become one of the country's most popular dances. See also Stuckey, *Slave Culture*, 65.

12. Lott, *Love and Theft*, 159.

13. Watkins, *On the Real Side*, 102.

14. Actually, Kersands was famous for his expert performances of a dance known as the "Virginia Essence," a direct forerunner of the soft shoe. See Stearns, *Jazz Dance*, 50–51. On Kersand's mouth, see Burton, *The Blue Book of Tin Pan Alley*, 22–23; see also Claghorn, *Biographical Dictionary of American Music*, 252. W. C. Handy's eyewitness account is in Watkins, *On the Real Side*, 113. The best biographical detail regarding Kersands is in Toll, *Blacking Up*, 254–61.

15. Toll, *Blacking Up*, 256.

16. "Aunt Jemima's Picnic Day," words by J. Will Callahan, music by F. Henri Klickman, McKinley Music Co., 1914; "Aunt Jemima Song," words by Raymond B. Eagan, music by Richard A. Whiting, Jerome H. Remick & Co., 1925.

The first appearance of Aunt Jemima I have found dates to 1855, in a song titled "Aunt Jemima's Plaster" by "M.A.I." and published by Lee & Walker of Philadelphia (The Newberry Library, Chicago). This Aunt Jemima is white. In the song she mixes up a batch of plaster so strong that her neighbor's cat gets stuck to the floor.

17. Toll, *Blacking Up*, 260.

18. Ibid., 256, 260–61, 201–2.

19. Stuckey, "Through the Prism of Folklore," 424; Brown, *The Negro Caravan*, 447. I am forever indebted to Dave Roediger, who pointed out the connection between the slave song and Aunt Jemima song.

20. Lott, *Love and Theft*, 27–28, 149; Davis, *Society and Culture in Early Modern France*, 128–31.

21. Gould, *Bully for Brontosaurus*, 96–97.

22. See the *St. Joseph Gazette*, 28 July 1889, 3, 1 Aug. 1889, 2, 2 Aug. 1889, 7, 26 Aug. 1889, 4, 7 Sept. 1889, 7. On Sam Lucas's career, see Toll, *Blacking Up*, 217–19.

23. *St. Joseph Gazette*, 22 Sept. 1889, 5, 5 Oct. 1889, 5, 2 Dec. 1889, 8.

24. Marquette, *Brands, Trademarks, and Good Will*, 143–45.

25. Norris, *Advertising and the Transformation of American Society*, 19, 97, 33–35, 43–45; Strasser, *Satisfaction Guaranteed*, 43–46, 93–94.

On the growth of advertising and its relationship to industrialization, transportation, and prices, see Galbraith, *The New Industrial State*, 206–20; Potter, *People of Plenty*, 166–88; Norris, "Toward the Institutional Study of Advertising," 59–73. For a summary of some of the conflicting views regarding advertising's rise and influence in American society, see Rotzoll et al., *The Role of Advertising in Contemporary*, 54–80. See also Pope, *The Making of Modern Advertising*, 22–29.

26. Strasser, *Satisfaction Guaranteed*, 18–26, 42–43, 51–57; Norris, *Advertising and the Transformation of American Society*, 13–20; Tedlow, *New and Improved*, 11–15.

27. Marquette, *Brands, Trademarks, and Good Will*, 144; Campbell, *Why Did They Name It . . . ?* 35; Kern-Foxworth, *Aunt Jemima, Uncle Ben, and Rastus*, 58.

28. Marquette, *Brands, Trademarks, and Good Will*, 144–46; Kern-Foxworth, *Aunt Jemima, Uncle Ben, and Rastus*, 58–60.

29. *Life of Aunt Jemima, the Most Famous Colored Woman in the World*, Lynn Burkett Collection, Hillsdale, Mich.; Marquette, *Brands, Trademarks, and Good Will*, 146–47.

30. Marquette, *Brands, Trademarks, and Good Will*, 148–49.

31. *JWT Newsletter*, 8 Jan. 1925, 10 Jan. 1924, 6, 17 Jan. 1924, 2.

32. The *Missouri Farmer* account is reprinted in *JWT Newsletter*, 3 Jan. 1924, 4.

33. Gannett News Service, 24 April 1994.

4. They Were What They Ate: James Webb Young and the Reconstruction of American Advertising

1. Stigler, "Domestic Servants in the United States, 1900–1940," 35.

2. Cowan, *More Work for Mother*, 28.

3. Dudden, *Serving Women*, 1, 72–79; Katzman, *Seven Days a Week*, 225–26.

4. Golden, "Female Labor Force Participation."

5. Dudden, *Serving Women*, 62–63.

6. Katzman, *Seven Days a Week*, 163.

7. Stigler, "Domestic Servants in the United States, 1900–1940," 39, 4.

8. Katzman, *Seven Days a Week*, 61.

9. Clark–Lewis, *Living In, Living Out*, 124.

10. Haynes, "Negroes in Domestic Service in the United States," 393–96; Katzman, *Seven Days a Week*, 221–22.

11. Thurber, "The Development of the Mammy Image," 99; Katzman, *Seven Days a Week*, 189; Stigler, "Domestic Servants in the United States, 1900–1940," 20–21.

12. Strasser, *Never Done*, 5–6.

13. Ibid.; Cowan, *More Work for Mother*, 58–62.

14. Cowan, *More Work for Mother*, 61–62.

15. Ibid., 38, 89.

16. Strasser, *Never Done*, 81.

17. Fox, *The Mirror Makers*, 13–39; Tedlow, *New and Improved*, 12–14.

18. Marchand, *Advertising the American Dream*, 22–29.

19. Lears, "From Salvation to Self–Realization," 19, 22–23.

20. *Ladies' Home Journal*, Dec. 1919, 32, Oct. 1923, 41, 59.

21. Marchand, *Advertising the American Dream*, 206–34.

22. Ibid., 203–5.

23. *Good Housekeeping*, Nov. 1926, 140; *Ladies' Home Journal*, Nov. 1921, 37.

24. Pierterse, *White on Black*, 188–210.

25. Strasser, *Never Done*, 78. For examples of postwar ads including maids, see Marchand, *Advertising the American Dream*, 194–205.

26. Fox, *The Mirror Makers*, 79, 81–90. Chapter 3 of *The Mirror Makers*, "High Tide and Green Grass," offers a detailed account of JWT's rise to prominence.

27. Marchand, *Advertising the American Dream*, 8–9, 12–13, 66–69.

28. *JWT Newsletter*, 23 April 1917, 1–2.

29. Marchand, *Advertising the American Dream*, 72. The "Colonel's Lady" refers to a character created by Rudyard Kipling and, according to Marchand, was an example of an upper-class woman who, despite her status, was expected to be the "same under the skin" as a lower-class woman (65–66).

30. "James Webb Young's Valedictory," JWT Archives, DU.

31. Ibid.

32. *JWT Newsletter*, 1 June 1928, 207; Fox, *The Mirror Makers*, 82.

33. Fox, *The Mirror Makers*, 87–88, 99.

34. *JWT Newsletter*, 1 March 1928, 93.

35. Fox, *The Mirror Makers*, 86–88.

36. James Webb Young Lectures, 4, JWT Archives, DU.

37. Reed, *Whistling Dixie*, 91.

38. Lears, *Fables of Abundance*, 124, 384.

39. "Brief Resume of Franklin Baker Coconut Advertising," JWT account files, JWT Archives, DU, 1–3.

40. *Ladies' Home Journal*, Nov. 1923, 84.

41. *Good Housekeeping*, June 1925, 133; *Ladies' Home Journal*, Sept. 1923, 66; Root and de Rochemont, *Eating in America*, 154, 235.

42. DMB&B Collection, oversized ads, 1936, DU.

43. "Brief Resume of Franklin Baker's Coconut Advertising," 7–8.

44. JWT account files, 1927.

45. Ibid.

46. JWT account files, 1926; DMB&B Collection, oversized ads, 1937, 1930.

47. Young is quoted in Fox, *The Mirror Makers*, 88. Although Fox said that the Maxwell House account came to JWT in 1928, the firm's account histories indicate that JWT began soliciting from Maxwell House in 1922 and won the account in 1924 (JWT account files, 1924).

48. Cheek-Neal account history, JWT Archives, DU. The account of the Klan meeting is in Folmsbee et al., *Tennessee*, 361.

49. Cheek-Neal account history, 3–4.

50. Ibid., 4–5.

51. Ibid.

52. *Ladies' Home Journal*, Jan. 1927, 70, Sept. 1926, 62, Aug. 1926, 53, July 1926, 53, June 1925, 66.

53. *Saturday Evening Post*, 1 May 1926, 118; *Ladies' Home Journal*, June 1926, 71; *Ladies' Home Journal*, March 1926, 66.

54. *Saturday Evening Post*, 24 July 1926, 83.

55. *Ladies' Home Journal*, Nov. 1925, 81.

56. Ibid., March 1925, 123.

57. *Saturday Evening Post*, 11 April 1925, 62; *Ladies' Home Journal*, Dec. 1926, 56, April 1925, 62.

58. Pieterse, *White on Black*, 189–94.

59. Folsmbee et al., *Tennessee*, 396.

60. *Saturday Evening Post*, 16 Jan. 1926, 120–21.

61. *Ladies' Home Journal*, July 1928, 51, Nov. 1928, 60.

62. DMB&B Collection, oversized advertisements, 1941.

63. Silber, *The Romance of Reunion*, 108–9.

64. *International Grocer*, Oct. 1928, 15.

65. *JWT Newsletter*, 26 March 1925, 3; 1 Dec. 1927, 493–94.

66. DMB&B Collection, oversized advertisements, 1933.

67. James W. Young biographical files, JWT Archives, DU.

68. James Webb Young Lectures, 49–50.

5. The Old South, the Absent Mistress, and the Slave in a Box

1. Bulgatz, *Ponzi Schemes*, 380–91. For Cargo Cults, see Cochrane, *Big Men*, and Worsley, *The Trumpet Shall Sound*.

2. Jennings, *N. C. Wyeth*, 6–17.

3. An example of the "ole swimmin' hole" ads can be found in the *Saturday Evening Post*, 6 July 1918, 61. American soldiers are depicted eating Aunt Jemima pancakes in the *Saturday Evening Post*, 28 Sept. 1918, 23 Nov. 1918.

4. *JWT Newsletter*, 14 May 1917, 1.

5. For examples of Cream of Wheat ads, see *Ladies' Home Journal*, Jan., Oct. 1919, Jan., April 1920, March, May 1921, July 1922, March 1923. The same ads ran in *Good Housekeeping* but not as prominently and often in black and white; see Jan. 1924, 117, Feb. 1924, 83, June 1927, 145, Aug. 1929, 141, July 1930, 130. In many of the ads, Rastus's image is minor.

6. Marquette, *Brands, Trademarks, and Good Will*, 105–10. For examples of Quaker ads, see *Ladies' Home Journal*, Aug. 1919, 84, Oct. 1919, 102, Nov. 1919, 96, Dec. 1919, 120, Jan. 1920, 112, Feb. 1920, 100, March 1920, 172, April 1920, 111, 120, May 1920, 70, 89, 109, June 1920, 83, 117, 128, Sept. 1920, 142, Oct. 1920, 106, 136, Nov. 1920, 84, Dec. 1920, 81, Feb. 1921, 50, Oct. 1921, 37, Dec. 1921, 44, Nov. 1922, 48, 84, Jan. 1923, 70, Feb. 1923, 61, March 1923, 71, 100, Nov. 1923, 51, Dec. 1923, 44, Jan. 1924, 44, Feb. 1926, 94, Nov. 1926, 103, Jan. 1927, 105, Feb. 1927, 44, 117, 135, March 1927, 53, Nov. 1927, 93, 95, Jan. 1928, 98, Feb. 1928, 90, 93, Oct. 1928, 78, Nov. 1928, 103, March 1930, 113, 216.

7. *Ladies' Home Journal*, Feb. 1921, 233, Oct. 1921, 102, Dec. 1921, 119, Feb. 1922, 142, Oct. 1924, 49, Nov. 1924, 49, Oct. 1925, 50, Nov. 1925, 55, Dec. 1925, 45, Feb. 1926, 42, Oct. 1926, 48, July 1928, 39, April 1929, 48, Feb. 1930, 47. The same ads ran in *Good Housekeeping* throughout the decade.

8. *Ladies' Home Journal*, Sept. 1920, 203, Oct. 1922, 124, Feb. 1923, 90; *Good Housekeeping*, Dec. 1927, 143.

9. *Ladies' Home Journal*, Feb. 1922, 86, Oct. 1922, 94, Dec. 1922, 93, Jan. 1922, 89, Feb. 1924, 74. See also "Gold Dust Twins Still Golden," *Black Ethnic Collectibles*, Spring 1991, 30–33.

10. *Saturday Evening Post*, 20 Nov. 1920, 112.

11. Ibid., 18 Dec. 1920, 40.

12. Silber, *The Romance of Reunion*, 39–65.

13. Lott, *Love and Theft*, 187–201.

14. *Saturday Evening Post*, 15 Jan. 1921, 66.

15. Ibid.

16. Ibid., 23 Oct. 1920, 85.

17. *Ladies' Home Journal*, Jan. 1920, 129.

18. Ibid., Oct. 1920, 173.

19. Ibid., March 1921, 86.

20. Ibid.

21. Ibid., Oct. 1925, 138, Dec. 1925, 111, Nov. 1928, 80.

22. *Saturday Evening Post*, 8 May 1920, 125.

23. Boydston, *Home and Work*, 145.

24. *Ladies' Home Journal*, Nov. 1919, 141.

25. Ibid., Dec. 1919, 141.

26. JWT account files, 1920, JWT Archives, DU.

27. *Ladies' Home Journal*, Jan. 1920, 143.

28. Ibid., March 1927, 153, Oct. 1924, 132; JWT account files, 1927.

29. *Ladies' Home Journal*, Oct. 1926, 94, Sept. 1926, 89, Nov. 1924, 152; *Pictorial Review*, Feb. 1922, 55.

30. *Ladies' Home Journal*, Aug. 1926, 84.

31. Mathews, *"Just a Housewife,"* 171.

32. *Ladies' Home Journal*, Aug. 1927, 80; *Woman's Home Companion*, March 1926, 55.

33. *Ladies's Home Journal*, March 1926, 196; JWT account files, 1927.

34. JWT advertising schedules, 1923–24, 1924–25, 1925–27, JWT Archives, DU.

35. *JWT Newsletter*, 15 Jan. 1928, 53, 59.

36. Fox, *The Mirror Makers*, 150–62; *JWT Newsletter*, 15 Feb. 1928.

37. JWT staff meeting transcripts, 15 Oct. 1929, 1–2, 16 April 1930, 3–4, JWT Archives, DU. Anyone hoping to learn much about the Aunt Jemima campaign during the 1920s will be disappointed by the transcripts of JWT staff meetings, in which the long-standing and successful account appears to have been discussed rarely. The content of the radio programs was discussed in the *JWT Newsletter*, 15 Dec. 1928.

38. Radio broadcasting estimates, *Phil Cook Program*, JWT account files, 1931.

39. *Good Housekeeping*, Sept. 1922, 133.

40. Ibid., Oct. 1922, 128.

41. Ibid., Dec. 1922, 202.

42. Ibid., Jan. 1923, 147.

43. Saxton, *Rise and Fall*, 165–70.

44. *Saturday Evening Post*, 5 June 1920, 130.

45. JWT account files, 1919–20.

46. Ibid., 1928, 1929, 1930, 1931.

47. Ibid.

48. *JWT Newsletter*, 15 Oct. 1927, 448.

49. Ibid., 15 Jan. 1928, 40–41.

50. *Woman's Home Companion*, Jan. 1933, 67, Oct. 1933, 56, Feb. 1933; *Cosmopolitan*, Jan. 1933, 115, Feb. 1933, 115; *American Weekly*, 15 Jan. 1933, 14 Jan. 1934, 23; *Ladies' Home Journal*, Jan. 1934, 83, April 1934, 68; *McCall's*, Oct. 1934, 87.

51. JWT account files, 1934.

52. Marquette, *Brands, Trademarks, and Good Will*, 139, 154.

53. *JWT Newsletter*, 9 June 1927, 301, 1 Sept. 1928.

54. Ibid., 20 April 1953, 1, 4 Jan. 1954, 1, 24 Oct. 1955, 1.

6. The Secret of the Bandanna: The Mammy in Contemporary Society

1. Ford, *Donovan of OSS*, 170; Powers, *Heisenberg's War*, 260.

2. *Crusader*, March 1919, 9.

3. Ibid., Oct. 1919, 10.

4. Ibid., Sept. 1918, 7.

5. Ibid., Dec. 1918, 4–5.

6. Robert A. Hill's introductory notes to the three-volume bound collection of the magazine, Robert A. Hill, ed., *The Crusader: A Facsimile*, xvi; *Crusader*, Nov. 1919, 11.

7. Hill, *Crusader: Facsimile*, xvi, xxii.

8. *Crusader*, Sept. 1920, 17.

9. Ibid., July 1920, 18.

10. Edwards, *The Southern Urban Negro as a Consumer*, 52, 96–97.

11. Ibid., 217–18, 229–30.

12. Ibid., 228–29, 234.

13. Bogle, *Toms, Coons*, 86–94.

14. Ibid., 162–66.

15. Abrahams, *Deep Down in the Jungle*, 19–21, 32–35. See also Abrahams, *Positively Black*, 39–42, and *Talking Black*, 44–45. On the African origins of playing the dozens, see Gates, *The Signifying Monkey*, 52–53.

16. Abrahams, *Deep Down in the Jungle*, 52, 56–57.

17. Kern–Foxworth, *Aunt Jemima, Uncle Ben, and Rastus*, 106–7; Jewell, *From Mammy to Miss America*, 61–62.

18. *San Francisco Examiner*, 16 Aug. 1966, 32, 35.

19. *San Francisco Call-Bulletin*, 11 Feb. 1938, 1G; *Nation* 158:23 (3 June 1944): 663; *San Francisco Daily People's World*, 24 April 1950, 5.

20. Malcolm X with Haley, *Autobiography*, 55, 243.

21. Ellison, *Shadow and Act*, 45.

22. Weems, "The Revolution Will Be Marketed," 93–107.

23. Marquette, *Brands, Trademarks, and Good Will*, 137, 157–58.

24. Kern-Foxworth, *Aunt Jemima, Uncle Ben, and Rastus*, 68–69.

25. Archer, *Black Images in the American Theatre*, 197.

26. Townsend, "Out of the Kitchen."

27. Archer, *Black Images in the American Theatre*, 206–8; *Crisis* 47:4 (April 1940): 1.

28. Jackson, *Hattie*, 50–51, 64–65, 99, 106–7, 112–13. On the rift between McDaniel and White, see also White, *A Man Called White*, 198–205.

29. See Archer, *Black Images in the American Theatre*, 183–262, 127–33.

30. *Papers of the NAACP*, pt. 1, reel 8: "The Press, the Pulpit, and Public Opinion," address by the Rev. R. L. Bradby, 1921 Detroit conference; "Public Opinion and the Negro," address by Harry H. Pace, 1921 Detroit conference; "The Value of the Press and Publicity in the Fight for Justice," address by Nahum Daniel Brascher, 1922 Newark conference; "The Value of the Press and Publicity in the Fight for Justice," address by Royal J. Davis, 1922 Newark conference; reel 9: "The Future Plan and Program for the NAACP," address by Walter White, 1935 conference; reel 10: "Proposed Resolutions," 1938 Columbus conference; "Final Resolutions," 1940 Philadelphia conference; reel 11: "Address by Walter White," 1942 Los Angeles conference; "Resolutions," 1946 Cincinnati conference; "Treatment of the Negro in Press, Radio, and Motion Pictures," address by George Schuyler, Detroit 1946 emergency meeting; "Statement to the Nation," Detroit 1946 emergency meeting; reel 12: "Resolutions," 1947 Washington conference; "Resolutions," 1948 Kansas City conference; "Resolutions," 1949 Los Angeles conference; "Resolutions," 1950 Boston conference.

31. Ely, *The Adventures of Amos 'n' Andy*, 239.

32. Ruth B. Loving to NAACP, 17 April 1956, NAACP Papers, Library of Congress.

33. "Poor Aunt Jemima," *Springfield Daily News*, 10 April 1956, 6.

34. John A. Sandifer to Dr. John Morrell, 28 Oct. 1959, NAACP Papers.

35. John Morrell to Henry Killingsworth, 9 Dec. 1959, ibid.

36. John A. Morrell to Jacob and Mervin Wineberg, 9 Dec. 1960, to Don Parsons, 22 Dec. 1960, 5 Jan., 13 Jan. 1961, Parsons to Morrell, 28 Dec. 1960, Frank T. Walker to Morrell, 7 Jan. 1961, ibid.

37. Sloan E. Williams to Gloster B. Current, 28 April 1963, to Sales Promotion Department, Quaker Oats Company, 28 April 1963, ibid.

38. Marguerite Eaglin and Carrie Lewis to Roy Wilkins, 31 Dec. 1964, ibid.

39. Virginia Harper to Leonard Carter, 5 Aug. 1964, ibid.

40. Forrest L. Tabor to Raymond Harth, 28 Oct. 1964, Harth to Rock Falls Chamber of Commerce, 22 Oct. 1964, ibid.

41. Raymond E. Harth to Robert Stuart, 22 Oct. 1964, ibid.

42. Kern-Foxworth, *Aunt Jemima, Uncle Ben, and Rastus*, 90–91; Jewell, *From Mammy to Miss America*, 47–48; *St. Louis Post-Dispatch*, 10 Aug. 1989, Style sec., 2.

43. *Chicago Sun-Times*, 21 Jan. 1924, Weekend Plus sec., 9; "Edith Wilson: Interview," *Cadence* 5 (Aug. 1979): 21.

44. Lyrics from the musical *Hair*, Northwestern University music archives, Evanston, Ill.

45. Kern-Foxworth, *Aunt Jemima, Uncle Ben, and Rastus*, 102–3.

46. Jewell, *From Mammy to Miss America*, 208.

47. Kern-Foxworth, *Aunt Jemima, Uncle Ben, and Rastus*, 103. The poem by Sylvia Dunnavant appeared in *An Affair of the Heart* (Madison, Wis.: National Minority Campus Chronicle, 1983).

48. Kern-Foxworth, *Aunt Jemima, Uncle Ben, and Rastus*, 63; Dubin, "Symbolic Slavery," 132; Haynes, *Sambo Sahib*, 163–64; Walker, "Giving the Party," 22–25.

49. No one knows how "valuable" Aunt Jemima might be today, but consider the fact that the Aunt Jemima brand is annually near or at the top of a category of breakfast food lines whose U.S. sales doubled in 1983–87. See *Supermarket News*, 9 Jan. 1989, 23.

50. *Kansas City Star*, 16 Dec. 1993, F1; *Economist*, 6 May 1989, 60; *Newsweek*, 14 Aug. 1989, 34.

51. *Chicago Tribune*, 15 Dec. 1989, sec. 2, p. 3.

52. *Advertising Age*, 26 June 1989, 24.

53. Public Enemy, *Fear of a Black Planet*, Def Jam/Columbia 1990 (45413); lyrics from Northwestern University music archives.

54. *Washington Post*, 25 July 1993, B1.

55. "Ads on Minorities Fall Short," *St. Louis Post-Dispatch*, 24 March 1994, 1B; Ricks, *Blunders in International Business*, 71–87. See also "Col. Sanders Cooks Up Comeback," *USA Today*, 15 May 1994, 4B; "Tobacco, Alcohol's New Foe: Black Ministers Target Ads," *Adweek*, 12. March 1990, 1, 60; "British Budweiser Ads Rankle American Indians," *Wall Street Journal*, 16. July 1996, B1.

56. *Wall Street Journal*, 11 Sept. 1995, A1; "Building a Better Betty Crocker," *Kansas City Star*, 11. Oct. 1995, E1.

57. *New York Times*, 11 June 1995, 4E.

58. *Saturday Evening Post*, 10 April 1920, 134; Omi and Winant, *Racial Formation*, 123–28; Goings, *Mammy and Uncle Mose*, 88–106.

59. *Wall Street Journal*, 16 Sept. 1994, B5; *Newsweek*, 17 Oct. 1994, 85; *Advertising Age*, 24 Oct. 1994, 27; *New York Times*, 29 Aug. 1994, D7.

60. *Ottawa Citizen*, 9 Nov. 1992, A1.

61. Cleaver, *Soul on Ice*, 162.

62. Fitzgerald, *The Great Gatsby*, 159.

Works Cited

Archival Collections

Hartmann Center, Special Collections, Duke University, Durham, N.C.
    D'Arcy, Masius, Benton & Bowles Collection
    J. Walter Thompson Company Archives
Library of Congress, Washington, D.C.
    Papers of the National Association for the Advancement of Colored People
Music Archives, Newberry Library, Chicago
Music Archives, Special Collections, Northwestern University, Evanston, Ill.
Special Collections, Brown University, Providence
State Historical Society of Missouri, Columbia
    Missouri Newspapers on Microfilm
    Peter Tamony Collection
Walt Disney Archives, Burbank, Calif.

Microfilm Collection

Papers of the NAACP, pt. 1, *Meetings of the Board of Directors, Records of Annual Conferences, Major Speeches, and Special Reports, 1909–1950*. Ed. adviser August Meier, ed. Mark Fox. Frederick, Md.: University Publications of America.

Magazine Advertisements

Good Housekeeping, Sept. 1922, 133; Oct. 1922, 128; Dec. 1922, 202; Jan. 1923, 147; Jan. 1924, 117; Feb. 1924, 83; March 1924, 233; June 1925, 133; Nov. 1926, 140; June 1927, 145; Dec. 1927, 143; Aug. 1929, 141; July 1930, 130.

Ladies' Home Journal, Jan. 1919, 2; Aug. 1919, 84; Oct. 1919, 2, 102; Nov. 1919, 96, 141; Dec. 1919, 32, 120, 141; Jan. 1920, 2, 112, 129, 143; Feb. 1920, 100; March 1920, 172; April 1920, 2, 111, 120; May 1920, 70, 89, 109; June 1920, 83, 117, 128; Sept. 1920, 142, 203; Oct. 1920, 106, 136, 173; Nov. 1920, 84; Dec. 1920, 81; Feb. 1921, 50, 233; March 1921, 2; May 1921, 2; Oct. 1921, 37, 102; Nov. 1921, 37; Dec. 1921, 44, 119; Jan. 1922, 89; Feb. 1922, 86, 142; July 1922, 2; Oct. 1922, 94, 124; Nov. 1922, 48,

84; Dec. 1922, 93; Jan. 1923, 70; Feb. 1923, 61, 90; March 1923, 2, 71, 100; Sept. 1923, 66; Oct. 1923, 41, 59; Nov. 1923, 51, 84; Dec. 1923, 44; Jan. 1924, 44; Feb. 1924, 74; Oct. 1924, 49, 132; Nov. 1924, 49, 152; Jan. 1925, 76–77; March 1925, 123; April 1925, 62; June 1925, 66; Oct. 1925, 50, 138; Nov. 1925, 55, 81; Dec. 1925, 45, 111; Feb. 1926, 42, 94; March 1926, 66, 196; June 1926, 71; July 1926, 53; Aug. 1926, 53, 84; Sept. 1926, 62, 89; Oct. 1926, 48, 94; Nov. 1926, 103; Dec. 1926, 56; Jan. 1927, 70, 105; Feb. 1927, 44, 117, 135; March 1927, 53, 153; Aug. 1927, 80; Nov. 1927, 93, 95; Jan. 1928, 98; Feb. 1928, 90, 93; July 1928, 39, 51; Oct. 1928, 78; Nov. 1928, 60, 80, 103; April 1929, 48; Feb. 1930, 47; March 1930, 113, 216; Jan. 1934, 83; April 1934, 68.

Saturday Evening Post, 6 July 1918, 61; 10 April 1920, 134; 8 May 1920, 125; 5 June 1920, 130; 23 Oct. 1920, 85; 20 Nov. 1920, 112; 18 Dec. 1920, 40; 15 Jan. 1921, 66; 11 April 1925, 62; 16 Jan. 1926, 120–21; 1 May 1926, 118; 24 July 1926, 83.

Woman's Home Companion, March 1926, 55; Jan. 1933, 67; Oct. 1933, 56; Oct. 1934, 104.

Nonfiction Books, Book Chapters, and Dissertations

Abrahams, Roger. *Deep Down in the Jungle: . . . Negro Narrative Folklore from the Streets of Philadelphia.* Hatboro, Pa., 1964.

——. *Positively Black.* New York, 1970.

——. *Talking Black.* Rowley, Mass., 1976.

Andrews, William L. *The Literary Career of Charles W. Chesnutt.* Baton Rouge, La., 1980.

Archer, Leonard C. *Black Images in the American Theatre: NAACP Protest Campaigns— Stage, Screen, Radio, and Television.* Brooklyn, N.Y., 1973.

Auerbach, Nina. *Woman and the Demon: The Life of a Victorian Myth.* Cambridge, Mass., 1982.

Ayers, Edward. *The Promise of the New South: Life after Reconstruction.* New York, 1992.

Bailey, Hugh C. *Liberalism in the New South: Southern Social Reformers and the Progressive Movement.* Coral Gables, Fla., 1969.

Baldwin, James. *Nobody Knows My Name.* New York, 1963.

——. *Notes of a Native Son.* Boston, 1955; rept., 1984.

Blassingame, John. *The Slave Community: Plantation Life in the Antebellum South.* Rev. and enlarged ed., New York, 1979.

Blottner, Joseph. *Faulkner: A Biography.* New York, 1991.

Bogle, Donald. *Toms, Coons, Mulattoes, Mammies, and Bucks.* New York, 1973.

Boydston, Jeanne. *Home and Work: Housework, Wages, and the Ideology of Labor in the Early Republic.* New York, 1990.

Brandimarte, Cynthia Ann. "Fannie Hurst and Her Fiction: Prescriptions for America's Working Women." Ph.D. diss., University of Texas–Austin, 1980.

Brown, Sterling. *The Negro Caravan.* New York, 1941.

Buchanan County History: The Heritage of Buchanan County, Mo. St. Joseph, Mo., 1981.

Bulgatz, Joseph. *Ponzi Schemes, Invaders from Mars, and More Extraordinary Popular Delusions.* New York, 1992.

Burton, Jack. *The Blue Book of Tin Pan Alley.* Watkins Glen, N.Y., 1950.

Campbell, Hannah. *Why Did They Name It . . .?* New York, 1964.

Carter, Dan T. "From the Old South to the New: Another Look at the Theme of Change and Continuity," in *From the Old South to the New: Essays on the Transitional South*, ed. Walter J. Fraser Jr. and Winfred B. Moore Jr. Westport, Conn., 1981.

Cash, W. J. *The Mind of the South.* New York, 1954.

Christian, Barbara. *Black Woman Novelists: The Development of a Tradition, 1892–1976.* Westport, Conn., 1980.

Claghorn, Charles Eugene. *Biographical Dictionary of American Music.* West Nyack, N.Y., 1973.

Clark-Lewis, Elizabeth. *Living In, Living Out: African American Domestics in Washington, D.C.* Washington, D.C., 1994.

Cleaver, Eldridge. *Soul on Ice.* New York, 1968.

Clinton, Catherine. "Caught in the Web of the Big House," in *Black Women in United States History*, ed. Darlene Clark Hine. 4 vols. New York, 1990. 1:230.

———. *Plantation Mistress: Woman's World in the Old South.* New York, 1982.

Cochrane, Glynn. *Big Men and Cargo Cults.* Oxford, 1970.

Collins, Patricia Hill. *Black Feminist Thought: Knowledge, Consciousness, and the Politics of Empowerment.* London, 1991

Cook, Raymond A. *Thomas Dixon.* New York, 1974.

Coontz, Stephanie. *The Way We Never Were: American Families and the Nostalgia Trap.* New York, 1992.

Cowan, Ruth Schwartz. *More Work for Mother: The Ironies of Household Technology from the Open Hearth to the Microwave.* New York, 1983.

Davis, Natalie. *Society and Culture in Early Modern France.* Stanford, Calif., 1975.

Davis, Thadious M. *Faulkner's "Negro": Art and the Southern Context.* Baton Rouge, La., 1983.

Dudden, Faye E. *Serving Women: Household Service in Nineteenth-Century America.* Middletown, Conn., 1983.

Edwards, Paul K. *The Southern Urban Negro as a Consumer.* New York, 1932.

Elkins, Stanley. *Slavery: A Problem in American Institutional and Intellectual Life.* Rept., Chicago, 1976.

Ellison, Ralph. *Shadow and Act.* New York, 1953.

Faulkner, John. *My Brother Bill.* New York, 1963.

Fishkin, Shelley Fisher. *Was Huck Black? Mark Twain and African-American Voices.* New York, 1994.

Folmsbee, Stanley J., et al. *Tennessee: A Short History.* Knoxville, Tenn., 1969.

Ford, Corey. *Donovan of OSS.* New York, 1970.

Foster, Gaines. *Ghosts of the Confederacy: Defeat, the Lost Cause, and the Emergence of the New South, 1865 to 1913.* New York, 1987.

Fox, Stephen. *The Mirror Makers: A History of American Advertising and Its Creators.* New York, 1984.

Fox-Genovese, Elizabeth. *Within the Plantation Household: Blacks and White Women of the Old South.* Chapel Hill, N.C., 1988.

Freud, Sigmund. *Jokes and Their Relation to the Unconscious.* Rept., New York, 1960.

Galbraith, John Kenneth. *The New Industrial State.* New York, 1985.

Gaston, Paul M. *The New South Creed.* New York, 1970.

Gates, Henry Louis. *The Signifying Monkey: A Theory of African-American Literary Criticism.* New York, 1988.

Genovese, Eugene. *Roll, Jordan, Roll: The World the Slaves Made.* New York, 1976.

Gerster, Patrick, and Nicholas Cords, "The Northern Origins of Southern Mythology," in *Myth and Southern History,* vol. 2, *The New South,* ed. Gerster and Cords. Urbana, Ill., 1989.

Gleick, James, *Genius: The Life and Science of Richard Feynman.* New York, 1993.

Goings, Kenneth. *Mammy and Uncle Mose: Black Collectibles and American Stereotyping.* Bloomington, Ind., 1994.

Gould, Stephen Jay. *Bully for Brontosaurus: Reflections in Natural History.* New York, 1991.

Gross, Theodore L. *Thomas Nelson Page.* New York, 1967.

Gutman, Herbert G. *The Black Family in Slavery and Freedom, 1750–1925.* New York, 1977.

Gwin, Minrose C. *Black and White Women of the Old South: The Peculiar Sisterhood in American Literature.* Knoxville, Tenn., 1985.

Harris, Trudier. *From Mammies to Militants: Domestics in Black American Literature.* Philadelphia, 1982.

Haynes, Elizabeth. *Sambo Sahib: The Story of Little Black Sambo and Helen Bannerman.* New York, 1981.

Hill, Robert A., ed. *The Crusader: A Facsimile of the Periodical,* ed. with a new Introduction and Index. New York, 1987.

Hine, Darlene Clark. "Rape and the Inner Lives of Southern Black Women: Thoughts on the Culture of Dissemblance," in *Southern Women: Histories and Identities,* ed. Virginia Bernhard et al. Columbia, Mo., 1992.

Hine, Thomas. *The Total Package: The Evolution and Secret Meanings of Boxes, Bottles, Cans, and Tubes.* Boston, 1995.

Hurst, Fannie. *Anatomy of Me: A Wonderer in Search of Herself.* New York, 1958.

Jackson, Carlton. *Hattie: The Life of Hattie McDaniel.* Lanham, Md., 1990.

Jenkins, Lee. *Faulkner and Black-White Relations: A Psychoanalytic Approach.* New York, 1981.

Jewell, Karen Sue. *From Mammy to Miss America and Beyond: Cultural Images and the Shaping of U.S. Social Policy.* New York, 1993.

Jones, Jacqueline. *Labor of Love, Labor of Sorrow.* New York, 1985.

Katzman, David. *Seven Days a Week: Women and Domestic Service in Industrializing America.* New York, 1978.

Kern-Foxworth, Marilyn. *Aunt Jemima, Uncle Ben, and Rastus: Blacks in Advertising, Yesterday, Today, and Tomorrow.* Westport, Conn., 1994.

Lears, T. J. Jackson. *Fables of Abundance: A Cultural History of Advertising in America.* New York, 1994.

———. "From Salvation to Self-Realization: Advertising and the Therapeutic Roots of the Consumer Culture, 1880–1930," in *The Culture of Consumption: Critical Essays in American History, 1880–1980,* ed. Richard Wrightman Fox and T. J. Jackson Lears. New York, 1983.

Leeming, David. *James Baldwin.* New York, 1994.

Levenstein, Harvey A. *Revolution at the Table: The Transformation of the American Diet.* New York, 1988.

Lott, Eric. *Love and Theft: Blackface Minstrelsy and the American Working Class.* New York, 1993.

Malcolm X with Alex Haley. *The Autobiography of Malcolm X.* New York, 1965.

Marchand, Roland. *Advertising the American Dream: Making Way for Modernity, 1920–1940.* Berkeley, Calif., 1985.

Marquette, Arthur F. *Brands, Trademarks, and Good Will: The Story of the Quaker Oats Company.* New York, 1967.

Mathews, Glenna. *"Just a Housewife": The Rise and Fall of Domesticity in America.* New York, 1987.

McClintock, Anne. *Imperial Leather: Race, Gender, and Sexuality in the Colonial Context.* New York, 1995.

McMillen, Sally G. *Motherhood in the Old South: Pregnancy, Childbirth, and Infant Rearing.* Baton Rouge, La., 1990.

Morton, Patricia. *Disfigured Images: The Historical Assault on Afro-American Women.* Westport, Conn., 1991.

———. "'My Ol' Black Mammy' in American Historiography," in *Southern Women,* ed. Caroline Matheny Dillman. New York, 1988. Pp. 35–43.

Moynihan, Daniel P. *The Negro Family: The Case for National Action.* Washington, D.C., 1965.

Norris, James D. *Advertising and the Transformation of American Society, 1865–1920.* New York, 1990.

Norris, Vincent P. "Toward the Institutional Study of Advertising," in *The Role of Advertising*, ed. C. H. Sandage and V. Fryburger. Homewood, Ill., 1960. Pp. 59–73.

Oates, Stephen. *William Faulkner: The Man and the Artist*. New York, 1987.

Oring, Elliott. *Jokes and Their Relations*. Lexington, Ky., 1992.

Packard, Vance. *The Hidden Persuaders*. New York, 1957.

Page, Thomas Nelson. *The Old South: Essays Social and Political*. New York, 1892.

Peters, Erskine. *William Faulkner: The Yoknapatawpha World and Black Being*. Darby, Pa., 1983.

Phillips, U. B. *American Negro Slavery: A Survey of the Supply, Employment, and Control of Negro Labor as Determined by the Plantation Regime*. Rept., New York, 1940.

Pieterse, Jan Nederveen. *White on Black: Images of Africa and Blacks in Western Popular Culture*. New Haven, 1992.

Pope, Daniel. *The Making of Modern Advertising*. New York, 1983.

Potter, David M. *People of Plenty: Economic Abundance and the American Character*. Chicago, 1954.

Powers, Thomas. *Heisenberg's War: The Secret History of the German Bomb*. New York, 1993.

Pyron, Darden Asbury, ed. *Recasting:* Gone with the Wind *in American Culture*. Miami, Fla., 1983.

Rawick, George. *From Sunup to Sundown: The Making of the Black Community*. Westport, Conn., 1972.

Reed, John Shelton. *Whistling Dixie: Dispatches from the South*. Columbia, Mo., 1990.

Render, Sylvia Lyons. *Charles W. Chesnutt*. New York, 1980.

Rhodes, James F. *History of the United States from the Compromise of 1850*. New York, 1900–1928. Vol. 1.

Ricks, David A. *Blunders in International Business*. Cambridge, Mass., 1993.

Roberts, Diane. *The Myth of Aunt Jemima: Representations of Race and Region*. New York, 1994.

Roediger, David R. *The Wages of Whiteness: Race and the Making of the American Working Class*. New York, 1991.

Root, Waverley, and Richard de Rochemont. *Eating in America: A History*. New York, 1976.

Rotzoll, Kim, et al. *The Role of Advertising in Contemporary Society*. Cincinnati, 1990.

Rutt, Chris L. *History of Buchanan County and the City of St. Joseph and Representative Citizens*. Chicago, 1904.

Saxton, Alexander. *The Rise and Fall of the White Republic*. New York, 1990.

Shaughnessy, Mary Rose. *Myths about Love and Woman: The Fiction of Fannie Hurst*. New York, 1980.

Smith, Lillian. *Killers of the Dream*. Rev. and enlarged ed., New York, 1961.

Smith, Valerie, et al., eds. *African-American Writers*. New York, 1991.

Spiniad, Leonard and Thelma, eds. *Treasury of Great American Sayings.* West Nyack, N.Y., 1975.

Stearns, Marshall and Jean. *Jazz Dance: The Story of American Vernacular Dance.* New York, 1968.

Stigler, George J. "Domestic Servants in the United States, 1900–1940," in National Bureau of Economic Research, *Occasional Papers* 24. New York, April 1946.

Strasser, Susan. *Never Done: History of American Housework.* New York, 1982.

———. *Satisfaction Guaranteed: The Making of the American Mass Market.* New York, 1989.

Stuckey, Sterling. *Slave Culture: Nationalist Theory and the Foundations of Black America.* New York, 1987.

Sundquist, Eric J. *To Wake the Nations: Race and the Making of American Literature.* Cambridge, Mass., 1994.

Tedlow, Richard S. *New and Improved: The Story of Mass Marketing in America.* New York, 1990.

Thurber, Cheryl. "The Development of the Mammy Image and Mythology," in *Southern Women: Histories and Identities*, ed. Virginia Bernhard et al. Columbia, Mo., 1992.

Toll, Robert C. *Blacking Up: The Minstrel Show in Nineteenth Century America.* New York, 1974.

Tucker, Susan. *Telling Memories among Southern Women: Domestic Workers and Their Employers in the Segregated South.* New York, 1988.

Turner, Patricia A. *Celluloid Mammies and Ceramic Uncles: Black Images and Their Influence on Culture.* New York, 1994.

Viguerie, Mary Patricia Robinson. "My Dear Ol' Mammy: The Enduring Image of the Mammy in Southern Literature." Ph.D. diss., University of Missouri, Columbia, 1993.

Watkins, Mel. *On the Real Side, Laughing, Lying, and Signifying: The Underground Tradition of African-American Humor That Transformed American Culture, from Slavery to Richard Pryor.* New York, 1994.

White, Dana F. "The Old South under New Conditions," in *Olmsted South: Old South Critic / New South Planner*, ed. Dana F. White and Victor A. Kramer. Westport, Conn., 1979.

White, Deborah Gray. *Ar'n't I a Woman? Female Slaves in the Plantation South.* New York, 1985.

White, Walter. *A Man Called White.* New York, 1948.

Wiener, Jonathan M. *Social Origins of the New South: Alabama, 1860–1885.* Baton Rouge, La., 1978.

Williamson, Joel. *A Rage for Order: Black-White Relations in America since Emancipation.* New York, 1986.

———. *William Faulkner and Southern History.* New York, 1993.

Woodward, C. Vann. *Origins of the New South*. Baton Rouge, La., 1971.

Worsley, Peter. *The Trumpet Shall Sound: A Study of "Cargo" Cults in Melanesia*. New York, 1968.

Fiction

Chesnutt, Charles W. *The Marrow of Tradition*. Rept., Ann Arbor, Mich., 1970.

Dixon, Thomas. *The Clansman*. New York, 1905.

——. *The Leopard's Spots*. New York, 1902.

Faulkner, William. *Go Down, Moses*. New York, 1942.

——. *The Sound and The Fury*. Rept., New York, 1956.

Hodgins, Eric. *Mr. Blandings Builds His Dream House*. New York, 1946.

Hurst, Fannie. *Imitation of Life*. Rept., New York, 1990.

Mitchell, Margaret. *Gone with the Wind*. Rept., New York, 1964.

Page, Thomas Nelson. *Red Rock: A Chronicle of Reconstruction*. New York, 1899.

Porter, Katherine Anne. *The Leaning Tower and Other Stories*. New York, 1944.

Twain, Mark. *The Tragedy of Pudd'nhead Wilson and Those Extraordinary Twins*. New York, 1922.

——. *The Unabridged Mark Twain*. Ed. Lawrence Teacher. Philadelphia, 1976.

Journal Articles

Anderson, James D. "Aunt Jemima in Dialectics." *Journal of Negro History* 61 (1976): 99–114.

Dormon, James H. "Shaping the Popular Image of Post-Reconstruction Blacks: The 'Coon Song' Phenomenon of the Gilded Age." *American Quarterly* 15 (1988): 450–70.

Dubin, Steven C. "Symbolic Slavery: Black Representations in Popular Culture." *Social Problems* 34 (1987): 122–40.

Du Cille, Ann. "The Occult of True Black Womanhood: Critical Demeanor and Black Feminist Studies." *SIGNS* 19 (1994): 591–629.

Fox-Genovese, Elizabeth. "Scarlett O'Hara: The Southern Lady as New Woman," *American Quarterly* 33 (1981): 389–411.

Golden, Claudia. "Female Labor Force Participation: The Origin of Black and White Differences, 1870 and 1880." *Journal of Economic History* 37 (1977): 87–108.

Haynes, Elizabeth Ross. "Negroes in Domestic Service in the United States." *Journal of Negro History* 6 (1923): 25–303.

Lemons, J. Stanley. "Black Stereotypes as Reflected in Popular Culture, 1880–1920." *American Quarterly* 29 (1977): 102–16.

McCauley, Lucy A. "The Face of Advertising." *Harvard Business Review* 67 (1989): 155–59.

Parkhurst, Jessie W. "The Black Mammy in the Plantation Household." *Journal of Negro History* 23 (1938): 352–53.

Stuckey, Sterling. "Through the Prism of Folklore: The Black Ethos in Slavery." *Massachusetts Review* (1968): 417–37.

Weems, Robert E. Jr. "The Revolution Will Be Marketed: American Corporations and Black Consumers during the 1960s." *Radical History Review* 59 (1994): 94–107.

Woodson, Carter G. "The Negro Washerwoman, a Vanishing Figure." *Journal of Negro History* 15 (1930): 269–77.

Magazine and Newspaper Articles

Abraham, Carolyn. "Not-So-Visible Minorities: Local Advertisers Are Reluctant to Tie Their Images to Non-white Models." *Ottawa Citizen*, 9 Nov. 1992, A1.

Brown, Robert J. "Aunt Jemima No Problem for Gladys Knight." *Advertising Age*, 24 Oct. 1994, 1, 27.

"Col. Sanders Cooks Up Comeback." *USA Today*, 15 May 1994, 4B.

"Danson in the Dark," *Spy* 8:4 (Feb. 1994): 21–24.

DePalma, Anthony. "Racism? Mexico's in Denial." *New York Times*, 11 June 1995, 4E.

Elliott, Stuart. "Gladys Knight Named National Spokeswoman for Aunt Jemima Products." *New York Times*, 29 Aug. 1994, D7.

Erickson, Julie Liesse. "Aunt Jemima Makeover." *Advertising Age*, 1 May 1989, 8.

Flannery, William. "Ads on Minorities Fall Short." *St. Louis Post-Dispatch*, 24 March 1994, 1B.

Griggs, Robyn. "Tobacco, Alcohol's New Foe: Black Ministers Target Ads." *Adweek*, 12 March 1990, 1, 60.

"Hattie McDaniel." *Crisis* 47:4 (April 1940): 1.

Hitt, Jack. "The Theory of Supermarkets." *New York Times Magazine*, 10 March 1996, 56–61, 94, 98.

Hokestra, Dave. "Original 'Aunt Jemima' Could Really Pour It On." *Chicago Sun-Times*, 21 Jan. 1924, Weekend Plus sec., 9.

Horwitz, Sari., "Pulling Together against Racial Stereotypes." *Washington Post*, 25 July 1993, B1.

Kasper, Shirl. "Product Figureheads Often Are Fanciful." *Kansas City Star*, 16 Dec. 1993, F1.

Key, Janet. "At Age 100, a New Aunt Jemima." *Chicago Tribune*, 28 April 1989, sec. 3, pp. 1, 6.

——. "Groups Say Quaker Must Widen Efforts among Blacks." *Chicago Tribune*, 15 Dec. 1989, sec. 2, p. 3.

Mabry, Marcus. "A Long Way from 'Aunt Jemima.'" *Newsweek*, 14 Aug. 1989, 34.

"Mammy's Makover." *Economist*, 6 May 1989, 60.

McLaughlin, Patricia. "Aunt Jemima: Today's Version Is a Working Grandmother." *St. Louis Post-Dispatch*, 10 Aug. 1989, Style sec., 2.

"A New Look for Aunt Jemima." *New York Times*, 1 May 1989, D10.

Ono, Yumiko. "Aunt Jemima Brand Hires Gladys Knight." *Wall Street Journal*, 16 Sept. 1994, B5.

Parker-Pope, Tara. "British Budweiser Ads Rankle American Indians." *Wall Street Journal*, 16 July 1996, B1.

"Poor Aunt Jemima." *Springfield (Mass.) Daily News*, 10 April 1956, 6.

"Quaker Oats Is Shedding New Light on Aunt Jemima." *Wall Street Journal*, 28 April 1989, B3.

Quick, Rebecca. "Betty Crocker Plans to Mix Ethnic Looks for Her New Face." *Wall Street Journal*, 11 Sept. 1995, A1.

Seligmann, Jean, and Allison Samuels. "Pancakes and Politics." *Newsweek*, 17 Oct. 1994.

Townsend, Chauncey. "Out of the Kitchen." *Crisis* 42 (Jan. 1935): 15.

Tucker, William. "All in the Family." *National Review* 47:4 (6 March 1995): 36–44, 76.

Walker, Alice. "Giving the Party: Aunt Jemima, Mammy, and the Goddess Within," *Ms.*, May/June 1994, 22–25.

Index

Page numbers for illustrations are in italics.

The American South Series

Anne Goodwyn Jones and Susan V. Donaldsen, editors
Haunted Bodies: Gender and Southern Texts

M. M. Manring
Slave in a Box: The Strange Career of Aunt Jemima